# THE GLOBAL VATICAN

# THE GLOBAL VATICAN

An Inside Look at the Catholic
Church, World Politics, and the
Extraordinary Relationship between
the United States and the Holy See

FRANCIS ROONEY
*Former Ambassador to the Holy See*

A SHEED & WARD BOOK
ROWMAN & LITTLEFIELD
*Lanham • Boulder • New York • London*

A Sheed & Ward Book
Published by Rowman & Littlefield
4501 Forbes Boulevard, Suite 200, Lanham, Maryland 20706
www.rowman.com

Unit A, Whitacre Mews, 26-34 Stannary Street, London SE11 4AB

Distributed by National Book Network

Copyright © 2013 by Rowman & Littlefield
First paperback edition 2015

British Library Cataloguing in Publication Information Available

**Library of Congress Cataloging-in-Publication Data**

The hardback edition of this book was previously cataloged by the Library of Congress as follows:

Rooney, Francis.
  The global Vatican : an inside look at the Catholic church, world politics, and the extraordinary relationship between the United States and the Holy See / Francis Rooney.
    pages cm
  Includes bibliographical references and index.
  1. Catholic Church—Foreign relations—United States. 2. United States—Foreign relations—Catholic Church. 3. Catholic Church—Foreign relations. I. Title.
  BX1406.3.R665 2013
  327.456'34073—dc23
                                                        2013018732

ISBN: 978-1-4422-2361-5 (cloth : alk. paper)
ISBN: 978-1-4422-4880-9 (pbk. : alk. paper)
ISBN: 978-1-4422-4881-6 (electonic)

∞™ The paper used in this publication meets the minimum requirements of American National Standard for Information Sciences—Permanence of Paper for Printed Library Materials, ANSI/NISO Z39.48-1992.

Printed in the United States of America

# CONTENTS

# FOREWORD

Many, if not most, U.S. diplomats have at least some dealings with their Vatican counterparts during the course of their foreign service careers. For my part, I witnessed the leadership role played by papal nuncios in assignments to three different countries in Latin America. At other postings, such as Vietnam in the 1960s and Iraq in the last decade, I witnessed the plight of Catholic populations, frightened and uprooted by ideological or sectarian conflict. And I was privileged to meet Pope John Paul II during his pastoral visits to three of my ambassadorial postings: Honduras, Mexico, and the Philippines. One has to personally witness such a papal visit to a predominantly Catholic country to appreciate the enormous spiritual and emotional influence these events can have on a country.

I first met Ambassador Francis Rooney in June 2007, when I accompanied President Bush on his visit to Rome and the Vatican. Both of us escorted President and Mrs. Bush on their call on Pope Benedict and, as it turned out, both of us were with the president after leaving the Vatican during those tense moments when his limousine momentarily stalled on the way to our next destination.

I appreciated then and have come to appreciate more, Ambassador Rooney's thoughtful, even scholarly approach to his assignment. What he has done in this book is to provide us with a very readable account of the U.S.-Vatican relationships since the founding of our nation. He also traces the growing importance over time of the Catholic Church in our country. Ambassador Rooney intertwines this very interesting history with relevant reflections and anecdotes from his tour of duty as our envoy to the Vatican.

In this era of globalization, it is key to remember that the Catholic Church has been a global institution for centuries. That fact, combined with the growing numbers of Catholics in the United States, now some 25 percent of the adult population, makes understanding the Vatican and its policies an ever more important part of our diplomacy. Ambassador Rooney's book is an important contribution to that understanding.

John Negroponte
Former Deputy Secretary of State
Washington, D.C.
June 2013

# PROLOGUE

## Introduction to an Education

### I.

M onsignor Caputo came to Villa Richardson on a bright morning in late October, two days after my wife, Kathleen, and I landed in Rome to begin my appointment as the U.S. ambassador to the Holy See. An aide led him up the short flight of stairs to the sunroom at the back of the residence, where we were still unpacking boxes. As I shook the monsignor's hand, he struck me as a man well suited to his position as the Vatican's head of protocol. He was tall, with neatly clipped black hair, and a calm demeanor, fully at ease yet not a bit informal. Like many Vatican officials, he had been educated in the Pontifical Ecclesiastic Academy, the esteemed three-hundred-year-old diplomatic school associated with the Vatican, and was fluent in four languages. His English, like everything else about him, was impeccable.

"Mr. Ambassador," he announced after we'd exchange a few pleasantries, "I have the honor of informing you that the Holy Father will grant an audience for your credentialing on the morning of Saturday, November 12."

I should point out that in the forty-eight hours between our arrival in Rome and Monsignor Tommaso Caputo's visit that morning I had already learned a few important lessons about this new job. I had learned, for example, that when a new U.S. ambassador to the Holy See lands at Rome's Fiumicino Airport, he is immediately escorted off the plane by Italian police and taken to a private lounge, where he is greeted by various dignitaries and the press and expected to deliver a coherent speech. Diplomacy is a serious matter in Italy and much attention is focused on any ambassador representing the United States.

Something else I had learned since our landing was that American ambassadors to the Holy See have many privileges, but the ability to move freely about Rome is not one of them. From the moment we arrived, every step outside the confines of the residence or the embassy had to be coordinated with the embassy's security detail. We would come to be highly appreciative of the embassy staff and the Italian secret service for their capable execution of the security regimen, but it took a bit of getting used to in those early days.

I knew the learning curve would be steep in Rome, but I had arrived as prepared as possible. My Catholic background, from my long-ago Sunday mornings as an altar boy at Sacred Heart Church in Muskogee, Oklahoma, through my education by the Jesuits at Georgetown Preparatory School and Georgetown University in Washington, was a good start. After law school and prior to the Vatican, I'd devoted most of my life, together with Kathleen, to building a family and a group of businesses. My career took me to many parts of the world, especially in Latin America, and gave me the opportunity to see, firsthand, the issues facing a church serving more than 1 billion members in 196 countries.

After President George W. Bush appointed me as ambassador to the Holy See in the winter of 2005, and prior to Senate confirmation and our departure for Rome, Kathleen and I had both launched into a crash course in church history and Vatican diplomacy, aided by a comprehensive reading list provided by the State Department. The State Department, of course, has a program for ensuring that incoming ambassadors receive the information they need to be effective upon arrival. This includes consultations with various policy experts in areas of concern to the Vatican mission and others within the department who work to support our missions abroad. There was also a two-week "ambassadors' seminar" conducted in the State Department's main building and at the George P. Shultz National Foreign Affairs Training Center in Arlington, Virginia, where Kathleen and I were joined by several other newly appointed ambassador-designates and their spouses. In addition to the State Department program, I was fortunate to receive generous help and advice from former Holy See ambassadors, church leaders, and scholars. By the time we landed in Rome, I was confident that I had a pretty good grasp of the task before me. But I also had plenty more to learn.

Back to that October morning in 2005: Monsignor Caputo was officially inviting me to my first official public function as ambassador, the occasion when I would present my credentials to Pope Benedict XVI and receive, in return, his sanction and blessing. Credentialing is a highly ceremonial affair, but is also substantive. A rare private audience with the pope, this would be an opportunity to make a positive first impression and articulate goals and objectives of the Bush administration which might resonate with the Holy See. This would be one of the most important days of my term as ambassador, and a remarkable moment for our family. So it was inconceivable for us to meet the pope without our children present. Our oldest son, Larry, was out of school and working at a new job in Chicago. His brother Michael and sister Kathleen were still in college.

"I'd sure like our children to come to this," I said to Monsignor Caputo. "Is there any chance we could do it during Thanksgiving break?"

The Monsignor gazed back at me blankly, as if he did not quite understand what I was asking. "If we moved it," I offered helpfully, "they wouldn't have to miss any classes." Should I have mentioned that Larry, Michael, and Kathleen attended the University of Notre Dame, a leading Catholic university in the United States? I doubt it would have helped.

"I understand, Mr. Ambassador," said Monsignor Caputo after a very quiet few moments, "but unfortunately November 12 is the date which is available in the Holy Father's agenda, according to the prefecture for the papal household." The look in his eyes told me this would not be a discussion worth pursuing.

"Right. Got it. November 12 it is then."

Lesson learned. A few days of classes would be missed. The professors at Notre Dame would probably understand.

★ ★ ★

This book is written in much the same spirit that I began serving at the U.S. Mission to the Holy See that autumn in 2005, at once hopeful to add value and to capably represent President Bush and our country but also humbly aware that there would be much to learn. What follows here is an effort to share what I have learned about the Holy See, particularly regarding its relationship with the United States, during my service.

Anyone who has served as ambassador to the Holy See would probably agree that this relationship is of vital importance to both America and the world. For me and our family, it was also an education. That term—*education*—calls to mind the great American historian Henry Adams and his classic *The Education of Henry Adams*, which I first read as an undergraduate at Georgetown. Adams went abroad at the start of a new century, at a time when the world was changing rapidly under a tide of new inventions and the industrial revolution. As the author of another classic of American literature, *Mont-Saint-Michel and Chartres*, and an accomplished medievalist, Adams believed that enduring truths can be just as sustaining and energizing as new discoveries; that times of great change, in fact, only make it more important to maintain alignment with fundamental moral and cultural principles. How enduring truths and human values are applied in the world is a big part of the long story of the Holy See. It is also one of the central themes of this book.

Before we continue, the terms "Vatican" and "Holy See" require clarification. The Vatican city-state is the physical place, the 109 acres of sovereign territory, where the pope and the Curia reside, and where St. Peter's Basilica and the Vatican museums are located. The term is commonly used to refer to church leadership and actions, much as the term "White House" is used to denote the executive branch of the U.S. government or "Washington" to denote the entire U.S. government. In fact, the governing body of the Catholic Church is the Holy See, not the Vatican. The Holy See enters into diplomatic treaties and exerts influence in world affairs, as described in this book. For simplicity's sake and in accordance with common usage, the terms Vatican and Holy See will be used more or less interchangeably here, but the distinction has important implications to be discussed in future pages.

## II.

The morning of the credentialing brought perfect autumn weather to Rome. Kathleen and I had been in town for about a month. I'd settled into my work at the embassy as Kathleen joined me in an almost nightly routine of diplomatic events. Our daughter and two sons had arrived from the States a day earlier, joined by my aunt from Pensacola, Florida, and my mother (my father had passed away in 1980), to make the Villa Richardson a real home for our family.

Everyone rose early that Saturday, filling the rooms with family voices and subdued excitement. Preparing for the credentialing visit to the Vatican was a simple matter for the women—all black, head-to-toe, veil-to-shoes—but more complicated for me, since Holy See protocol requires use of the "frac," a white tie outfit with black vest. Once we were prepared, we gathered in the front hall at the bottom of the stairs. We were soon joined by staff members from the embassy. A fleet of black Mercedes sent by the Vatican pulled into formation in the porte cochere. Along with the cars came several Gentlemen of His Holiness, high-level officials dispatched by the Vatican to escort us to the pope. (There are established protocols in all countries for credentialing but the Vatican is especially attentive to these.) I entered the front car with one of the Gentlemen. Kathleen, accompanied by her own Gentleman, followed in a second Mercedes, as the rest of the family piled into a third. The embassy staff brought up the rear. In a convoy we took off for Vatican City, led by a squadron of leather-clad motorcycle police—the *Stradali*—and the usual armed guards in back.

Descending from the top of the Janiculum Hill, we passed a statue of Garibaldi marking the site of the Italian revolutionary's 1849 battle against French troops who fought on behalf of Pope Pius IX. Looking to the east, beyond the steeple of San Pietro in Montorio (where St. Peter was crucified) and across the Tiber, I could see the domes and bell towers of central Rome, a city that had been ruled by popes, saved by popes from barbarian plunder, and, occasionally, sent popes fleeing into exile. There is almost no place you can go in Rome without encountering the two-thousand year history of the papacy, and we were about to visit the most extraordinary place of them all.

Two distinct thoughts ran through my head as we sped north along the Tiber toward Vatican City. The first concerned the incredible fact that we were on our way to meet the pope, humbling beyond description for someone from rural Oklahoma, a state where Catholics comprise a mere 3 percent of the population. The other thought was that I had been given an important mission and intended to successfully accomplish what the government and the president expected of me. On my lap, in an envelope, was the prepared statement which I would hand to Pope Benedict XVI when we met, just as he would deliver one to me. This meeting was an opportunity for me to move beyond the formal statement, though, and establish a basis for an open, expansive, and productive dialogue with the Holy See.

★ ★ ★

This papal audience and, more generally, the timing of my assignment to the Holy See, came at an important moment in history of both the United States and the Catholic Church. America was four years out from 9/11 and locked in difficult wars in two countries, including a conflict in Iraq of which the Holy See had strongly and vocally disapproved. The Bush administration was making headway in bringing democracy, freedom, and stability to Iraq and Afghanistan, but it was a difficult struggle on both fronts. One of my tasks at the Vatican would be to explain our positions on Iraq and Afghanistan and to achieve as much alignment as possible about the way forward. Our primary goal was to focus attention on those areas where the embassy and State Department were confident that we could work with the Holy See productively.

The Holy See had its own series of challenges and frustrations that autumn. The first of these facing Pope Benedict XVI was succeeding Pope John Paul II, one of the most beloved and extroverted pontiffs in modern history. The new pope's academic background and his cerebral, seemingly introspective approach made the contrast especially apparent. "He is at heart a teacher, an academic," is how Thomas Reese, a Jesuit scholar and author of *Inside the Vatican*, described Pope Benedict to me. "He is a shy person running the biggest organization in the world."

Benedict had been pope for only six months when I arrived in Rome, but he was already enmeshed in several controversies. These included the ongoing scandal of priests charged with sexual abuse, which predated his papacy. The American Church had been especially affected by allegations and law suits, prompting "the greatest crisis in its history," as the theologian George Weigel noted. Before becoming pope, Cardinal Ratzinger, in his role as head of the Congregation for the Doctrine of the Faith, put in place several important new measures to streamline procedures for assessing abuse allegations, to assure that they were dealt with promptly, and to engage the civil authorities in a timely manner. These were important steps, but the church remained under incessant attack from those who believed it had been negligent.

Beyond the impact of the scandals, the church was suffering a decline in active participation in much of the Western world. Of approximately 65 million American Catholics, for example, less than 30 percent regularly attended mass at the start of 2005, and that number was dropping by the year. A similar wave of secularism was emptying churches across the traditionally Catholic counties of Europe. Seventy-six percent of France's citizens still professed to be Catholic in 2005, but just 12 percent attended mass regularly. Ireland remained 90 percent Catholic, at least nominally, but regular church attendance, once uniform, had fallen to 50 percent. The situation was even more troubling in Italy: 97 percent of Italians identified themselves as Catholic, but just 30 percent regularly attended mass. Spain and Germany, the pope's homeland, were trending in the same precipitous direction. The dangers undermining families, religions, and governments in these increasingly secular societies would become a major emphasis of Pope Benedict's personal diplomacy.

★ ★ ★

Whatever challenges and changes each faced, the United States and the Holy See remained two of the most significant institutions in world history, one a beacon of democracy and progress, the other a sanctum of faith and allegiance to timeless principles. Despite the obvious differences between the first modern democracy and the longest surviving Western monarchy, both were founded on the idea that "human persons" possess inalienable natural rights granted by God. This had been a revolutionary concept when the Catholic Church embraced it 2,000 years ago, and was equally revolutionary when the Declaration of Independence stated it 1,800 years later.

Given our mutual respect for human rights, it is natural, even inevitable, that we should be friends and collaborators. Why it took nearly two hundred years for us to establish formal diplomatic relations is a question explored at some length in these pages. The answer lies in our respective histories, particularly in the evolution of each one's attitude toward the other. The short answer is that both the United States and the Holy See had to overcome deeply held convictions and perceptions—entrenched anti-Catholicism on the part of Americans; antidemocratic, monarchical reflexes on the part of the Holy See—and that neither managed to do so until the latter half of the twentieth century. "Congress will probably never send a Minister to His Holiness," wrote John Adams (great-grandfather of Henry Adams) in 1779, voicing the opinion shared by many of his compatriots. Nor, added Adams, should Congress accept a nuncio from the pope, "or in other words, an ecclesiastical tyrant which, it is to be hoped, the United States will be too wise ever to admit into their territories."

Some Americans still question our diplomatic relations with the Holy See. They do so by either citing the Establishment Cause of the First Amendment—that it is unconstitutional for the U.S. government to accord diplomatic status to a religious body—or assuming that, as a matter of *realpolitik*, the relationship is inconsequential.

I earnestly hope that this book shows the error of those views. President Reagan established full diplomatic relations with the Holy See in 1984 because, among other reasons, he realized that he could have no better partner than the Pope John Paul II in the fight against communism—and he was right.

Since the fall of the Berlin Wall, the Holy See has continued to play an important role as a diplomatic force while maintaining formal relations with 179 countries, a number surpassed only by the United States. The church is one of the leading advocates and providers for the poor in the world, fights against the scourge of human trafficking, and advances the cause of human dignity and human rights more than any other organization in the world. The Holy See also plays a significant role in pursuing diplomatic solutions to international problems, whether promoting peace between Israel and Palestine, for example, or helping end the civil war in Lebanon, or obtaining the release of nearly one hundred political prisoners from Cuba in 2010—or numerous other examples discussed in this book.

Why is the power and influence of the Holy See underestimated? Part of the answer lies in the fact that it is an extraordinarily complex and unique institution and is therefore easier to dismiss than to understand. A benevolent quasi-monarchy tucked into a corner of a modern democracy, the Holy See is at once a universally recognized sovereign—representing more than a seventh of the world's population—and the civil government of the smallest nation-state on earth. It has no military and only a negligible economy (the Vatican's fungible assets are worth about a billion dollars, a mere drop in the bucket compared to, say, Harvard University's $27 billion endowment), but it has greater reach and influence than most nations.

The word "catholic" originates from the Greek word *katholikos*, meaning universal. The church has been earning that description since the days of the Roman Empire, when Christianity spread like wildfire through Europe, northern Africa, and the Arab Peninsula. Today, the church remains a singular supranational force, operating effectively in more places and cultures than any other international body, with the possible exception of the United Nations. Actually, I would argue that the Holy See has the longer, deeper reach. Unlike the United Nations, which often imposes itself on local cultures from the outside, the Catholic Church is *part* of any place it is present, whether a Nigerian village, an Ecuadorian farming community, or a middle-class American suburb.

It's not simply the number or variety of people that the Holy See represents that gives it relevance; it's also the moral influence of the church, still considerable despite secularization and scandals. The Holy See advocates powerfully for morality in the lives of both Catholics and non-Catholics, and in both individuals and nations. One may disagree with some of the church's positions and yet still recognize the value—the real and practical value—of its insistence that "right" should precede "might" in world affairs.

The historian Arnold Toynbee has made the argument that it is religion, specifically Christianity and its organized framework for defining and advancing moral principles, which distinguishes Western civilization from prior ones, driving it forward and preventing its degeneration into amorality. The universal Catholic Church continues to provide such a framework. The world, I would argue, is better off for it.

Of course, the church has been disparaged at times throughout its long history, and sometimes for good reason. Critics can point to instances in which its power has been misapplied, from the Crusades through the Inquisition, right up until the current abuse scandals. It is important to contextualize historical actions: rather than apply contemporary standards to, for example, the twelfth century, we must align actions in a given period with the social and political mores of that time and thereby create a balanced perspective. Nonetheless, it is clearly the case that the church, being a human enterprise, has occasionally fallen short of its best ideals. But these lapses do not overshadow the good it has accomplished in the past and—more to the point of this book—can accomplish in the future.

On the whole, the church is a powerful and unique source of *soft power*, to borrow a phrase coined by the political scientist Joseph Nye. Soft power is noncoercive. It moves people to do the right thing by appealing to ideals and shared values, rather than to fear and brute force. Soft power is sometimes dismissed by hardcore "realists" as a distraction, but who wants to think and act as if hard power is the only answer in a nuclear twenty-first century? When the master of *realpolitik* diplomacy Dr. Henry Kissinger notes in his recent book, *On China*, that a "congruence on values" is "generally needed to supply an element of restraint" in international relations, he is giving a nod of respect to soft power. My friend Dr. David Abshire, former ambassador to NATO and special counselor to President Reagan, has spoken of a form of soft power that he and others call "people power." This is a phenomenon that became quite interesting and visible during the "Arab Spring" of 2011, when hundreds of thousands of protestors were mobilized by the social media sites like Facebook. People power is really nothing new. The Holy See has been supplying it for centuries. Even now, the Catholic Church is more powerful as a source of people power than any new technology. This is evident in the church's ability to reach out and appeal to its faithful. The communication flows the other way, too. The Vatican is a top-down hierarchy, but it's also a grassroots organization, with deeply embedded sources from which to extract different views of events and attitudes around the world. Its extensive and reliable network of clergy and parishes, of nuns and leaders of Catholic nongovernmental organizations (NGOs) give it a clear understanding and granular feel for world events, sometimes to the surprise of our own State Department or CIA.

III.

As our convoy swung onto the Via della Conciliazione, the wide cobblestone avenue that runs from the banks of the Tiber to the gates of the Vatican, I saw the dome of St. Peter's gleaming in the distance before us.

I was, I realized, a bit nervous, not an inappropriate sensation under the circumstances. Later, an Italian diplomat would tell me that President Bush had been visibly moved the first time he met Pope John Paul II, so I was in good company. The diplomat said this to me with great appreciation and respect that "the most powerful leader in the world" obviously cared so much about the pope and the Holy See's role and effectiveness.

Police had closed down the street for our motorcade to pass. Crowds of tourists watched from the sidewalks as we sped toward St. Peter's Square. Arriving at the piazza, the motorcycles peeled off and the convoy slowed to a stop. We entered Vatican City through the Arch of Bells. Once on Vatican territory, we crept through a labyrinth of narrow alleys, dipping into subterranean passages, rising into small courtyards, then wending our way through more narrow alleys. Many of the structures we passed dated back to the Middle Ages or earlier, and the modern hubbub of Rome could have been a thousand miles and a thousand years away. The effect was transporting and not insignificant. To borrow that famous Marshall McLuhan phrase about television ("the medium is the message"), the atmosphere is the message in the Vatican. As I'd been warned by numerous Vatican observers, anyone wanting to understand the workings of the Holy See should begin with the fact that the pope, cardinals, and Curia view time differently than most of us in the Western world. They act in the context of centuries, even millennia, not days and hours. Probably only the Chinese have similar perceptions of time. Kissinger's description of Chinese diplomacy—"the meticulous preparation, the complexity of argumentation, the capacity for long-range planning, and the subtle sense for the intangible"—is equally applicable to the methods of the Holy See.

What this means for diplomats working with the Holy See is, first, that they must proceed with patience no matter how eager they are to move the ball forward. People operating on a millennial time scale do not feel pressure to move quickly the way an American might, especially one who has spent most of his life in business. This explains why the Vatican tends to favor precedent and continuity over political expediency. Plenty of Vatican policies might seem questionable when viewed in light of contemporary Western values, which is to say popular opinion. The church's ban on artificial birth control, for example, is ignored by 98 percent of American Catholics. However, the church sets standards that do not shift according to popularity. An argument that begins with concern for broad-based acceptance will not get very far in the Vatican.

This is not to imply that the Vatican is out of touch with the modern world. It's not Silicon Valley, but it is far from the technological Dark Ages.

Along with troves of Renaissance art, baroque fountains, medieval walls, and the rare manuscripts in the Vatican's library—including some of the earliest versions of the New Testament and the oldest Hebrew text known to exist—are several communication towers and a robust website which attest to an active global communications network. The pope even has his own Twitter account, implemented under Benedict XVI and now active under Francis.

## IV.

The car stopped in Cortile San Damaso, at the foot of the entrance to the Apostolic Palace. We were met at the entrance by Prince Hugo Windisch-Graetz, a Gentleman of His Holiness. Escorted to the palace by Hugo and several other Gentlemen, we passed a dozen or so Swiss Guards mustered at attention, then entered a loggia, where we encountered additional Gentlemen and guards. Among the people waiting to greet us was a warm and familiar face, Archbishop (later made Cardinal) James Harvey, formerly of Milwaukee and serving as the prefect of the papal household, a position that made him a well-recognized face at the Vatican. After a quick elevator ride, our procession followed Archbishop Harvey through the grand halls of the palace toward the papal suite.

For such a small territory, the Vatican contains an amazingly extensive labyrinth of halls, corridors, and rooms. We walked on floors of inlaid marble and under vaulted ceilings, passing wall-to-wall frescoes many centuries old. Advancing through various rooms where more Swiss Guards stood at solemn attention, we arrived in the Sala Clementina, the anteroom of the pope's chambers. To my right, I saw a familiar-looking painting.

"That looks like an El Greco," I said quietly to Archbishop Harvey.

"That is an El Greco," the archbishop responded. "We've got lots of art like that around here."

There were more halls and rooms—a red one, and then a yellow one where the pope's white marble throne sits (unused since Paul VI ended the practice)—and ultimately a gold room called the Sala degli Ambasciatori. The doors opened and Pope Benedict XVI stepped out to greet us.

Benedict's reputation as a reserved intellectual notwithstanding, he had kind and welcoming eyes that exuded pleasure and kindness. He was seventy-eight years old and worked hours that would exhaust a man half his age, and yet he seemed rested and focused. He ushered me into his library. A few more photographs were taken, and then the room was cleared, the doors were closed, and we were alone in the serene grandeur of the papal library. We sat for a moment in silence. The pope was waiting for me to speak. I was waiting for myself to speak, too. No words were coming out.

"I'm sorry, Holy Father," I finally managed. "I'm nervous. I imagine that happens a lot here."

"It does." He smiled patiently, as if to assure me we had all the time in the world, and waited for me to find my voice.

★ ★ ★

What follows is some of what I might have discussed with the pope if we really did have all the time in the world. It's the voice of an American Catholic who remains grateful for the opportunity he had to represent the United States and President George W. Bush before such an important institution as the Holy See.

It is also a consideration, from one observer's perspective, of a pope who seemed an enigma to many people throughout his papacy, right down to his startling resignation in February 2013. The view I offer here will contrast somewhat with the narrative that began taking shape immediately after Benedict announced his resignation, when various pundits cast him as ineffectual and unassertive, a man generally out of his element in the papacy. I don't dispute that certain administrative lapses occurred in the Vatican during Benedict's reign, nor can anyone dismiss the toll the pedophilia scandals have taken on the church. But I suspect history will ultimately judge Benedict XVI as strong-minded, farsighted, and committed to the best interest of the church and the world, even at the expense of his own short-term popularity.

Mainly, this book tells the story of a relationship between two of the most extraordinary powers in human history. To understand the forces behind this diplomatic alliance, I begin in the turbulent past, at a moment in history when the United States first came together and the Holy See seemed to be coming apart. I will examine the Holy See's evolution as a soft power, including its crucial claims on sovereignty and moral authority, and its development as a diplomatic force, particularly vis-á-vis the United States of America. From the past, we will move into recent events, including my time as ambassador and those of my predecessors. In the end, I hope this book will enlighten readers not only about what was and is, but what still can be.

*I*

# FAITH AND REVOLUTION

# 1

# THE GREATEST OF
# EVILS TO BE FEARED

By reputation, the United States is a Protestant country and
Catholics were asserted to be unsuited for it. Yet virtually every Catholic writer or thinker who visited America since 1607
has been excited by the country's extraordinary consonance
with Catholic faith.

—Michael Novak

I.

The first question any author writing about the Vatican asks is: where to
start? The Catholic Church has been around for more than two thousand very eventful years. To put the longevity of the church in perspective,
consider that the United States of America is currently on its 44th president;
the church is on its 265th pope. This is a sweep of time so vast and rich that
no single volume could do it justice.

This volume obviously intends no such thing. We are interested here
in the church primarily as a diplomatic entity, particularly in relation to the
United States. The 1,800 years of Catholicism that preceded the birth of
the United States will not be ignored, for no aspect of the church can be
isolated from its long history. Given this project's scope, though, the distant
past will be treated only briefly. And while much of what is told here will
be compelling in its own right, touching upon some of the most important
human events of the last few centuries, this is history with a purpose. In
part, that purpose is to give American readers insight into the nature of the
Holy See, its guiding principles, and its legacy of engagement in the affairs
of states. One primary purpose is to answer a question that I have been

3

asked many times since serving as ambassador: why, given the obvious congruence of our values, did it take until 1984 for the United States and Holy See to recognize each other formally? In the answer lies an understanding of this most singular relationship.

There is no better place to begin this inquiry than on the campus of my alma mater, Georgetown University. Just inside the main gates of Georgetown, rising from the circular lawn in front of Healy Hall, is a statue I have walked by hundreds, maybe thousands, of times since first stepping onto campus more than forty years ago. I'm sure that many mornings in my undergraduate years I raced by the bronze figure on my way to class with barely a glance. These days it never fails to grab my attention.

The subject of the statue, as every good Hoya knows, is John Carroll, the first Catholic bishop in the United States and Georgetown's founder.

Most Americans have forgotten the name John Carroll. Also largely forgotten are the once-celebrated names of his brother, Daniel, a framer of the U.S. Constitution, and his cousin, Charles, a signer of the Declaration of Independence. You won't find much in history textbooks about this once-prominent American Catholic family. In fact, you won't find much about Catholics *at all* in histories of early America. Today's histories include a wider variety of people—Native Americans, African Americans, Dutch, Jews—than just Pilgrims and Puritans, but still not much about Catholics, and even less about the Carrolls. This is unfortunate. The Carrolls were not only important founding fathers of the United States; they were also—and this applies to John Carroll especially—critical early links between the new nation and the Catholic Church in Rome.

As depicted in the sculpture at Georgetown, John Carroll sits in a chair perched atop a granite pedestal. He is dressed in the flowing robe of a bishop's vestments and his expression is pensive and dignified. I have no idea if Carroll the man looked anything like Carroll the statue, but the pose is striking. Carroll's face turns slightly to his right, as if he's gazing through the buildings and trees of the campus and down the Potomac River toward swampy Washington, D.C. (The nation's capital was *literally* a swamp in Carroll's day.) He appears to be contemplating the future. Or maybe it's the opposite: maybe he is looking further downriver, toward the distant Chesapeake Bay, recalling the difficult past.

One of the unsettling truths about the America in which Carroll was born and lived is how inhospitable it was to Roman Catholics. The colonies were populated overwhelmingly by Protestants, and though many of them came to escape persecution in the Old World, they did not extend their hopes for religious liberty to Catholics in the New World. Massachusetts Bay Colony set the tone in 1647 when it banished, under threat of death, any "Jesuit or ecclesiastical person ordained by the authority of the pope." Virginia had a law excluding "popish recusants" (Catholics who persisted in practicing their faith) from a host of occupations and rights. Some version of this law was on the books in nearly every colony, including John Carroll's birthplace, the Province of Maryland.

Initially, Maryland was intended to be the exception to the rule. The colony was founded by a Catholic Englishman, Cecil Calvert, better known as the second Lord Baltimore. Calvert's father, George, the first Lord Baltimore, had been granted a charter by King Charles I in 1632 to form a settlement along the Potomac River. While never conceived as an exclusively Catholic enclave, Maryland was meant to be a place where Catholics might enjoy "mutual love and Amity" with Protestants, "free from persecution on account of their religion." George Calvert died shortly after receiving the charter and it was left to Cecil to organize the settlement, which he did in 1634, when the *Ark* and *Dove* landed in Maryland's Chesapeake Bay, carrying Jesuit missionaries along with Catholics and Protestant settlers.

The spirit of amity held for a number of years. In 1649, the Maryland assembly took a historic step, ensuring the right of Catholics and Protestants to practice their respective religions. Maryland's "Toleration Act," limited as it was—no allowance was made for Jews or other non-Christian faiths—is widely considered a template for the establishment and free exercise clauses of the First Amendment that would be adopted by the United States 140 years later.

But Maryland did not turn out to be a happy refuge for Catholics. Five years after its passage, the Toleration Act was tossed out in a Protestant coup within the colony. Catholics soon regained control and reinstated the law, but by 1692, after the "Glorious Revolution" in England (when the Catholic King James I was replaced by the Protestant William of Orange), they had lost power again. Protestant orthodoxy became the law of the land. Talk of religious toleration did not resume for another eighty years.

The persecution of Catholics varied in degree during these years, but it was persistent. "Anti-popery" laws restricted Catholics' rights to celebrate mass publicly and to baptize their children, as well as their rights to vote or hold public office, and generally dismissed Catholics as misguided and possibly seditious aliens whose faith precluded full citizenship. Having been tempered by years of persecution, Maryland Catholics learned to accommodate their faith to reality. Some prospered financially in spite of such indignities as a double tax on their land, enacted in 1756. The Carroll family managed to become one of the largest and wealthiest landholders in all the colonies.

Rich or poor, Catholics worshipped quietly in homes or in small private chapels, a function both of the illicitness of public mass and the scarcity of churches. Most of their priests were itinerant missionaries who traveled great distances through the countryside, showing up in towns between long intervals to perform baptisms, weddings, burials, and other rites. "You must not imagine that our chapels look as yours do," one Jesuit missionary wrote home to England in 1764, "they are in great forests, some miles from any House of Hospitality. . . . Swamps, runs, miry holes, lost in the Night, as yet and ever will in this country attend us." Given these obstacles, it's a good bet that the man who later became the first bishop of the United States seldom met a priest as a young boy.

II.

John Carroll was born in Upper Marlborough, Maryland, on January 8, 1735. Not much is known of Carroll's childhood. He was probably educated at home as a young boy, as were many Catholic children, since Catholic education outside the home was prohibited. At age twelve, he attended a semicovert Jesuit school at Bohemia Manor, on the upper Eastern Shore of the Chesapeake Bay. A year later, in the summer of 1748, thirteen-year-old "Jackie" said farewell to his family and sailed out of the Chesapeake, following a route across the Atlantic taken by many Maryland Catholic boys in the eighteenth century. Accompanying him was his eleven-year-old cousin, Charles, the future signer of the Declaration of Independence. Neither would see home again until they were grown men.

The Carroll cousins landed in London, then made their way across the channel and north through France to Flanders. A Jesuit school there, in the town of St. Omer, had been educating Catholic boys since the late sixteenth century. The school offered an extraordinary education for an American, deeper and more cosmopolitan than any colonial Protestant was likely to receive at the time, albeit one earned by exile from home and family. "Most of our Merylanders do very well," John's cousin Charles would write home in 1750, "and are said to be as good as any, if not the best boys in the house."

Given events on the political horizon in the late eighteenth century, the curriculum at St. Omer was notable. Along with Latin and Greek classics, students were given a steady diet of Catholic theology as interpreted by the intellectually probing Jesuits. They would have been exposed to Thomas Aquinas's writings from the thirteenth century, but also to the works of sixteenth century Jesuit thinkers such as Spaniards Francisco Suarez and Juan de Mariana and Italian Robert Bellarmine. These authors were, in their way, as rousing as John Locke on the subject of liberty. In *Summa Theologica*, Aquinas distinguished between just and unjust government, proposing that subjects had a right to rise up against an unjust tyrant, and even commit tyrannicide, in certain extraordinary circumstances. The Jesuit writers took this line of thought a little further, expanding the conditions for resistance against corrupt monarchs. Rulers ruled with the consent of the people, the Jesuits argued, and lost legitimacy when they lost consent. Such ideas did not sit well with Europe's monarchs and would eventually haunt the Jesuits. In the meantime, the education at St. Omer armed its students well, both intellectually and morally, for the looming battle for liberty.

★ ★ ★

John's cousin, Charles Carroll, left Europe and returned to Maryland in 1764 to take his place as his father's heir. By the early 1770s, Charles was caught up in the political fervor in the colonies. He engaged in a widely publicized debate in a Maryland newspaper, emerging as a brilliant and inspiring proponent for the cause of liberty under the pseudonym "First Citizen." Charles's entry into politics was remarkable given that he and his fellow Catholics still had no right to vote in Maryland.

John Carroll took a different route after St. Omer. He remained in France and entered a Jesuit seminary. Ordained a Jesuit priest in 1759, Carroll took his final vows in 1771. His timing could not have been worse. This was precisely the moment when Europe's Catholic monarchs, including rulers from France, Spain, Portugal, and Sicily, decided they had had enough of what they perceived to be the Jesuit's meddling and seditious behavior. On August 16, 1773, Pope Clement XIV buckled under the monarchs' demands to put the religious order out of business. Deciding that the Jesuits were more trouble to the church than they were worth, he issued a papal bull known as *Dominus ac Redemptor*. The Society of Jesus was thereby "suppressed."

The bull was "one of the unfairest pontifical acts in the history of the papacy," one biographer of John Carroll has written. The papal historian Eamon Duffy calls it "the papacy's most shameful hour." For John Carroll, the suppression was a devastating blow. "I am not, and perhaps never shall be, recovered from the shock of this dreadful intelligence," he wrote home to his brother, Daniel. "The greatest blessing which in my estimation I could receive from God, would be immediate death."

But God had other plans for John Carroll. In 1774, hoping to escape the despair that Europe had come to represent to him, he boarded one of the last passenger ships to leave England for the Chesapeake Bay before the Revolutionary War.

III.

We have to imagine how difficult his homecoming must have been for John Carroll. He was forty years old, well into middle age, and had been away for twenty-seven years. His religious family, the Jesuits, had been condemned and outlawed by the pope. His father had passed away a few years earlier. His mother, whom he had not seen since he was twelve, failed to recognize him when he first returned. And while much had changed in Maryland in the years that he'd been gone, the colony still refused to grant him and his fellow Catholics the right to practice their religion as they pleased. Practically a stranger in a strange land, Carroll moved in with his mother at Rock Creek, Maryland, where he built a small wooden chapel to serve local Catholics, and began a peripatetic ministry to more distant Marylanders and Virginians.

Meanwhile, the winds of revolution were sweeping across the colonies. The Boston Tea Party occurred a year before Carroll's return, in December 1773. By 1774, delegates of the colonies, spurred by the Intolerable Acts (a series of laws passed by Parliament after the turmoil in Boston), were meeting in Philadelphia to discuss tactics against Britain. The first shots were fired in Lexington and Concord in the spring of 1775, and Bunker Hill came two months later.

The American Revolution was initially a mixed blessing for Roman Catholics living in the colonies. On the positive side, all the talk of liberty raised the promise of new freedoms, including freedom of religion. One auspicious sign: Charles Carroll, though *still* unable to vote, attended the First Continental Congress in Philadelphia in 1774. The fact that Marylanders were apparently putting their faith in a Catholic was a step in the right direction.

But along with anti-British sentiment came, ironically, a new wave of anti-Catholicism. This was generated mainly by the Quebec Act, passed by Parliament in the summer of 1774. The Quebec Act (usually lumped among the Intolerable Acts) was a blatant attempt by the British Parliament to seek support from the Canadian provinces. Recognizing that much of settled Canada was still French-speaking and very much Catholic, as it had been under French dominion, the British offered the Canadians the right and freedom to practice their faith, provided they profess allegiance to King George. The act also included a provision to hand over frontier territory to Quebec's Catholics; land that many Americans believed was rightfully theirs (and which would eventually become part of the United States).

The response to the Quebec Act in the colonies was outrage. Anti-British rhetoric now blended with long simmering fears of "popery." In October 1774, the Continental Congress, in an address written by John Jay—later the first chief justice of the U.S. Supreme Court—issued dire warnings of a conspiracy between the English monarchy and the Roman Catholic Church. Citing the church's propensity for "impiety, bigotry, persecution, murder and rebellion," Jay insinuated that the pope intended to help Britain enslave Americans.

Jay was hardly alone among the Founders in promoting anti-Catholicism. Even so fair-minded a man as John Adams scorned Catholics as "poor wretches fingering their beads," as he wrote home to his wife, Abigail, after attending a mass in Philadelphia the same October that John Jay issued his address. In the immediate wake of the Quebec Act, Adams encouraged Protestant preachers to use their pulpits to inflame feeling against the Catholic Church. His Boston cousin, the rabble-rousing Sam Adams, went even further, denouncing popery as "the greatest of evils to be feared."

But then, quite abruptly, the attitudes of the Americans began to shift. One important indication of the new direction was an order issued by George Washington to the Continental army on November 5, 1775, in anticipation of an annual holiday known as Pope's Day. Marking a Catholic plot to blow up the House of Parliament in 1605, the holiday—called Guy Fawkes Day in England, after its most infamous conspirator—was traditionally celebrated in America by burning the pope in effigy. General Washington condemned "that ridiculous and childish custom," as he put it, "so monstrous as not to be suffered or excused."

Washington was moved by his real sense of decency, but he was also being pragmatic. Just a year after the Quebec Act, the patriots had come to realize that they needed the French Canadians on their side. Burning popes in effigy was not going to win friends in Quebec.

Regretting earlier outbursts, the Continental Congress decided to send a special committee of ambassadors on a diplomatic mission to Montreal to make amends and try to lead their northern neighbors to the colonial cause. The Congress named Benjamin Franklin to lead this committee. Franklin would be accompanied by two other delegates to Congress, the Marylanders

Samuel Chase and Charles Carroll. Though Franklin brought his prestige and fame to the mission, Charles Carroll was the indispensable man. Not only would he be religiously agreeable to the French Canadians, but he also spoke fluent French. John Adams, who had so recently dismissed Catholics as "simple and ignorant," had to admit that Charles Carroll was neither. In a letter to Abigail, dated February 1776, Adams described Carroll as a man "of great Abilities and Learning," as well as a "zealous Supporter of the Rights of America, in whose Cause he has hazarded his all."

Before sending the expedition off to Canada, Congress also resolved that Charles Carroll would ask his cousin, Fr. John Carroll, to accompany the group. Like Charles, John spoke fluent French and Latin, which would be useful. Nor would it hurt that he was a Catholic priest. John Carroll appreciated the "distinguished and unexpected honour" of the invitation, but he had doubts about the chances of the mission's success and his own credentials as a diplomat. Despite his hesitations, he agreed to go.

The four Americans departed from Philadelphia in the early spring of 1776 to commence an arduous journey, north over land to New York, then along the Hudson River to Albany and across Lake Champlain to Montreal. The orders they carried from Congress instructed them to promise the Canadians that if they cooperated, the Americans would treat them as equals and leave Catholics alone to practice as they chose.

John Carroll's concerns turned out to be warranted. The Canadians were in no mood to help the colonists who had so recently maligned them. The committee persevered in Canada for several months but to no avail. When Ben Franklin's health turned poor, John Carroll accompanied him home to Philadelphia. "I find I grow daily more feeble and think I could hardly have got so far, but for Mr. Carroll's friendly assistance and tender care of me," Franklin wrote in a letter along the way home. By the end of the journey, the two men were close friends.

Here was at least one fruit of an otherwise futile sojourn: a relationship that would have a crucial effect on Carroll's future life and the future of the American Catholic Church.

## IV.

The mere fact that Charles and John Carroll had stuck out their necks for the American cause was evidence that their religion, whatever its perceived flaws, produced good and reliable patriots. Over the next several years, many more Catholics would give their hearts and lives to the cause of liberty, proving themselves to be as American as any Protestant. Eventually, of course, America would ask France, a Catholic nation, for help. The Victory at Yorktown in the autumn of 1781—and, more generally, independence itself—would never have been possible without the support of nearly eight thousand French troops and Admiral de Grasse's blockade.

Yorktown was still very much in the future in the spring of 1776, but the Carrolls returned from Canada to a land already undergoing extraordinary changes, some of which would have been inconceivable in the colonies even a few years earlier. That July, Charles Carroll joined fifty-five other Americans in signing the Declaration of Independence and endorsing these words: "We hold these truths to be self-evident, that all men are created equal, that they are endowed by their Creator with certain unalienable Rights, that among these are Life, Liberty and the pursuit of Happiness." As the only Catholic signer, Carroll could not endorse that passage without understanding very personally what these unalienable rights entailed: freedom to worship as he saw fit.

Right up until the Revolution, no colony, with the exception of Pennsylvania, had allowed Catholics to celebrate mass. Now, one by one, the former colonies began passing laws that extended to Catholics full rights of citizenship and religious freedom. As the constitutional scholar Leo Pfeffer points out in his book *Church, State, and Freedom*, the Americans were practically forced by their own logic to grant religious freedom; they could not insist on "self-evident" "unalienable Rights" while denying some fellow citizens that most self-evident of unalienable rights, the freedom to worship as they pleased. "Thoughtful persons could not fail to see the inconsistency," Pfeffer writes, "between the practices of religious discrimination and the natural-rights doctrines of freedom and equality set forth in the Declaration of Independence."

One hundred and eighty-nine years after the signing of the Declaration of Independence, the Second Vatican Council would pass its own breakthrough Declaration on Religious Freedom, known as *Dignitatis Humanae*. The Catholic Church, having deemed itself the only legitimate religion on earth for centuries, finally, in 1965, recognized other religious faiths as worthy of respect and freedom of worship. Drafted by an American Jesuit named John Courtney Murray, *Dignitatis Humanae* would be a striking case of America's experiment in democracy influencing Catholic thought.

Long before church leaders learned about liberty from America, though, the American Founding Fathers were learning such lessons from the Catholic Church.

To be sure, the Founders' debt to the church was an inherited one, which they probably did not even know they owed. Thomas Jefferson credited his influence for the Declaration to John Locke, the English philosopher who despised Catholicism so intensely that he neglected to include it as a religion deserving of toleration. Jefferson had his own concerns about the Catholic Church, considering it antidemocratic. "History, I believe, furnishes no example of a priest-ridden people maintaining a free civil government," he wrote to Alexander von Humboldt on December 6, 1813. Nonetheless, Jefferson joined James Madison and other Founders in composing a constitution that extended freedom of worship to *all* religions, including Catholicism. The Founders recognized, as John Locke never did, that the logic of human rights demanded the acceptance of *full* religious freedom.

Bringing this full circle, if the Founders owed their inspiration to John Locke, Locke himself probably owed more to influences that preceded him—*Catholic* influences, that is—than he would ever have admitted. The renowned Medievalist scholar Brian Tierney has shown that precedents for natural rights theory go back to twelfth-century Canon Law and include Aquinas's expression of the social compact of the consent of the governed, noted earlier. From these evolved the modern concept of God-given, self-evident rights possessed by all individuals by virtue of their being born human, and which all humans can recognize by virtue of their capacity for reason. Among the Lockian-sounding ideas considered in earlier Catholic theology, particularly by Jesuit thinkers, were, first, that rulers rule by the consent of the ruled and, second, that rulers themselves are subject to the rules of natural law.

American ideals, in other words, may owe more to Catholic thought than most of us recognize, for the simple reason that Western thought *was* Catholic thought for millennia; this was the philosophical and theological tradition from which Locke's, and then Jefferson's, ideas arose.

I am hardly the first person to notice commonalties between the Declaration of Independence and Catholic theology. In the 1920s, at a time when anti-Catholicism was flaring up yet again in America, a number of Catholic scholars attempted to polish their patriotic credentials by making the case that the Declaration was shaped *directly* by the Catholic tradition of natural law. Some even suggested that Thomas Jefferson had read Catholic literature. The evidence for this seems thin. Nonetheless, Jefferson's words *are* strikingly similar in some cases to those of St. Thomas Aquinas and Robert Bellarmine, to name just two. In 1930, a Catholic priest named John C. Rager made the comparison explicit in a side-by-side comparison. One of these concerned the natural rights of humans:

> Jefferson (eighteenth century): "All men are created equal; they are endowed by their Creator with certain inalienable rights."
>
> Bellarmine (sixteenth century): "All men are equal, not in wisdom or grace, but in the essence and nature of mankind."
>
> Aquinas (thirteenth century): "Nature made all men equal in liberty, though not in their natural perfections."

Another of the comparisons concerned governments:

> Jefferson (eighteenth century): "Governments are instituted among men, deriving their just powers from the consent of the governed."
>
> Bellarmine (sixteenth century): "It depends upon the consent of the multitude to constitute over itself a king, consul, or other magistrate. This power is, indeed, from God, but vested in a particular ruler by the counsel and election of men."
>
> Aquinas (thirteenth century): "Therefore the making of a law belongs either to the whole people or to a public personage who has care of the whole people."

Does the fact that many of Jefferson's arguments and phrases echo Catholic theology mean that the Declaration of Independence was in origin a Catholic document? Certainly not. Neither the Founding Fathers, who were mostly Deists, nor the Vatican, which had little sympathy for revolutions or democracy or Enlightenment thought at the time, would have been comfortable with that description. Nonetheless, the similarities should be recognized if for no other reason than to highlight the irony—and the absurdity—of what followed. Rather than find common ground and join forces, the United States and the Vatican spent the next 150 years caught up in a web of prejudices and suspicions. Anti-Catholicism would continue to cast a shadow in America deep into the twentieth century. It was, according to the historian Arthur M. Schlesinger Sr. (not to be confused with his son, Arthur M. Schlesinger Jr., who served as aid to John F. Kennedy, America's first Catholic president), "the deepest bias in the history of the American people."

Meanwhile, the Catholic Church was about to undergo a jolt, making it even more wary than it already was of the democratic ideals from which the American experiment had sprung.

# 2

## THE LAST POPE

When we reflect on the tremendous assaults which she has survived we find it difficult to conceive in what way she is to perish.

—Thomas Babington Macaulay

### I.

As consequential as the American Revolution would be to world history, and to the future of the Roman Catholic Church, the Holy See seemed to give it little thought as it was occurring. This is not all that surprising when we consider that the number of Catholics in the distant American colonies, just twenty-five thousand, comprised a small fraction of the Vatican's flock of more than 100 million, and that the regime from which the Americans were attempting to break—Britain—was Protestant and historically at odds with the Holy See. The pope at the time, Pius VI, had more important things on his mind than a Protestant dispute more than four thousand miles from Rome.

There is an intriguing story—I've never been able to confirm it myself—that suggests Pius VI was at least mildly interested in the events in America. He apparently asked his nuncio in Paris, Giuseppe Doria Pamphili, to procure a copy of the Declaration of Independence from Benjamin Franklin. This would have occurred about two years after Pius became pope (in early 1775) and a short time after Franklin landed in Paris (in late 1776) to solicit French help for the American cause. Franklin apparently obliged the nuncio and a copy was delivered to Rome.

If Pius VI did in fact receive a copy of the Declaration, how ironic it would have been for him to read it in the light of one of the great windows of the Quirinal Palace, the residence of popes until 1870 and the ultimate symbol of monarchism. One might imagine Pius VI, an Italian deeply schooled in Old World Europe, carefully sounding out these distinctly New World words: "When, in the course of human events, it becomes necessary for one people to dissolve the political bands which have connected them with another, and to assume among the powers of the earth, the separate and equal station to which the laws of nature and of nature's God entitle them."

Quite likely, the pope's reaction would have been mixed. He would have applauded the Declaration's implicit promise of religious freedom for Catholics in America. He would have approved, too, the hints of Catholic natural law sprinkled through the document. But other parts would have troubled him. Whatever it shared with Catholic theology, the Declaration of Independence was unmistakably a product of the Enlightenment; and the Catholic Church, in 1776, was far from ready to embrace Enlightenment thought. Behind Thomas Jefferson's eloquent phrases were the inimical ideas of John Locke—the same John Locke who attacked the church in England with his 1689 treatise *Letter Concerning Toleration*; the same John Locke who argued that all religions should be treated with toleration *except* Catholicism. In league with Locke's ideas were the disturbing provocations of Voltaire, Hobbes, and a host of other skeptics, rationalists, empiricists, and freethinkers who embraced the age of reason and disparaged the Catholic Church.

While the philosophers of the Enlightenment inflicted their wounds by pen than by sword, the injury was real. They steadily undermined the authority of the church and the faith of its flock, making room for secularism to grow and giving Europe's monarchs license to wrest religious control from Rome. Later, Enlightenment ideas would haunt the monarchs themselves. Momentarily, the decline of faith left a gap. As power abhors a vacuum, government moved in to fill it.

The worst offenders were the Catholic monarchs. The Bourbons in Spain and France, the Hapsburgs in Austria, the Braganzas in Portugal—these rulers envied their Protestant counterparts, who had full control of their national churches. Why, the reigning Catholics wondered, should the pope dictate religious practice in *their* countries when no one told the King of England how to run the Anglican Church in *his*? Catholic kings believed they had a right to make ecclesiastical appointments as they pleased—to appoint their own bishops and cardinals, to even elect their own popes. The monarchs were encouraged by a number of movements within the Catholic Church, such as Gallicanism in France and Febronianism in Germany, promoting national, as opposed to Roman, control of the church.

The end of the eighteenth century found the Holy See nearly stripped of its power. At one time the monarchs had considered the pope as an equal or superior partner in guiding Europe. Now the monarchs had the upper hand. The suppression of the Jesuits was but one poignant example of the new balance of power. In that case, the monarchs essentially arranged the election of Pope Clement XIV, with the understanding that he would rid them of the meddlesome and subversive Society of Jesus. When he hesitated, the monarchs threatened and badgered until he complied. Pope Clement seemed to grasp more than anyone how much was lost under his papacy. He died September 1774, a year after ordering the suppression, humiliated, haunted by depression and paranoia.

Pius VI, installed as pope in February 1775, appeared at first to be a man born to lead the church through troubled times. He certainly looked the part of a great pontiff, handsome and dignified. He was endowed with highly regarded skills as a diplomat, which he put to use not only in relations with Catholic monarchies, but in reaching out to Protestant governments. Pius's willingness to treat with representatives of rival sects was a turning point in the diplomatic history of the church. Indeed, Fr. Robert A. Graham, SJ, in his classic study of the Holy See, *Vatican Diplomacy*, locates the start of modern papal diplomacy in the reign of Pius VI, "when non-Catholic states, instead of only those states in communion with the pope, began to be represented at the Roman Court."

For all of his notable qualities, Pius VI was a flawed pope. Reverting to old papal foibles like nepotism and ostentation, he drained the coffers of the Vatican and reinforced stereotypes of the Catholic Church as obsolete and out of touch—"a venerable anachronism more and more identified with political and social structures doomed to collapse," as historian Thomas Bokenkotter describes a common late eighteenth-century perception of Pius VI.

The church was in trouble, and the trouble was about to get worse. Still, as Pius VI pondered what these strange new ideas of liberty might mean for the church, he must have found consolation in the past. Because if the Catholic Church has shown one attribute through history, it is endurance.

Endurance: that's the word that came to mind when I first entered the Vatican to meet the pope in 2005, gliding through years of permanence in the narrow alleys and courtyards leading to St. Peter's and the Apostolic

Palace. It struck me again and again, as it would anyone who goes to the Holy City, how much history has accumulated there. You see it gazing down from the frescoes on the walls and the marble eyes of the statues that populate those halls and salons. It's represented in the millions of volumes of manuscripts and books contained in the Vatican's library and Secret Archives, and in the very stones of the walls themselves. It's a message of continuity, and it speaks to an essential truth: the Catholic Church has not simply *been around* a long time; it has *endured*.

Those who live surrounded by the long history of the church have a special perspective that informs the way they think. They are keenly aware of the church's resilience. Kingdoms have come and gone—nations have been born and died; dynasties have flourished and faded—but the church is still here. From the persecutions of the Roman Empire to the barbarian invasions of the Dark Ages; from the Great Schism of the Middle Ages through the Reformation of the sixteenth century, the church has endured. It has faced countless wars and famines and plagues. It has suffered the reigns of the tyrants of other nations and its own self-inflicted tyrants—and yet it has endured. In fact, no single institution in history has lasted longer than the Roman Catholic Church.

Surely this knowledge has fortified the faith and courage of popes who led the church through hard times. It must have fortified Pius VI, who was about to lead the church through some of its darkest days.

II.

The not-so-secret secret of the church's survival comes down to two great traditions that have sustained it through history. These can be broadly categorized as *theology* and *diplomacy*. Although diplomacy is the focus of this book, theology and fundamental teachings of the church cannot be ignored.

Catholic theology, as understood in general terms, encompasses the church's capacity to define—and refine—its message through the ages, achieving balance between constancy and renewal. Starting with the first great ecumenical council at Nicaea in 325, the church sought to express a clear and unified creed. However, Catholicism was never simple. Any religion founded on the belief that a man born of God also *is* God is profound and invokes serious reflection. (In fact, that very issue—whether Jesus was both man and God—was on the agenda at Nicaea.) Countless councils after Nicaea, from Trent (1545–1563) to Vatican II (1962–1965), were devoted to defining exactly what Roman Catholicism is and is not. While many people dislike certain aspects in the doctrinal rulings of the Catholic Church, no one can deny that, over time, the church has done a remarkable job of preserving the integrity of its message—its core values, its immutable beliefs—while adapting, albeit gradually, to progress and change.

In some respects, the Catholic Church can be compared to the ship of Theseus. What happens to the identity of an old ship, this ancient paradox poses, when the parts of it that have rotted or worn out are replaced? The ship, inevitably, changes as its parts change. What becomes of the ship if, over time, nearly all the original material is replaced? Is it still the same ship? In the case of the Catholic Church, the answer is a resounding *affirmative*. Though the church has been renewed countless times, has evolved and adjusted through the course of history, it is unmistakably the same ship that set sail from the Holy Land two thousand years ago. In his first Christmas Address to the Roman Curia, Pope Benedict XVI, the successor of St. Peter whose very person represents the continuity of the Holy See, described the church as "a subject which increases in time and develops, yet always remaining the same, the one subject of the journeying People of God." Cardinal James Harvey, the first American ever to serve as the prefect of the papal household, told me that despite all the years and evolutions of the church in the world, "the basic principles stay the same."

Holy See diplomacy is a means of applying those basic principles to real life problems in the world of nations, states, and communities. Through the exercise of its diplomacy the Holy See seeks to advance freedom, safeguard human dignity, and protect the human condition in a variety of contexts. In the words of Cardinal Jean-Louis Tauran, one of the Vatican's most respected and distinguished diplomats, "The Holy See, which enjoys international juridical status, is . . . presented as a sovereign and independent moral authority, and as such takes part in international relations. Within nations its action as a moral authority, aims at furthering an ethic of relations between the different protagonists of the international community." The Holy See expresses and elaborates upon its principles and values in a most secular context, the affairs of states. As such, the Holy See brings a unique perspective to international relations. Here is Fr. Robert Graham again, quoting a definition of ecclesiastic diplomacy from an Italian guide to diplomacy:

> The science and art . . . which is directed towards ordering the reciprocal rights and duties resulting from the coexistence of the church with the various states and which, while tending constantly to the advancement of

the interests of the Holy See, at the same time promotes and preserves peaceful relations between the two powers.

Church officials have always known how important diplomacy is to them. That is why they have been studying and teaching it for hundreds of years in the Pontifical Ecclesiastical Academy, the world's first professional school for diplomats, founded by the Vatican in 1701.

Archbishop Pietro Sambi, Apostolic Nuncio to the United States from 2005 until his death in 2011, once explained the three key principles of Holy See diplomacy as follows: the first is *truth*, because "if you don't know truth you cannot build peace"; the second is *justice*, the concept of which "in the modern times . . . is a little bit lost"; and the third is *freedom*, "something that at the time was a surprise in the church itself." Of all freedoms, said Archbishop Sambi, "first is religious freedom and freedom of conscience."

The church's status as a diplomatic entity was questioned throughout history. Some of the church's own bishops dismissed it as a distraction from the Holy See's pastoral mission. The last major internal challenge to papal diplomacy came during Vatican II. Pope Paul VI answered it eloquently and effectively. In fact, he had already mounted a defense of diplomacy years before he became pope, in a 1951 speech made on the 250th birthday of the Pontifical Ecclesiastical Academy. Holy See diplomacy, he declared then, is "the art of creating and maintaining the international order, which is . . . the art of establishing human relationships, reasonable law between nations, and not through force or of inexorable contrast and balance of interests." Diplomatic engagement "is not exclusive to defend the interests of [a] nation, but instead [is] of mutual benefit, common interest and universal value."

On June 24, 1969, Paul VI further established the basis for the Holy See's diplomatic engagement with the world in his landmark apostolic letter *Sollicitudo Omnium Ecclesiarum:*

> It is true that the aims of Church and State are of a different order and both are perfect societies, equipped with their own means, and independent in their respective spheres of action, but it is also true that the one and the other act for the benefit of a common subject, man, called by God to eternal salvation and [offered] a place on earth to enable him, with the help of grace, to pursue a life of work, leading him to be in peaceful coexistence with others.

It follows that certain activities of Church and State are in a sense complementary, and that the good of the individual and the community of nations requires an open dialogue and a genuine understanding between the Church on the one hand and the States on the other hand, in order to establish, foster and strengthen relationships of mutual understanding, mutual coordination and cooperation, and to prevent or remedy any disagreements, in order to achieve the implementation of great human hopes, peace between nations, the domestic tranquility and progress of each country.

Well before the eighteenth century, the church proved capable of organizing its foreign relations and negotiating its way through the intrigues and rivalries of Europe's dynasties. Having no standing military to project or protect its interests, the church drew its strength from religious faith and moral suasion, both intangible but real. It relied on the premises noted earlier, which were taught in the academy and practiced by papal nuncios positioned around the civilized world. Napoleon Bonaparte would call these assets the pope's "lever of opinion"—a tool that could also be used, if needed, as a blunt instrument. "Deal with the Pope as if he had two hundred thousand men at his command," Napoleon instructed an aide in 1801, converting papal influence into military currency.

Not so prescient was Joseph Stalin, who once derisively dismissed the Vatican for its lack of firepower. "How many divisions has the Pope?" Of course, Stalin's regime is now long gone. So is Napoleon's. And the Catholic Church? It endures.

## III.

The diplomacy that has allowed the church to survive and often thrive is a function, by definition, of its compatibility with temporal governments, whether monarchies or democracies, whether Catholic or not. A concern in some quarters, as old and enduring as the church itself, is that the Vatican will overreach. During the mid-twentieth century, when John Kennedy explicitly disavowed papal influence during his run for the presidency, many Americans were convinced the church had designs on the United States. As I write this, I have before me a book published in the United States in 1949 entitled *The Vatican in World Politics*, in which author Avro Manhattan claims that the church was "feverishly engaged in a race for the ultimate spiritual conquest of the world," a Vatican plot "as indisputable and as inextricably a part of contemporary history as the rise of Hitler, the defeat of Japan, the existence of Communism."

It might have surprised the excitable Mr. Manhattan, along with countless others who have ascribed hegemonic aspirations to the Holy See, to learn that the church historically has been dedicated to preserving the distinction between church and state. In fact, the very idea of separation of powers is Christian in origin. "Render unto Caesar the things which are Caesar's," said Jesus, "and unto God the things that are God's." Canon law of the early Middle Ages made great strides in distinguishing between matters over which the state appropriately ruled and those best left in the hands the church.

Ideally, church and state worked together in a dynamic partnership of equals, each knowing its place and function. In practice, relations were a bit thornier through much of history, as a brief retrospective of church-state alliances will illustrate.

★ ★ ★

The story begins with the conversion of Roman emperor Constantine at the beginning of the fourth century. Constantine brought Christianity to the forefront and ended rounds of grisly persecutions and martyrdoms that had been Christians' lot since the time of Jesus. He also took an interest in church structure and dogma. It was Constantine who called for the council at Nicea in 325. Though acting in some ways as the church's leader, Constantine recognized that authority over spiritual matters belonged to the pope, Sylvester I, who was represented at Nicea by a legation from Rome. As it happened, this papal legation marked the debut of the diplomatic corps of the Holy See, which has been in business more or less uninterrupted ever since.

Even as he ruled from his new capital city in Byzantium, Constantinople (later Istanbul), Constantine built basilicas in Rome, including the original St. Peter's. These benefactions were not just charity; they were also strategy. "When they are free to render supreme service to the Divinity," Constantine said of clerics he supported, "it is evident that they confer great benefits upon the affairs of state." The church enjoyed the sanction and protection of Constantine; Constantine aligned himself with the moral legitimacy and powerful message of Christianity.

The Christian Church suffered from the onslaught of barbarian invasions when the Roman Empire collapsed in the fifth century. In the absence of emperors, who followed Constantine's example of ruling from Constantinople, popes dissuaded barbarians from sacking Rome, as Pope

Innocent I did in 408, when he met with marauding Visigoths at the city walls and convinced them—with the help of a tidy ransom—to end their siege. Pope Leo I (Leo the Great) did much the same in 452, when he talked Attila the Hun out of marching into Rome. This was survival diplomacy at its best, and a number of early popes were masters of it.

In 496, one of Europe's tribal chiefs, after conquering Gaul (France), converted to Christianity and allied himself with the church. The baptism of this man, King Clovis, marked the beginning of the Merovingian dynasty in France, ensured the survival of the Catholic Church in the Dark Ages, and inaugurated an extraordinary alliance between Rome and France that would last nearly fourteen centuries. In 754, another French ruler, the Carolingian King Pepin the Short—better known as the father of his tall son, Charlemagne—increased the power of the church by giving it parcels of conquered land in Italy. The Donation of Pepin added real estate to the church's domain—the papal states—and made the pope a temporal sovereign and spiritual leader, changing forever the nature of the papacy. In return, Pope Stephen II enhanced Pepin's authority by anointing him "King by the Grace of God."

But it was Charlemagne, at the end of the eighth century, who brought the two powers fully into the symbiosis that would define Western civilization for millennia to come. After fully embracing Christianity as the faith of his realm, Charlemagne had himself crowned under the title Holy Roman Emperor by Pope Leo III in St. Peter's on Christmas Day in 800. The round porphyry stone on which this event took place can still be seen, and walked over, in the floor near the main entrance of St. Peter's. "Western Christendom," the church historian Joseph McSorley wrote of Charlemagne's coronation, "was now composed of an empire and a church—*Regnum* and *Sacerdotium*—distinct from, yet complimentary to, each other."

Planted in that coronation, ironically, were the seeds of forthcoming conflict. If a king needed the blessing of a pope to be truly a king, then which of them had the greater power? Popes and kings would argue this question for centuries to come.

Pope Gregory VII, also known as Hildenbrand, gave his own unambiguous answer in *Dicatatus papae*, a brief he issued in 1075: supreme authority rested in *him*, the Holy Father. He was the ruler of rulers, with God as the only higher authority. Gregory's claim was tested by Henry IV, king of Germany and Holy Roman Emperor. The issue was investiture, the appointment of bishops and other clerics within the empire. Henry believed that he had the right to make such appointments; Gregory insisted the right belonged to the pope alone.

Investiture may seem a dry and arcane matter of church administration, but it was at the heart of many centuries' worth of disputes between popes and monarchs. Incredibly, arguments about investiture continue even today, notably in China. The Chinese government has ordained several Catholic bishops without obtaining the approval of the pope, contrary to church law. In response, the Vatican has threatened to excommunicate all participating clergy. (We will explore contemporary Chinese–Holy See relations in chapter 12.)

In investiture disputes, a crucial principle is at stake, one at the very heart of the relationship between the Holy See and other sovereign powers. By claiming the sole prerogative to make ecclesiastical appointments, the pope is essentially insisting on the separation of church and state. Once other sovereigns appoint bishops, those appointments become political: the bishops are beholden to the temporal ruler; they serve the state and its ephemeral needs before they serve the church and its timeless ideals, and the line between the two domains dissolves. One reason the church still has a resonant voice in the twenty-first century is its refusal to submit to that dissolution in centuries past.

No pope has ever personified the refusal to submit more completely than Gregory VII. An unimposing man in the flesh—short, stubby, and thin-voiced—Gregory's physical attributes belied an extraordinary will. When Holy Roman Emperor Henry IV had the temerity to name his own man as archbishop of Milan, Gregory gave him an ultimatum: either withdraw the appointment or face excommunication. The king lashed back: "Descend and relinquish the apostolic chair," he chided the pope. "Descend, descend to be damned throughout the ages." Gregory responded by excommunicating Henry. The king was given one year to mend his ways and apologize; after that, the excommunication would be permanent.

The pope's excommunication took a heavy toll on Henry. He quickly found his legitimacy undermined and his authority diminished. His own nobles turned from him, while his enemies circled and began planning for his successor. Henry realized he had no choice but to submit to Gregory. Thus commenced one of the most extraordinary acts of contrition in history, the so-called Walk to Canossa. Accompanied by his wife and infant son, Henry set out on an arduous trek from the German town of Speyer to a fortress in Canossa, Italy, where Gregory had repaired for the winter of 1077. Barefoot and clad in a penitent's hair shirt, Henry and his party crossed the snowy Alps in early January, nearly freezing to death along the way. They arrived at the hilltop fortress later in the month. For three days, the pope made the king stand in the snow outside the castle doors. Finally,

Gregory allowed Henry to enter, whereupon the king fell to the pope's feet and begged forgiveness. The pope reluctantly granted absolution and withdrew his excommunication.

The conflict did not end there. Henry still had to fight to secure his throne from eager enemies; and several years later, after the pope excommunicated him a *second* time, he laid siege to Rome and brought an end to Gregory's papal reign. But Gregory's stand had long-term consequences. Future popes would recall Canossa as a model for strong church leadership.

The tug-of-war between popes and kings never ceased. Kings had powerful armies to assert their will, but popes had the threat of excommunication and hell—and enough spiritual authority to inspire thousands of Europeans to risk their lives and homes on crusades to the Holy Land, as they occasionally did between the end of the eleventh century and the end of the thirteenth century. When push came to shove, kings settled matters by marching against popes, as King Philip IV of France did against Pope Boniface VIII in 1303. Incredibly, though, popes held their own, and sometimes better, against lay sovereigns in Europe for more than five hundred years.

When did the Holy See's temporal power first begin to erode? One unhappy milestone is the papal schism of the fourteenth century when, for nearly seventy years, Europe had two distinct and competing lines of popes, one in Rome and the other in Avignon, France. Two popes divisively claiming the authority of the papacy understandably diminished the office as a whole.

Shortly after the schism was resolved, a new crisis overtook the church in the form of the Reformation. The challenge mounted by Martin Luther and others in the sixteenth century was the first true existential threat to the papacy itself, for at root of the Reformation were plans to dispense with the pope. But it was not until the end of the Thirty Years' War of the seventeenth century, in which Protestants and Catholics battled to control Europe, that the church was finally forced to deal with the changed world in Europe. The treaty ending the war in 1648 increased the power of nation-states over the church, and likewise increased the power of Lutherans and other Protestants *within* those states, marking "nothing less than a complete revolution in the relations that had existed hitherto between Church and State," as stated by church historian Rev. James MacCaffrey. Popes would now be burdened by "the terrible responsibility of governing the Church during the one hundred and fifty years that elapsed between the Peace of Westphalia and the outbreak of the French Revolution."

When Pius VI inherited the papacy in 1774, the Enlightenment was in full swing, the French Revolution was on the horizon, and the church was beginning to live in a new world of religious pluralism. It would rise to the challenges.

IV.

As the Vatican struggled to adjust to its declining temporal status in Europe, clergy in the newly minted United States were organizing an American Catholicism that would reinvigorate the church in Rome. For the moment, the Vatican was too preoccupied with problems at hand to offer much support or guidance, which suited American Catholics perfectly.

The Revolution brought two significant changes to the lives of American Catholics. The first and most obvious was the freedom they now enjoyed to practice their faith in the open. Not every state in the union immediately embraced religious freedom. New Jersey and North Carolina, for example, still prohibited Catholics from holding public office. Only with the passage of the U.S. Constitution in 1787 did the federal government fully relinquish the power to promote or curtail a particular religious belief. But the standing of Catholics rose well before that.

The second change concerned the governance of American Catholic clergy. Prior to the Revolution, the Americans had been overseen by a Vicar-Apostolic—an English Bishop who ruled from London. That would no longer be acceptable, not to American Catholics and not to their Protestant compatriots. Nor would it be acceptable to have the Vatican administer the American Church from abroad. After a long and bloody war in which Americans fought to throw off the yoke of London, Catholics in the new nation would not now submit, or even appear to submit, to the yoke of Rome. Doing so would countermand the hard-won new principles of liberty and self-rule, and would reignite the old prejudices against Catholics and popery.

No one understood this better than John Carroll. Fr. Carroll quickly became the voice and de facto leader of American Catholics, as well as middleman and interpreter between the Vatican hierarchy and the United States. In the years after the Revolution, Carroll frequently expressed to the Vatican the need for American autonomy. He was always respectful in his communications with Rome, but his bitter experience during the suppression of the Jesuits must have made him especially wary of Vatican interference.

"You are not ignorant that in these United States our Religious system has undergone a revolution, if possible, more extraordinary than our political one," Carroll wrote to a friend in 1783, in a note accompanying a brief to Pope Pius VI. Catholics now enjoyed freedoms and rights as never before in America, but they were obliged to behave "as subjects zealously attached to our government and avoiding to give any jealousies on account of any dependence on foreign jurisdictions more than that which is essential to our religion." American Catholics would gladly acknowledge the pope's spiritual leadership over the Christian world, Carroll implied. Otherwise, the less Rome interfered, the better for all.

Rome did not initially embrace the concept of a semi-autonomous American Church, much less grasp the concept of "America." This strange new nation with its unnerving ideas about liberty and democracy presented a challenge to the Vatican. The church's concern was evident in its efforts to appoint somebody to lead the American Church.

In 1783, the papal nuncio to France—the same Doria Pamphili who had supposedly procured a copy of the Declaration of Independence for Pius VI—was instructed to consult with Benjamin Franklin regarding the wishes of Congress, as per normal Vatican diplomatic protocol. Given the lengths to which European nations continually went to control religion within their borders, the Vatican naturally assumed the U.S. government would expect to have a say in the matter.

Franklin took Pamphili's query to Congress. The response, dated May 11, 1784, is preserved in a folio in the archives of the Propaganda Fide section of the Vatican. Who knows how the Vatican came to possess a copy, but it must have delivered quite a shock when it arrived. "Resolved, that Doctor Franklin be desired to notify to the Apostolic Nuncio at Versailles, that Congress will always be pleased to testify their Respect to his Sovereign and State; but that the subject of his Application to Doctor Franklin being purely spiritual it is without the jurisdiction and powers of Congress who have no authority to permit or refuse it."

Franklin duly informed Pamphili that Congress was utterly indifferent and disinterested on the subject of clergy appointments. But when Pamphili solicited his suggestions for the leader for the church in America, Franklin was not above giving private advice. He insisted there was just one man for the job: his old friend Fr. John Carroll.

In the summer of 1784, Carroll was named "Superior of the Mission in the thirteen United States." Six years later, in 1789—the same year, coincidentally, that George Washington was elected as the first U.S. president—Carroll would be approved by Pope Pius VI as bishop of Baltimore, thereby becoming the first Catholic bishop in the United States. One of Bishop Carroll's first important acts was the creation of a new college, at Georgetown, near the banks of the Potomac River, to educate young American men who could join the priesthood and minister to the quickly growing Catholic flock in America.


## V.


Even as American Catholics found their footing under the guidance of John Carroll, the ground beneath the Roman Catholic Church was starting to tremble. The eighteenth century brought grave challenges to the papacy. Now, in 1789, the same year Carroll became bishop and Washington became president, a revolution in France threatened to topple it forever.

The French Revolution did not appear to be aggressively anti-Catholic in the first spring days of 1789. For all the damage done by the Enlightenment, France was still a Catholic country, as it had been since King Clovis ruled in the fifth century. The French clergy, honored as the First Estate, enjoyed high regard among most French citizens. Higher clergy, members of the *ancien regime*, were against the revolution from the start, since it threatened the privileges to which they had grown accustomed, but *curés*—the common parish priests—supported the revolution as an overdue corrective to the inequalities in French society. The cry of the revolutionaries—"Liberty! Equality! Fraternity!"—was a slogan they could initially embrace. Indeed, for many good French priests, the turn to republicanism, already thirteen years old in America, seemed late in coming.

Very quickly, though, French priests went from fanning the flames of revolution to getting caught in them. By the spring of 1790, France's revolutionary government appropriated church lands and wealth. This was partly a Gallican effort to nationalize the church and partly an effort to fill the coffers of a bankrupt government. That summer, the assembly tightened its control over the church, imposing a "Civil Constitution of the Clergy." Henceforth, by law, the French church would be entirely subject to the state. Clergy would be elected, rather than appointed, and paid wages, as if they were civil servants. As for investiture, the pope would no longer have any say in choosing clergy. He would be informed of appointments after the fact.

By the time the revolutionary government began demanding that French clergy swear an oath of loyalty to the Constitution, most *curés* had grown disenchanted with the revolution. Only a third swore the oath. Of the nonjuring clergy, many fled the country, while others were deported to French Guyana. Some remained in France to keep ministering, albeit covertly and at great risk to their freedom and lives. Prison, followed by execution, was often their fate.

As the new rules went into effect in France, the pope was caught between silent acquiescence and useless rebukes. He could say nothing and watch the French church slip from the fold of Roman Catholicism, or he could object strenuously and risk worse—total schism, annexation of papal lands in Avignon (which did occur later), or even the total suppression of Catholicism in France (which occurred in England in the sixteenth century). When the pope privately condemned the Constitution in a letter to Louis XVI—still three years from losing his head but already stripped of real power—the king tried to negotiate with the pope to save the French church. Under the circumstances, this was little more than a pathetic demonstration of how drastically both of their stations had fallen. The king and the pope could negotiate all they wanted, but the revolution made them irrelevant.

Louis XVI's demise in January 1793 only added more blood to destruction in France. The Catholic religion was condemned as a cult and driven underground in France. Churches and cathedrals were vandalized and shuttered, or they were converted, like Notre Dame in Paris, into "Temples of Reason." Those priests who remained were pressed to marry, in defiance of their vows. When an envoy was dispatched to the Vatican in the winter of 1793, his instructions made clear how little regard the secular government of France had left for the pope: "As the supreme head of a religion he has become a stranger to us. We no longer have a clergy. In the ministers of the various cults we recognize only citizens." Pius VI refused to meet the envoy.

★ ★ ★

The terror soon sputtered out in France, but the worst was yet to come for the pope. The final insult was delivered by the little general from Corsica, Napoleon Bonaparte, just launching a military career that would soon make him the dictator of France and the conqueror of Europe. In 1796, Bonaparte invaded Milan, from which he announced his intention to advance south and take Rome. In exchange for not invading, he demanded a huge ransom from the pope, including cash and hundreds of rare manuscripts and paintings from the Vatican's collections. Of course, this was not the first time the Vatican had been plundered—Charles V had done much the same as Napoleon back in 1527—but for sheer hubris and greed Napoleon had few equals.

In February 1798, while Napoleon was away preparing his invasion of Egypt, the French army entered Rome and declared a new Roman Republic, this one without a pope. Pius VI, now eighty years old and critically ill, was put into a carriage to be exiled from the city forever. When the pope begged to die in Rome, the French commander only scoffed. "A man can die anywhere." Anywhere turned out to be a military citadel in Valence, France, where Pius VI, after being hauled roughly across the Alps, spent his last days in captivity. When he passed away in August 1799, the French refused to give him a Catholic burial.

Some prognosticators saw the end of the papacy in the undignified death of Pius VI: that he might be the last pope to ever serve. This turned out not to be the case. Understandably, though, it would be a very long time before anyone inside the Vatican was able to look at what France had done to the Catholic religion and not suspect that the real meaning of the phrase "liberty, equality, and fraternity" was "atheism, chaos, and brutality."

## 3

# RETURN TO ROME

Does he imagine that his excommunication will make the weapons fall from the hands of my soldiers?

—Napoleon Bonaparte

I.

The eighteenth century, to paraphrase Charles Dickens, had been the best of times and the worst of times. The era inspired great leaps of human thought and aspiration, but also disrupted a system of spiritual faith and moral values that sustained people for millennia. It gave life to a revolution in America that resulted in the first true democratic republic in the world, but it also spawned a revolution in France that wreaked violence and injustice throughout Europe. Across its stage strode a great general, George Washington, who led America to victory over the British then served the nation as its first democratically elected president. But it also marked the debut of another remarkable general, Napoleon Bonaparte, who tried and failed to conquer the world.

It's one of those interesting quirks of history that the last month of the last year of the century—December 1799—saw the convergence of several milestones, almost as if the century intended to go out with a bang. On December 12, Napoleon Bonaparte, just thirty years old, assumed the title of First Consul and became virtual dictator of France. Two days later, on December 14, George Washington, at sixty-seven, passed away at Mount Vernon and sent the United States into mourning. Meanwhile, at a Benedictine monastery on an island near Venice, the conclave of Roman Catholic cardinals met to elect a new pope. The outcome of their deliberations would not be certain for several more months, but one thing was already clear: the last pope, Pius VI, would not be the *last pope* after all.

Many striking changes accompanied the turn from the eighteenth century into the nineteenth century, as the age of revolution lurched into the age of Napoleon, but perhaps the most surprising was the shift in the fortunes of papacy. Popes were hardly in for smooth sailing in years to come—quite the contrary—but the dawn of the new century brought a resurgence in the power and moral authority of the church that nobody would have predicted a decade earlier. The modern Holy See was born in the dying days of the French Revolution.

One of Napoleon's first official acts in those final days of 1799 was to order funeral honors for Pius VI, who still lay unburied in a sealed coffin in Valence. Having dragged the pope to his death—or at least made the final earthly journey as unpleasant as possible—the French, under Napoleon, now seemed to have a change of heart.

Another indication of Napoleon's new attitude toward the church came six months later, in June 1800. By this point, the new pope, a former Benedictine monk who took the name Pius VII, had been crowned and had taken up residence in Rome. Three hundred miles to the northwest, in a cathedral in Milan, Napoleon delivered a speech to local clergy:

> I wished to see you all gathered here that I might have the satisfaction of disclosing in my own person the feelings which I entertain for the Catholic Apostolic Roman religion. I am convinced that this religion is the only one that can bring true happiness to a well-ordered community, and lay firm the foundations of government. I assure you that I shall strive to guard and defend it at all times, and by all means.

Napoleon had maligned Catholicism in the past, but apparently no longer. "France has had her eyes opened through suffering and has seen that the Catholic religion is her single anchor amid the storm."

Napoleon's sentiments echoed a theme George Washington raised in his Farewell Address of 1796. "Of all the dispositions and habits which lead to political prosperity, religion and morality are indispensable supports," Washington wrote. "The mere politician, equally with the pious man, ought to respect and to cherish them."

In the case of France, the people, not the politicians, first grasped how indispensable religion was to a country that had been Roman Catholic since the days of Clovis. Whatever his own spiritual beliefs (his most constant object of worship seemed to be himself), Napoleon recognized that Catholic piety was already reawakening across France, and that most of his countrymen were eager to return to the old faith. Facing a populace weary of years of revolution and chaos, Napoleon realized he needed the church. "My political method," Napoleon once said on the subject of religion, "is to govern men as a majority of them want to be governed."

Napoleon not only wanted to restore the Catholic faith; he wanted the new pope to *help* him restore it. The French clergy who survived the revolution were bitterly divided between those who had signed the Constitution and those who had refused. The only person who could reconcile these two groups, Napoleon understood, was the pope. "Go to Rome," he told an emissary, "and tell the Holy Father that the First Consul wishes to make him a gift of thirty million Frenchmen."

Realizing that Napoleon, a man of extraordinary political acumen on one hand and intolerance for rivals on the other, was willing to deal with the pope says a great deal about his estimation of the importance of Catholicism. "There has seldom been a more convincing tribute to the underlying strength of the Church," wrote E. E. Y. Hales in his highly regarded history of Catholicism.

Over the next months, representatives of Napoleon and Pius VII worked on a concordat, setting the terms of Catholicism's restoration in France. The concordat had to overcome the objections of both French Jacobins, who could not bear the return of Catholicism to France, and conservative cardinals, who could not abide making peace with a government that deeply harmed the church. Napoleon pressured the pope's secretary of state, Ercole Consalvi, to accept his conditions by threatening to break off from the Catholic Church completely. "If Henry VIII, who had not a twentieth part of my power, could successfully change the religion of his country, surely I can do the same." After a meeting lasting twenty consecutive hours, the two sides managed to draft an agreement, only to have Napoleon throw it into the fire in a fit of pique. Finally, an understanding was reached. The concordat was signed on July 15, 1801.

No sooner was this accomplished, however, than Napoleon had second thoughts. He began unilaterally to amend the concordat, attaching seventy-seven "organic articles" to the original document, most of which severely abridged the pope's authority and left no doubt who controlled the church in France.

Pius VII was an exceptionally thoughtful, good-hearted, and open-minded man. He read the works of John Locke and Diderot's *Encyclopedia* when most of his fellow clergy did not dare to wade into the perilous waters of the Enlightenment. He shocked some of his more reactionary colleagues in 1797 when, as bishop of Bologna, he announced that democratic forms of government were not necessarily incompatible with the Catholic religion—the first and last time, for a very long while, that any church official, much less a future pope, would suggest as much. He was a man, in other words, who believed in reasoned compromise. This was a belief Napoleon would severely test.

For the moment, Pius reluctantly accepted the First Consul's conditions. He made a tactical decision that restoring the church in France was more important than asserting his authority over it. Moreover, the French, perhaps unwittingly, actually granted important new authority to the pope. In resolving the issue of the divided French clergy, the concordat called for the pope to dismiss *all* bishops and start with a clean slate. The First Consul would choose the new episcopate, but the appointments would not be valid until approved—*invested*—by the pope, who would also have the right to depose them. In other words, the concordat affirmed the principle, never before conceded by the French government, that the pope was the ultimate authority over ecclesiastical appointments. This would have the important long-term consequence of centralizing, once again, church authority in the person of the pope.

The publication of the concordat was celebrated in Notre Dame on Easter Sunday, 1802. Napoleon and his retinue poured into the cathedral for mass, and the bells of Notre Dame rang over Paris for the first time in a decade.

## II.

Pius VII himself entered Notre Dame several years later, on December 2, 1804. Accompanied by six cardinals, ten bishops, and a hundred horses, the pope traveled to Paris to preside over the coronation of Napoleon. Not content with the title of First Consul, Napoleon had decided to make himself emperor, a more fitting position for a man who intended to rule the world. To give the new title its full legitimacy, he summoned the pope to administer his crowning, as Pope Leo III had done for Charlemagne a thousand years earlier. Pius VII, despite his misgivings about Napoleon, agreed to attend, perhaps sensing that he, like Leo, would gain something in the bargain. Making the same calculation that led him to accept Napoleon's altered concordat, the pope targeted a long-term opportunity for the Holy See's diplomatic engagement with France, even if it risked a short-term perception of weakness.

Napoleon made sure to put the pope in his place at Notre Dame. He arrived an hour late, then set the crown upon his own head as the pope watched. But Pius VII had already won a moral victory over the emperor since arriving in Paris. Having learned upon his arrival in Paris that Napoleon and his wife Josephine were married in a civil ceremony, he issued an ultimatum: they would submit to the wedding rites of the church or he would refuse to attend the coronation. Napoleon had conceded; he and Josephine had been privately married by a priest in the Tuileries the previous afternoon.

Much like the crowing of Charlemagne, the coronation did as much to elevate the pope as it did to legitimize the emperor. Pius VII's presence in Paris raised his profile and prestige. The French flocked to him, and Napoleon later came to regret it. "Nobody thought of the Pope when he was in Rome," he complained. "My coronation and his appearance in Paris made him important."

Over the next ten years, as he warred with much of Europe, the emperor seemed intent on making the pope pay for the impertinence of upstaging him at his own coronation. A prime opportunity came in 1806. Napoleon demanded that Pius VII show his fealty by supporting a blockade against France's enemies and closing papal ports to English and Russian shipping. Pius VII refused; supporting a blockade would contradict the neutrality of the papacy and would make him party to war that was not his to fight. Napoleon responded furiously—and vengefully—by moving his troops into Rome and seizing the papal states in central Italy. "Your Holiness is the sovereign of Rome," he reminded the pope, "but I am its Emperor; all my enemies ought to be yours."

Pius VII's patience was finally strained to the limit; he issued a general excommunication against enemies of the Holy See, including Napoleon (not by name but by description). The pope had to know that he would pay a price for this, and he did. French soldiers broke into the Quirinal Palace in the early hours of July 6, 1809, abducted the pope and his secretary, and whisked them away before dawn. Now, like Pius VI before him, Pius VII became a prisoner of the French. He was placed under house arrest in a palace on the Italian coast.

The pope bore his captivity stoically. He prayed constantly, read, washed and mended his own clothing, cut his own hair, and spent much of his time in solitude, much like the young Benedictine he had once been. Cut off from Rome, he had little power. But he did ably deploy the one bit of leverage that remained to him. He refused to approve any of the bishops that Napoleon nominated for the French church. When Napoleon tried to invest the bishops himself, the nominees refused to serve. For all the discord among the clergy within the French church after the Revolution, on this at least they agreed: they were not bishops until they received blessing of the pope.

Napoleon ordered that Pius VII be transferred to him at Fontainebleau. He intended to talk sense into the "imbecile old man," as he had taken to calling the pope, and put an end to this insubordination. At midnight on June 9, 1812, the pope was removed from the palace on the coast of Italy that served as his prison. The operation was undertaken with great stealth, the wheels of the pope's carriage covered in cloth to muffle their sound in the night. Like his predecessor, Pius VII was now subjected to a grueling journey over the Alps. He became gravely ill en route and came so close to death that he was given last sacraments by a fellow priest.

Pius survived the journey, arrived in Fontainebleau in shattered health, and then proceeded to wait for Napoleon—for six months—while the emperor waged war in Russia. It's doubtful that Pius VII spent this time praying for the emperor's military victory, as Pope Leo III had done for Charlemagne a thousand years earlier. That December, Napoleon suffered one of the worst military defeats in history, returning home to France with merely ten thousand of the four hundred thousand men he took to Moscow. There were mutterings among French clergy that the emperor's defeat was the judgment of God.

The loss in Russia taught Napoleon nothing about hubris or vanity. Returning to Fontainebleau on January 18, 1813, he attempted to bully Pius VII into signing a new concordat, the terms of which were far less favorable to the Holy See than the concordat of 1801. The pope resisted, but his bargaining position was weak. A prisoner in France, suffering poor health, cut off from friends and confidants, and unaware that Napoleon's own position was crumbling, Pius succumbed and signed a draft agreement. One of the stipulations was to move the seat of the papacy from Rome to France. The agreement also required the pope to surrender the papal states, relinquishing the temporal sovereignty that the Holy See had exercised since the rule of Pepin the Short in the eighth century.

Almost immediately after signing, Pius recovered his strength and wits, and renounced the Concordat of Fontainebleau. Napoleon insisted it was binding, even in draft form. How this dispute was ultimately resolved is unclear, but soon it was swept away by larger currents of history. Napoleon's loss in Russia, followed by another defeat in Leipzig in October 1813, had shattered his invincibility. His enemies were closing in, and he had no more will to fight the pope. He tore up the concordat in January 1814 and sent the pope back to Italy. Pius's captivity was over.

By the time Pius VII returned to Rome on May 24, 1814, Napoleon was out of power, soon to be exiled to Elba. All of Rome greeted the long lost pope when he arrived at the city gates. Children waved palm fronds along the way as thirty young men from Rome's noble families pulled Pius's unhitched carriage through the city to St. Peter's, where Pius VII, after six years absent, resumed his throne. The pope would have to flee once more, when Napoleon escaped from Elba and reemerged as the emperor of France in the spring of 1815, but this coda—the 100 Days, as it's known—was short lived, and soon the pope was back in Rome in the Quirinal Palace.

As Europe's rulers met in Vienna to redraw Europe in the aftermath of Napoleon, Pope Pius VII focused on rebuilding a Catholic Church badly damaged by a quarter century of continuous revolution and war. Despite illness and frailty, the pope showed great moral fortitude, standing up to Napoleon as other monarchs fell by the wayside. The papacy survived.

## III.

One of Pius VII's first acts to restore the church after the Revolution and Napoleon was as symbolically potent as it was practical: he lifted the ban on the Society of Jesus. After forty years in exile, the Jesuits were back in business.

John Carroll's reaction to the reinstatement of the Jesuits is undocumented, but it must have been emotional. These were exuberant days for Catholics, and they must have been especially gratifying for Bishop Carroll, who turned eighty at the start of 1815, the final year of his life.

Carroll and his countrymen were far removed from the Napoleonic Wars, but they were not unaffected. The War of 1812, indirectly prompted by England's blockade against Napoleon's France—a response to Napoleon's own blockade against England—was one notable sideshow of the European drama. Carroll himself witnessed the British bombing of Baltimore in the late summer of 1814.

Carroll also had one odd but not insignificant brush with the Bonaparte family during Napoleon's reign. This came in 1803 when the bishop presided over the wedding of a seventeen-year-old Maryland belle, Elizabeth Patterson, to her twenty-two-year-old sweetheart, a French naval captain named Jerome Bonaparte—Napoleon's youngest brother. Carroll can hardly be blamed for the wedding, held in Baltimore Cathedral on Christmas Eve 1803, but it later became a matter of contention between Napoleon and Pope Pius VII. Disgusted by his brother's youthful folly, Napoleon demanded that the pope annul the marriage. Pius's refusal added to the score the emperor later tried to settle by imprisoning him.

When not attending to weddings and other pastoral duties, Carroll spent his time overseeing the expanding American Church, which now included, in addition to Baltimore, diocese in New York, Boston, Philadelphia, and Louisville, Kentucky (where a number of Maryland Catholics migrated). His view of the American Church had evolved. Immediately after the American Revolution, Carroll favored a distinctly indigenous church, unencumbered by Rome's interference. Later, as a bishop, he steered the church in a more conservative and recognizably Roman direction. He remained a strong advocate of the separation of church and state, and of religious pluralism—both inherent American values—but sought to organize and centralize the American hierarchy and, increasingly, to echo the European model of Catholicism.

The shift in Carroll's attitude reflected a conservative trend throughout Western society after the "anarchy and insurrection" (in Carroll's words) of the French Revolution. The American Catholic Church experienced a large influx of European clergy, particularly French, in the late eighteenth and early nineteenth century. Many of these priests were refugees of the French Revolution with a different experience of liberty and Catholicism than the native-born priests. Inevitably, their preference for tradition and order was absorbed into American Catholicism.

John Carroll died in Baltimore on December 3, 1815, as the papacy was being reborn in Rome. He left behind an American Church strong enough to stand on its own, yet leaning increasingly toward the Vatican, drawn by renewed papal gravity. It was still a small church—just 2 percent of the population—but within just a few decades, the American Catholic experience would change into something that John Carroll could hardly have anticipated. He would have been pleased by the remarkable growth of the Catholic population in the United States. But he would have been shocked by the new wave of anti-Catholicism that swept across the country after his death.

★ ★ ★

John Carroll's cousin, Charles Carroll, outlasted the bishop by another eighteen years. Following the simultaneous deaths of John Adams and

Thomas Jefferson on July 4, 1826, Charles Carroll, at eighty-eight, became the last surviving signer of the Declaration of Independence.

Charles Carroll was still robust six years later, in 1831, when the French traveler Alexis de Tocqueville visited him. De Tocqueville was delighted to meet this living, breathing relic of American history, and found Charles Carroll to be a man of intelligence and culture. His feelings for Carroll might well have influenced the long passage Tocqueville later included in his classic, *Democracy in America*, in which he described American Catholics as "fervent and zealous in the belief of their doctrines" and yet "the most republican and the most democratic class in the United States."

De Tocqueville's assessment notwithstanding, anti-Catholicism was already sweeping through the country by the time Charles Carroll died, at ninety-five, on November 14, 1832. Catholic immigrants started arriving in large numbers from Ireland and Germany. To nativists, these immigrants seemed alien and menacing, soldiers on the front lines of an obedient papal army that intended to conquer America. Such sentiments were fanned by groups like the American Tract Society, founded 1825, which published anti-Catholic pamphlets. Several popular and scurrilous books published in the 1830s, including *Six Months in a Convent* and *Awful Disclosures of the Hotel Dieu Nunnery of Montreal*, added fuel to the fire.

More damaging than the pamphlets or the books were the preachers who spewed anti-Catholic rhetoric. Perhaps the most famous—and egregious—of these was Lyman Beecher, a fiery New England Calvinist who moved his family to Cincinnati, Ohio, in 1832, the same year Charles Carroll passed away in Maryland. Beecher was already well known by the time he moved west. Several of his children would eventually become even more famous than he, including Lyman's daughter, Harriet Beecher Stowe, future author of *Uncle Tom's Cabin*.

Beecher's move to Cincinnati was prompted by his belief that the "moral destiny" of the nation would be decided in the west. At the time, "west" meant primarily the Ohio Valley, where both natives and immigrants, including some Catholics, were starting to settle. The future of America must be saved from "Catholics and infidels," preached Beecher. His twenty-one-year-old son, Henry Ward Beecher, who later became famous—then infamous—as a Brooklyn minister, warned in a Cincinnati newspaper that the pope was *intentionally* sending Catholics to America to extend his power. The younger Beecher admonished native-born Protestants to "arouse themselves and shake off the drowsy stupor that has long blinded their eyes to the fact that Catholics are assuming a stand prejudicial to the liberties of *our* country."

The general theme of these attacks from the Beechers and others was that Catholicism and America were incompatible. As De Tocqueville had understood, this view was completely unfounded but it gained traction in nineteenth century America, and it became even more entrenched as numerous Catholic immigrants poured into the country from Europe. Ironically, the more Catholic that America became, the greater the distance between its shores and the Holy See.

## II

# THE MODERN WORLD

# 4

# PIO NONO AND THE
# TURNING POINT

If, with Shakespeare, we were to choose for our title the suffering tragic hero . . . then the middle of the century would
be called the age of Pio Nono.

—E. E. Y. Hales

## I.

The man known to the world as Pio Nono arrived in Rome in the late
spring of 1846 on a current of optimism. Since the death of Pius VII in
1823, the papacy had been filled by popes who ruled the church and its terrestrial domains with iron-fisted orthodoxy. Each of these popes (Leo XII,
Pius VIII, and Gregory XVI) had lived through the terrible years of French
Revolution and the indignities of Napoleon. As a result, their reflexive
response was to reject anything even hinting of liberality or reform. The
last of these, Gregory XVI, despised newness so intensely that he banned
railroads in the papal states. By the time Gregory died in 1846, the College
of Cardinals was ready for a change. The Conclave chose Gregory's successor after just two days of deliberations.

The new pope's given name was Giovanni Mastai-Ferretti. For his
papal appellation he took the name Pius IX, in honor of Pius VII, the
pope held captive by Napoleon. In Italian, Pius IX translated as *Pio Nono*.
The Italian version resonated so well that the rest of the world soon adopted it.

Pius IX was neither as brilliant nor as erudite as some of his predecessors, but he was widely admired for his industry, charity, good humor, and,

most notably, his moderately liberal views. He was also, at fifty-four, a relative youngster among popes when he assumed the throne of St. Peter. An infant during the height of the French Revolution, he had not been seared by the fires of Paris. He seemed just the man to move the church beyond the difficulties of the past and find an accommodation with the fast-changing political and economic landscape of mid-nineteenth century Europe.

The first months of Pius IX's reign were exuberant and hopeful. In contrast to the reserved and severe pontiffs of recent years, Pius was a natural *bon vivant* who hosted garden parties, loved to laugh, enjoyed an occasional pinch of snuff and conversing with women. His humanity only added to his esteem among the Italians. He was a pope, yes, but he was also a man: a man of the world, a man of the people.

Pius IX immediately undertook a number of reforms to modernize the papacy. Mainly, these reforms pertained to the governance of the papal states. The papal states were the terrestrial patrimony held by popes since the donation of Pepin in the eighth century. By the mid-nineteenth century they included about sixteen thousand square miles of land, a sizable portion of central Italy covering Romagna, Marche, Umbria, and Lazio. The city of Rome, too, remained under the rule of the papacy, as it had been, with occasional interruptions, for centuries. These combined territories made the pope a temporal sovereign as well as a spiritual leader.

This duality was the problem with the papal states. Popes had tended not to be very good temporal rulers. Poor administration and draconian laws combined to produce resentment and poverty in the papal states which, in turn, undermined the position of the church as a paragon of spiritually and charity. Pius IX seemed determined to change this. He introduced a constitutional framework that allowed lay people greater representation in local politics. He granted amnesty to more than a thousand political prisoners. He relaxed restrictions on the press and ended some obnoxious burdens imposed on Roman Jews by previous popes, such as exclusion to walled ghettoes and required attendance at weekly Christian sermons. He brought gas lighting to the streets of Rome, welcomed modern ideas in education and agriculture, and allowed construction of the railroads Pope Gregory XVI had so despised.

Not everyone approved of the pope's reforms. Among Pius IX's most vocal detractors was Prince Metternich, the archconservative foreign minister of the Austrian Empire and architect of post–Napoleon Europe, who dismissed the pope as "warm of heart and weak of intellect." To Metternich, a liberal pope was an oxymoron destined to fall upon his own contradictions. For the moment, though, the popular reaction remained mostly adulatory, not only in Italy but in all of Europe. Pius IX was praised as a hero of reform at a moment when social and economic revolutions were occurring throughout the world.


## II.

The United States was not immune to the excitement surrounding the new pope. Given their own positive experience with democracy and independence, Americans generally supported the pope's transformations and his apparent embrace of liberal ideals. Pius IX's greatest fans included prominent American Protestants whose ancestors had despised all things "papist" or "Romish." Charles Edwards Lester, author and ordained Presbyterian minister—and grandson of Calvinist preacher John Edwards—declared Pius "the man Heaven seemed to have chosen to lead the human race out of the house of bondage." *New York Tribune* correspondent Margaret Fuller wrote from Rome to herald the new pope as "a man of noble and good aspect, who . . . has set his heart on doing something solid for the benefit of Man," while her celebrated editor, Horace Greeley, joined thousands of New Yorkers at the Broadway Tabernacle to pay tribute to the pope's "enlightened policy and liberal measures." A laudatory letter from Secretary of State (and future President) James Buchanan was read aloud at the Tabernacle, along with letters from former president Martin Van Buren and other dignitaries.

In the midst of all this good feeling, Secretary Buchanan received a letter from Nicholas Brown, the American consul to Rome. The letter was dated June 1, 1847:

> You may recollect that some time since I informed you that on several occasions persons holding high official stations in the Papal Govt. had expressed to me a desire that diplomatic relations might be established between the U. States & the Papal Govt., on a footing similar to those which exist between the Papal States & countries where the Romish Religion is not the prevalent sect.

This was not the first time relations between the United States and the Holy See had been discussed. Indeed, America had intermittently employed consuls to the pope since 1797. These men worked essentially as freelance business agents, overseeing minor American trade with the papal states. Now, after reading Brown's letter, Secretary Buchanan approached President James K. Polk with a proposal to formalize relations with the papal states and send a *chargé d'affaires* to the Holy See. The *chargé* would not have the status of a full-fledged ambassador, but he would be a *de jure* representative of the U.S. government, a big step up from a mere consul. President Polk approved the idea. On December 7, 1847, in his third annual message, he informed Congress that "interesting political events" in the papal states, as well as "a just regard to our commercial interests," made an appointment of a *chargé d'affaires* to the Holy See "highly expedient."

Inevitably, perhaps, the debate in Congress over funding a legation to the papal states became mired in anti-Catholic rhetoric. Leading the opposition was Rep. Lewis E. Levin, a "Know Nothing" from Pennsylvania who made a career of dividing Protestants and Catholics. On March 8, 1848, in the House of Representatives Levin gave a long speech attacking the Catholic Church with insinuation and innuendo. His point seemed to be that placing a legation in Rome would aid the church's supposed scheme to seize control of the United States by sending hordes of Irish Catholics to U.S. shores. Although the U.S. Constitution might stand in the way of Catholics establishing a theocracy on the federal level, Levin warned that nothing prevented individual states from succumbing, one by one, to the Catholic conspiracy. "This, sir, in itself explains the secret of this extraordinary flood of Roman Catholic population now pouring into our country." As for who was behind the plot, Levin blamed dark forces in the Catholic hierarchy, especially the Jesuits.

Another representative from Pennsylvania, C. J. Ingersoll, rose to scold Levin. He suggested that his fellow congressman accompany him across town to Georgetown College and dine with some actual Jesuits, whom he might discover to be good, patriotic, and freedom-loving men. Levin thanked Ingersoll for the invitation but declined. He was suffering from dyspepsia, he announced on the House floor. "Suppose I should go and should be seized with one of those unfortunate attacks of cramp and should die; nothing would satisfy my constituents that I had not been poisoned by Jesuits."

In the end, Ingersoll and others won the argument with an appeal to common sense and American ideals. The legation would cost taxpayers a mere $9,000 and would reward them with a small but potentially lucrative trade with the papal states in cotton, sugar, and tobacco. Not incidentally, the American presence would be fortuitous at a time when the pope was introducing reforms. As another Pennsylvania congressman, Rep. Brown, put it that day, "Did not the American heart beat in unison with that of Pope Pius in his efforts for the amelioration of the condition of the Italians?" The American heart apparently did: an amendment to strike the papal legation from an appropriations bill was easily defeated, 137–15 in the House, 36–7 in the Senate. Funding was approved.

Secretary Buchanan nominated Jacob L. Martin to fill the post. Though not well known today, Jacob Martin was a man of considerable reputation and influence in mid-nineteenth-century America. He served in numerous capacities in the State Department. For two days in 1841 he even filled in as interim secretary of state. A Catholic convert from North Carolina, Martin spent much of his adult life abroad, including the previous four years with the American legation in Paris. In addition to his work as a diplomat, Martin had earned minor literary fame. An 1871 anthology entitled *Choice Specimens of American Literature* includes his poem, "The Church of Santa Croce, Florence."

> Tomb of the mighty dead, illustrious shrine
> When genius, in the majesty of death,
> Reposes solemn, sepulchred beneath

And so on—a gloomy poem which unfortunately set the stage for what happened to Jacob Martin when he arrived in Rome the following August. For the moment, though, in that still hopeful April 1848, no hint of ill fortune was apparent. Expecting only success, Secretary Buchanan sent Martin his official instruction. Buchanan made clear that the mission to the Holy See was limited in scope, as dictated by the U.S. Constitution:

> There is one consideration which you ought always to keep in view in your intercourse with the Papal authorities. Most if not all the Governments which have Diplomatic Representatives at Rome are connected with the Pope as the head of the Catholic Church. In this respect the Government of the United States occupies an entirely different position. It possesses no power whatever over the question of religion.

Martin's assignment would be to pursue good relations and economic opportunities for the United States, not to interfere in the internal affairs of the papal states. Nonetheless, the *chargé* was expected to let the pope understand where the United States stood. As Secretary Buchanan wrote to Martin, "the American people can never be indifferent to the cause of constitutional freedom and liberal reform in any portion of the world."

Martin responded from Paris on May 1, 1848. He would indeed avoid religious issues and direct interference, he assured the secretary of state, while informing the pope of the "moral sympathies" of Americans. "I am fully aware of the interest which is felt by the President and the People of the United States, in the efforts of the present Pope to introduce wise and judicious reforms in the country over which Providence has called him to rule." Martin shared with Buchanan his own high hopes for Pius IX, who appeared "resolved to invigorate that ancient establishment with the animating principle of liberty."

III.

Even as Jacob Martin was writing to Secretary Buchanan, the Pope's popularity in Italy was diminishing rapidly, along with the perception that Pius IX was committed to the principle of liberty. By the time Martin arrived in Rome to assume his duties three months later, the hero of 1847 was the villain of 1848. The sudden shift in the pope's fortunes and intentions must rank as one of the quickest turnabouts in modern world politics.

Pius IX was caught up in the historical currents which converged into a political tsunami that swept across much of the world in 1848. In France, the king abdicated and the streets of Paris filled with protests, a flashback to 1789. Revolutions simultaneously broke out in Budapest and Warsaw, over much of Austria (where the conservative Metternich was driven out of power), and in large parts of Germany. Meanwhile, that same fateful year, a young German named Karl Marx published *The Communist Manifesto*, a book inspiring further revolutions for more than a century to come.

Among the loudest stirrings of 1848 were those heard in Italy, where the *Risorgimento*—the resurgence—exploded in a series of revolts and riots. The goals of the *Risorgimento* movement, under the leadership of Giuseppe Mazzini and Giuseppe Garibaldi, were Italian nationalism and democratic reform. Achieving these meant, first, kicking the Austrians out of northern Italy, where they ruled for fifty years, and, second, unifying the dozens of independent Italian states under a single republican government.

Metternich's warning about liberal popes now came due. Because Pius had allowed himself to be cast as a reformer, the Italian revolutionaries naturally assumed that he was in sympathy with their goals. They expected him to cheer the unification movement and throw his weight into the fight against Austria, ignoring the fact that Pius had done little to support these expectations. Simply by *appearing* sympathetic he raised the hopes of reformers.

The truth was that the pope, a monarch who ruled over much of central Italy, could not possibly back a movement that was antimonarchist and aimed to unify the country. Doing so would require him to give up the papal states. Not only would this be a betrayal of the church patrimony handed down to him, but it would strip him of his temporal sovereignty, which he believed to be critical to his spiritual sovereignty. Nor was he willing to support a war against Austria, a Catholic country long allied with the Holy See. Pius IX might have been willing to tweak the status quo, but he had no interest in overthrowing it.

Realizing he had been misunderstood, Pius now made his position clear. On April 29, 1848, he issued an *allocation* declaring his opposition to the unification of Italy and the expulsion of Austria. The response to this was instant outrage, as revolution-minded Italians turned on the pope with fury.

The unfortunate Jacob Martin arrived on August 2, 1848, during a wave of "canicular heat," to find the city in "the greatest agitation, and threatened with riot if not revolution." The pope was too occupied to see Martin at once, so the American found lodging on the ground floor of a residence near the Pincian Hill and waited. Martin's audience with the pope finally came on Saturday, August 19. Pius IX was "cordial in a high degree" and very pleased that the United States had agreed to diplomatic relations. The pope took Martin's hand and escorted him around one of the Vatican's vast marble-floored salons, speaking first in French and then Italian, the pope expressing delight at the American's presence, Martin expressing admiration for the pope's "wise and liberal" policies.

The following day, Martin wrote a long letter to Secretary Buchanan. Noting the "imprudent attacks upon the character and office of Pius IX," he suggested that Italian revolutionaries were recklessly overreaching. "Young liberty should not exhaust her efforts against this rock of ages," wrote Martin. "She should conciliate what is an immense if not irresistible moral power. The alliance of freedom and religion were wiser than their conflict." Martin did not seem hopeful that such an alliance would be formed anytime soon. Nor would there be much opportunity to pursue American interests in the papal states at a moment when Rome was "intent now only upon questions affecting its very existence."

★ ★ ★

The heat and chaos of Rome soon took their toll on Martin. Within days of meeting the pope he came down with a serious illness, probably malaria. On the morning of August 26, exactly a week after composing his letter to Secretary Buchanan, Jacob Martin died. The secretary of the legation, who visited him just before he collapsed, attributed his death to "bad air" and "Roman fever."

Untimely death saved Martin from witnessing what followed in the months and years ahead, events that would have been profoundly disillusioning to him. Relations between the pope and the liberals continued to deteriorate as summer turned to fall. The breaking point came one November evening a few months after Martin's death. Pius IX's chief minister, Count Pellegrino Rossi, had just stepped out of a carriage in front of the *Cancelleria*—the Council Chamber of the Holy See—when he was surrounded by a gauntlet of revolutionaries. A man lunged forward with a knife and stabbed Rossi to death. The following day, a violent crowd descended on the Quirinal Palace. Gunfire rang out; one of the pope's prelates was shot through a window.

The city had become too dangerous for the pope. A week later, on November 24, 1848, in a carefully plotted escape involving his valet and several foreign ambassadors, Pius IX disguised himself as an ordinary priest and slipped out of the palace through a secret passage. He fled by carriage over the Alban hills, leaving the city in the hands of a revolutionary government. He took refuge in a castle in Gaeta, a Mediterranean town seventy-five miles southeast of Rome.

Pius's exile was short lived. Like many a pope before him, he prevailed upon friends for aid. In this case, the French responded and won Rome back. Returning to the Quirinal palace in the spring of 1850, Pius was much changed from the youthful man crowned four years earlier. Any liberal sentiments he had once indulged were now extinguished. Never again would he entertain such ideas as republicanism, nationalism, or progress.

## IV.

Italian issues dominated his long reign, but Pius IX found time and energy to devote to other church matters. In the ecclesiastical realm, he opened more dioceses than any pope in history. He also pursued a very active diplomacy, signing new concordats with Russia, Spain, Austria, and several Latin American republics, while hosting ambassadors from nations around the world.

The United States, too, commanded his attention. Just as Pius IX was the first pope to receive official diplomatic recognition from the United States, he was likewise the first pope to take a serious interest in the young nation. In part, this was a simple matter of arithmetic. The number of American Catholics was rising rapidly, as thousands of Irish and German immigrants flowed into the country. By 1850, 1.75 million Catholics lived in the United States. Ten years later, the number doubled, and Catholics comprised 10 percent of population, the largest single religious denomination in the country. As the Catholics grew in numbers, so did the clergy to serve them. The ranks of priests would rise from about seven hundred when Pius entered the papacy to six thousand when he left three decades later.

In 1859 Pius IX acted on his understanding of the importance of the growing American Church by arranging the acquisition of a convent near the Gregorian University in Rome. This would be used to house priests from the United States who came to Rome to study, and would be an encouragement for more American priests to do the same. The pope was taking subtle, implicit steps to align the church in the United States with Rome. The acquired property became, and still is, the Pontifical North American College, now referred to as the Casa Santa Maria to distinguish it from a second facility of the college built in the 1950s on the Janiculum Hill.

★ ★ ★

If the church's stance toward America was more paradoxical than ever, so too was the stance of the American people toward Catholicism. As the country became increasingly Catholic, it continued to become more vocally *anti*-Catholic. Many native-born working-class Protestants objected to the rapid influx of Catholic (mainly Irish) foreigners, whom they resented not just on religious grounds but as competitors who flooded the labor market and stole jobs. These American nativists were precisely the constituency to which Rep. Levin and other Know-Nothing politicians appealed with their speeches about the Jesuits' plots. Educated Americans, who would never associate with Know-Nothings, had their own reasons to worry as Pius IX returned to the absolutist ways of his predecessors. "The Catholic Church," proclaimed the popular Harvard-graduated Unitarian minister Theodore Parker in 1854, "opposes everything which favors democracy and the natural rights of man." Therefore, being essentially un-American, the church was "the foe of all progress" and "the irreconcilable enemy of freedom."

At the government level, at least, relations between the United States and the Holy See remained cordial for a time after Jacob Martin's death, ministered by the mostly capable men who succeeded Martin as *chargé d'affaires*. The warmth of these relations was occasionally cooled by awkward incidents. One of these occurred when the Pius IX was still in Gaeta in 1849 and inadvertently became the first pope to step onto U.S. territory. What he stepped onto, actually, was an American warship, the USS *Constitution*. The ship was visiting Gaeta and the captain invited the pope aboard. Since any ship of the U.S. navy was technically American territory, this act constituted insubordination on the part of the captain, who had no authority to issue such an invitation, which unwittingly implied diplomatic recognition of a foreign government with which the United States was not in agreement, and a serious breach of diplomatic protocol by the pope.

A more significant crimp in Holy See–U.S. relations came in 1853, when Pius IX sent a personal envoy and close associate, Archbishop Gaetano Bedini, to the United States. Ostensibly, Bedini was passing through on his way to South America, where he was to become papal nuncio to Brazil. In fact, the visit, which ended up lasting eight months, was a chance for the pope to conduct reconnaissance on the state of the American Church and exert some Roman influence over it.

Bedini arrived in June 1853 in New York, then immediately traveled to Washington to meet President Franklin Pierce and present a letter from the pope. He was welcomed in both cities with all due ceremony and respect, but no one was really too happy to see him. Anti-Catholic Protestants considered him an interloper sent by Rome to stick his nose in the business of the United States. Catholic clergy worried he would inflame anti-Catholic feeling and interfere with their independence.

After meeting the president, Bedini journeyed across the country, stopping in cities with large Catholic populations such as Baltimore, Philadelphia, and Milwaukee. At first, the visits were politely received, but that soon changed. A rumor that Bedini, while serving as nuncio to Bologna, had participated in the 1849 execution of a beloved left-leaning priest (Ugo Bassi) picked up steam and pursued him city to city. In Pittsburgh and Wheeling torch-wielding mobs surrounded the cathedrals where he spoke. In Cincinnati, the city Lyman Beecher had so adamantly cultivated with his anti-Catholic preaching, Bedini found his nastiest greeting. On the day of his arrival in December 1853 a local newspaper urged his assassination. On Christmas night, shortly after 10:00 p.m., a mob of hundreds, carrying banners and placards, marched through town and burnt him in effigy. The demonstration ended with a violent melee in which one man died and many more were wounded.

In early February 1854, having completely worn out his welcome and fearing for his life, Bedini was smuggled out of New York harbor in row boat under cover of night. Clearly he did not leave the United States an affectionate admirer. In a report to the pope, he wrote of his distaste for American democracy, where "popular whim is everything" and conviction counted for nothing. Altogether, the visit was a setback for Catholic-Protestant relations in the United States, "a blunder from every point of view," as one American archbishop declared.

Perhaps the strangest episode of anti-Catholic mischief occurred a month after Bedini left, during the construction of the Washington Monument. Like other dignitaries around the world, Pius IX donated a stone to the monument, to be set in the obelisk as a token of the pope's admiration for George Washington. The stone was a block of marble three feet long and eighteen inches high, reportedly taken from the ruins of an ancient Roman temple. It was stored with other stones in a shed, or "lapidarium," at the base of the half-finished monument. In the dark early hours of March 5, 1854, a group of Know-Nothings broke into the shed and stole the block. The culprits were never apprehended. Pieces of the block were found scattered on the shores of the Potomac River. At least one small chunk was later discovered by a diver on the bottom of the river, where fragments may still rest, undisturbed, to this day.

## V.

Controversy surrounding the destruction of the pope's stone was soon washed away by the great national drama of the Civil War. Catholics, like all Americans, were divided between north and south, and Catholic men were well represented on both sides of the battlefields. Unlike the American Revolution, the Civil War occupied—and deeply troubled—the mind of the pontiff. In the fall of 1862, he wrote letters to the archbishops of New York and New Orleans, urging them to broker peace between their respective congregations.

As Pius IX made clear many times during this war, his official position in the conflict was neutral. Yet conjecture has persisted ever since about which side he really favored. According to Leo Francis Stock, noted historian of nineteenth century Holy See–U.S. relations, "the papal government never wavered in its sprit of loyalty to the Federal government." The pope's Cardinal Secretary of State, Giacomo Antonelli, said at the time that he personally favored preservation of the Union and believed the Confederate's rebellion to be unconstitutional.

The only evidence that Pius IX preferred the South is a correspondence between him and Jefferson Davis in late 1863. Davis wrote to Rome in September of that year to express his thanks for the pope's efforts to "favor peace." He also took the opportunity to explain that the fault of the war belonged to the North, which the Confederacy only asked "to let us live in peace under the protection of our own institutions." This letter, now preserved in the Vatican's Secret Archives, is an intriguing document. Davis was eagerly seeking recognition of the Confederacy by a European power. Having failed to find support elsewhere, he hoped the Pope would oblige; hence the letter, a baited hook. In the opinion of some, he got exactly what he wanted. Pius IX opened his response by addressing Davis as "Illustrious and Honorable Sir, Jefferson Davis, President of the Confederate States of America" (was this not arguably a recognition of Davis's legitimacy?) and closed by beseeching God to "illumine your Excellency with the light of his divine grace, and unite you with ourselves in perfect charity."

It would take some wishful thinking to draw from these writings a formal, diplomatic recognition, or even approbation, of the Confederacy. Contextualizing papal writing of this period shows the pope's expressive language to be typical Vatican diplomatic prose, extravagant and polite but noncommittal. The Confederacy's secretary of state, Judah P. Benjamin, dismissed the letter as diplomatic largesse rather than any sort of formal recognition. Others read more into it. Certainly, Jefferson Davis believed he received Pius's blessing. He later recalled the pope as "the only prince in the world that really wished well to our cause, and sent us his blessing."

The perception that the pope favored the Confederacy crystallized after the war when fugitive John Surratt, one of the alleged conspirators behind Lincoln's assassination, showed up in Rome in 1866. He was discovered living under a pseudonym and serving as a member of the Papal Zouaves, a small army of Catholic volunteers from around the world committed to defending the pope. Although the Vatican cooperated fully in obtaining Surratt's arrest and extradition back to United States (despite the lack of an extradition treaty between Rome and Washington), such measures did not dampen the impression that the church knowingly gave sanctuary to a treasonous conspirator.

Early the following year came a final damning incident. A rumor passed through the American press, and into the halls of Congress, that the Vatican had forbidden Protestant Americans to worship within the city of Rome. The American *chargé d'affaires* to Rome, Rufus King, insisted that the rumor was false but this did nothing to stop its spread. "The only government in the world that recognized the rebel Confederacy was that of the Sovereign of Rome," began a *New York Times* editorial on January 25, 1867. "The only Government in the world that denies today the right of worship to American Protestants within its capital is that of the Sovereign of Rome." By the end of the month Congress voted to kill the appropriations for the mission to the Holy See.

For Rufus King, a former general in the Army of the Potomac, the news that Congress was ending his mission was confounding. He was "at a loss" as to how to proceed, he wrote to Secretary of State William Seward on May 7, 1867. How was he to tell the Vatican that Congress withdrew funds, not for any good reason but based on rumors and innuendo? The idea was so absurd that King himself rejected it. Pending instructions to the contrary, and "in view of the fact that Congress . . . was misled by an utterly false report and will, doubtless, avail itself of an early opportunity to revise the proceeding," he informed Seward, he intended to stay at his post. "The question of 'compensation' I leave to the justice of my County."

Unfortunately for King, a man of no independent means, compensation was not forthcoming. He finally had to call it quits on January 1, 1868. "I did my best," he wrote to Seward after returning home, "and have endeavored, repeatedly, since, to correct the misapprehensions which prevailed on the subject, but, apparently, without the slightest effect."

Awkwardly, a twenty-year chapter in Holy See–U.S. relations ended. To many Americans, the end was long overdue. The excitement surrounding Pius IX's early days as pope was a distant memory. Now his days appeared to be numbered, if not as pontiff then as temporal sovereign, as the forces of revolution closed in. "Rome is about to pass off the stage of history," observed an editorial in the *New York Tribune*, the same newspaper that had so lauded Pius Nino in his early days. "Pope Pius is about to go out of business."

"[A]ll the better for him," added the *Tribune*, "and the world."

# 5

# THE NEW CONCEPT
# OF SOVEREIGNTY

What the Pope has already destroyed by his liberalism is his
own temporal power; what he is unable to destroy is his spiritual power; it is that power which will cancel the harm done
by his worthless counselors.

—Prince von Metternich

It was necessary that the whole world should have means of
knowing that the head of Catholicism was free. It was not
enough for him to be free; he also had to be seen to be free.

—Fr. Robert A. Graham, SJ

## I.

They filed into St. Peter's on a dreary December day, seven hundred soggy bishops. They came to Rome from dioceses around the
world—from Antioch to Zamora, from Adelaide to Zaku; from Camerino
and Granada and Limerick and Malta; from Baltimore and Milwaukee and
a dozen other American cities—and took their places under the vaulting
ceiling of the great basilica. Outside, despite a steady rain, crowds packed
the streets and the square, drawn by the spectacle of the largest gathering of
Catholic hierarchy in the history of the church. Bells rang from St. Peter's.
The cannons of Castel Sant'Angelo thundered from the banks of the Tiber.
The date was December 8, 1869, and the First Vatican Council—only the
twentieth ecumenical council in the church's history, and the first since the
Council of Trent in 1545—was convened.

For all the ceremonial grandeur of the surroundings, this council, like Trent, meant business. The pope was marshaling his bishops against threats to the church. In the case of Trent, those threats were unleashed by Martin Luther and the Reformation. This time, the threat was more immediate and palpable. It was represented by the armies arrayed against the church; armies which intended to deprive the pope of every last acre of land under his territorial domain. Nine years earlier the papal states of central Italy had been taken at gunpoint from the Holy See by the soldiers of King Victor Emmanuel II, ruler of Piedemont-Sardina and would-be king of Italy. Now Victor Emmanuel sought to take the Eternal City from the church and designate it as the capital of his unified nation.

The fact that Rome still remained in the hands of the pope owed a little to the Papal Zouaves and a lot to the protection of the French army. The emperor of France, Louis Napoleon III, was committed to saving Rome for the pope, a penance, perhaps, for the sins of his uncle, Napoleon Bonaparte, against prior popes. French troops were garrisoned in the city, keeping the pope's enemies well outside the gates. Victor Emmanuel would not dare attack so long as the French remained.

Excluding the opinions of Pius IX and his closest advisors, the conventional wisdom held that the pope was living on borrowed time. Whoever thought he might give in, however, did not know this pope. The greater the odds, the more defiant he became—defiant not just against his immediate enemy, but against, seemingly, all the modern world. His first salvo was an extraordinary document entitled the *Syllabus of Errors*. Issued on December 8, 1864—five years to the day before the start of the Vatican Council—the *Syllabus* was a list of eighty "principal Errors of our times." Among these was the proposition that non-Catholics should have the right to practice their faiths in Catholic countries. More shocking was the last error on the list: "the Roman Pontiff can and should reconcile himself to and agree with progress, liberalism and modern civilization."

The *Syllabus* was met with dismay through much of the civilized world. To his detractors, the pope was dragging the church back into the Dark Ages. For Americans, especially, the *Syllabus* read like a detailed rejection of everything for which the United States stood. But the document was not quite what it seemed to be. In his 1954 biography of Pius IX, E. E. Y. Hales, while acknowledging the *Syllabus* to be "irritating" and "indigestible," explained it as Pius's reaction to the political situation in Italy, where *modern* meant *anti-church*. The long list of errors was a manifesto from a pope fighting for the life of the church.

Five years had now passed since the *Syllabus*, and the church was under greater threat than ever. This great council was a conspicuous show of strength to reinforce the primacy of Rome to the Catholic Church, and of the Catholic Church to Rome. The agenda for the bishops in St. Peter's was to refine Catholic dogma in the face of spiritual challenges, much as the Council of Trent had done. As the council proceeded through the winter of 1869–1870, though, bishops would be asked to support one doctrine in particular: *Infallibility*. The doctrine of Infallibility held that statements of the pope were beyond question or repudiation. This did not mean that popes were assumed to be perfect as human beings; but pronouncements issued from their office as Supreme Pontiff, *ex cathedra*, carried the seal of the divine. Infallibility was a not really new idea; most Catholics already assumed it as a matter of course. An explicit declaration, however, was something quite different.

To say that the world beyond the Vatican was amazed by Pius's position would be an understatement. The British foreign minister described papal infallibility as a "monstrous assault on the reason of mankind." Prime Minister William Gladstone saw the doctrine as an attempt to the reassert the "universal monarchy" of the pope, while other European leaders detected a papal desire to return to the days of Gregory VII, when a pope could make a king kneel before him. Did not an assertion of infallibility assume a prerogative to interfere in the affairs of other, more fallible, sovereign nations? Would not the Catholic citizens of those nations be required to demonstrate their spiritual allegiance by heeding the pope's every infallible directive? Napoleon III, the pope's ally and protector, warned Pius IX that the doctrine was a mistake. Germany's Otto von Bismarck urged his fellow European leaders to demand a noninterference pledge from the pope to let him know, in Bismarck's words, "We will not go to Canossa."

A number of Catholic prelates expressed their own concerns about the new doctrine. The French bishop Felix Dupanloup worried it would antagonize rulers and inflame Protestants. "This question has already set Europe on fire," he wrote to the pope. If infallibility were hastily pushed forward at the council, "the fire will become a conflagration." That prospect did not seem to bother the Pius IX. His official position on infallibility was neutral, but where he stood was clear. When one cardinal suggested that infallibility went against tradition of the church, Pius stormed: "I *am* the tradition! I *am* the Church!"

The pope's strongest supporters were adherents of a Catholic movement called "Ultramontanism." An antidote to Gallicanism, which had advocated for the decentralization of ecclesiastical authority, Ultramontanism equated the strength of the church with the primacy and centrality of the Roman Pontiff. Many of the staunchest Ultramontanes, surprisingly, came from Protestant-majority countries. Cardinal Manning, archbishop of Westminster, was among the church's firmest believers in "the beauty of inflexibility," as he so memorably put it, that derived from papal absolutism. Of course, Ultramontanism was not just a theological or rhetorical position in the context of 1869. It was also a political strategy. What the loss of the papal domains might subtract in the pope's temporal power, infallibility would add to his moral authority.

Just as the council had commenced with inclement weather in December 1869, so it climaxed six months later, on the morning of July 18, 1870. Sheets of rain ripped across St. Peter's Square. Bolts of lightning ruptured the dark sky over the basilica as thunder rattled the windows. Inside, the bishops gathered under flickering candles to cast their votes on infallibility. The motion passed by an overwhelming majority, its opponents having either come around to support it or, in some cases, stayed away to avoid casting a ballot. Just two bishops voted against it. One of these was an American, Edward Fitzgerald, of Little Rock, Arkansas. Immediately after the vote, Fitzgerald fell to his knees and declared his consent to the pope.

★  ★  ★

The pope was now doctrinally infallible, but he was not invulnerable. This was demonstrated the very next day, July 19, 1870, when France declared war on Prussia. The culmination of long simmering hostilities, the Franco-Prussian War marked the beginning of the end for popes' temporal power. The French garrison that had been protecting the pope from King Victor Emmanuel's army was withdrawn from Rome to join the fight against Prussia, leaving the city undefended but for the small force of Zouaves. Victor Emmanuel massed his troops and waited to see how the French fared. The answer came soon: on September 2, Napoleon III was overwhelmed by the Prussians and was captured with his army. The king ordered his troops to move on Rome.

Even Pius accepted now that Rome was lost, but he remained unbowed. He would not give up the city without a fight. "If the Lord wants me to lose the Papal States," he explained, "then let him take them away. I cannot hand them over." Because he did not want bloodshed to delay a *fait accompli*, he ordered the Zouaves to make only a show of resistance, enough to indicate the pope's defiance but no more.

The attack began at 5:30 a.m. on September 20, 1870, when Italian forces began pounding the ancient Aurelian walls with artillery. At 7:00 a.m., diplomats from Austria and France and elsewhere began arriving at the Vatican in carriages to receive the pope's formal protest and witness history in the making. Pius IX said mass in his private chapel. Lost in prayer, he barely noticed the thuds of distant cannon fire.

Italian troops entered the city through a breach in the walls near the Porta Pia at mid-morning. A white flag rose to the top of the Castel Sant'Angelo; another appeared fluttering over the cupola of St. Peter's. More than eleven hundred years after the Donation of Pepin, the church was stripped of its last earthly domain. Rome was lost. The temporal role of the Holy See came to an end.

## II.

The world's reaction to the pope's temporal downfall was mixed. In the United States, newspapers registered conflicted feelings. "The great scandal of the ages is wiped out," exulted one New Hampshire journal, "and the deeds of violence, blood and shame, enacted by an ecclesiastical prince, are to be known no more except in history." Other papers carried reports of anguished Catholics congregating to protest the "spoilation" of the pope's domain, including a "monster demonstration" in Philadelphia and a march of five thousand in Covington, Kentucky, to condemn the "usurpation."

Not all Catholics were sorry to see the pope's temporal power end. Many viewed the loss of Rome as a blessing in disguise, believing, in the words of the *New York Times*, "that the Pope as head of the Christian world would be much more powerful than in his capacity as the Sovereign of Rome." An editorial in the *Times* put it this way: "Pope Pius IX, as simple head of the Catholic Church, will be a greater man than he who combined that office with the kingship of a small, badly-governed and disaffected territory."

This line of reasoning was not new. As Fr. Robert Graham, SJ, points out in his book on Vatican diplomacy, it had been entertained decades earlier by no less a church authority than Cardinal Bartolomeo Pacca, one of the heroes of the Holy See in its struggles against Napoleon Bonaparte. When Napoleon tried to separate the papal states from Pius VII, Cardinal Pacca urged the pope to stand firm against the emperor's demands. Pacca was captured and thrown into prison by Napoleon's forces in 1809. He had plenty of time to reflect during his four-year incarceration. Among his epiphanies was that the loss of the papal states might not be all bad. "For one thing," writes Graham (paraphrasing Pacca),

> the end of the papal states would end or weaken the blind jealously or antipathy which existed in so many places against the clergy and Court of Rome. The Sovereign Pontiffs, freed of their heavy burden of temporal affairs, could devote all their time henceforth to the spiritual good of their flock.

History has shown that Pacca was right. Popes gained much more than they lost with the end of the temporal sovereignty. To quote a more recent scholar, George Weigel, "it would take a particular kind of obtuseness, combined with over-the-top romanticism, to think that the loss of the Papal States was anything other than a tremendous blessing for the Catholic Church."

Does this mean that Pius IX's efforts to keep the papal states were not only in vain, but counterproductive? Maybe not.

Pius's defiance, doomed as it may have been, established an extraordinarily important precedent: *the pope and the church would yield to no earthly power.* Though it was not ultimately useful to the church's spiritual mission for the pope to rule over a large temporal domain, it would have been far worse for him to submit to the sovereign rule of *another* temporal power. Had Pius IX caved to King Victor Emmanuel II—or, to take another example, had Pope Pius VII caved to Napoleon Bonaparte—the pope would have admitted dependence on a foreign potentate, and the church would have suffered an irreparable abridgment of its independence, neutrality, and ultimately its inherent sovereignty. Since the church is meant to be international and universal—to serve God and all humankind, not the whims of a particular king, president, or premier—it *must* operate as its own sovereign and independent power. Here again is Fr. Graham, who understood and wrote about the political status of the Catholic Church with great insight:

> The supreme head of the Church recognizes no territorial boundaries in the scope of his mission and his religious role is liable to be suspect to any given portion of his flock by being himself the political subject of any one prince. In order to be free in his religious work he had also to be politically free. It was necessary that the whole world should have means of knowing that the head of Catholicism was free. It was not enough for him to *be* free; he also had to *be seen to be* free.

★ ★ ★

Despite Pius IX's excommunication of the king, Victor Emmanuel II considered himself a pious Catholic, and he was determined to be as respectful to the pope as he could be under the circumstances. He did not boast about conquering Rome, nor did he rush in to personally claim it. He waited almost a year, until July 1871, to enter the city and declare Rome the capital of Italy.

In the meantime, his government offered the pope generous terms in the Law of Guarantees. The law gave the pope nearly all the privileges and immunities he had enjoyed as a temporal sovereign. He would no longer possess territory, but he would be granted exclusive use of the Vatican and would have his own post office and telegraph service. In addition, he would be paid the large sum of 3,500,000 lire to compensate for the confiscated territories. Perhaps most important, given the history of investiture, he would have total control over all ecclesiastic appointments.

Pius IX refused the deal. The Law of Guarantees was an insult to him. The thieves, having stolen the farm, were offering a carrot. "Never will I accept it from you by way of reimbursement," the pope responded, "and you will obtain no signature which might seem to imply an acquiescence in or a resignation to the Spoilation." As an ultimate act of defiance, he then withdrew into the Vatican and shut the gates behind him. Like his namesake, Pius VII, he became a "prisoner," albeit one by his own volition. He never stepped foot outside the Vatican walls again. Nor would any pope for decades to come.

★ ★ ★

Pius IX died on February 7, 1878, after thirty-one years as pope, the longest pontificate in history. He was a man beloved by some and reviled by many. For three days after his death, crowds of grieving Romans filed past his dead body in the chapel of the Blessed Sacrament in St. Peter's. When his body was moved for final burial three years later, a mob of Romans—perhaps some of the same Romans who had paid their respects at his death—flung mud at his casket and attempted to throw his remains into the Tiber. They loved him as a father, but hated him as a tyrant.

Even now, Pius IX remains a complicated case. He refused to give an inch—"Pio No! No!" Yet the same clarity and sense of purpose that frustrated his contemporaries preserved the independence and efficacy of the church. In time, just as some predicted, the church would become stronger when freed from its earthly bonds, but this was only made possible by Pius's insistence that the church be its own master—and the Holy See its own sovereign.

"He had the grittiness and determination to say, 'I may have lost my land, but now the Papacy will become the foremost moral and spiritual authority in the world,'" is how Cardinal Timothy Dolan of New York described Pius IX to me. "It's almost like Pio Nono is saying, 'you may be taking my property away and I resent that, but now you have a spiritual leader that you will have to contend with.' He might have been the first who realized the clout of what is now called 'soft power.'"

## III.

The question, in the last decades of the nineteenth century, was how this soft power would be deployed, and whether it would be any kind of power at all. Would the church drop off the world stage and become a mere spectator to secular events, or would it find new ways to matter? Pius IX gave the church structure and strength by drawing a line in the sand and refusing to let the tides of progress wash it away, but how did his absolutism reconcile with the modern world? Where did the church fit into a world rapidly embracing new political and economic systems that promised greater rights and higher standards of living, on one hand, yet threatened the familiar patterns of faith, family, and community on the other?

Fortunately for the Catholic Church, the College of Cardinals found the right man at the right time to fill Pius IX's shoes. The new pope, born Gioacchino Vincenzo Pecci sixty-eight years earlier, took the name Leo XIII, an unlucky number but a fortunate pick. The first pope born after French Revolution, Leo would also be the first to survive into twentieth century. He would lead the church into the modern world.

Leo XIII was really no less conservative or ultramontane than Pius IX. He was a proponent of the *Syllabus of Errors* and supporter of the infallibility doctrine. Like Pius, too, Leo refused to leave the Vatican, preferring to remain a "prisoner" than concede the loss of Rome. But Leo did not turn his back on the modern world. Well educated and well traveled, he was a man of great intellectual acuity and diplomatic experience. Like Thomas Aquinas, whose long neglected teachings he revived, he looked to reason as the natural companion of faith. Knowledge, too, could be a path that led *into* faith, not away. Leo embraced science, especially astronomy, and encouraged scientific research at the Vatican. He also encouraged Catholic scholars to write objectively of church history, and he opened the Vatican's

Secret Archives for first time to non-Catholic scholars. He was the first pope to allow electricity into St. Peter's and the first to have his moving image captured on film.

Most importantly, Leo XIII addressed in very specific terms the political and economic issues that dominated the late nineteenth century, giving Catholics a picture of how their faith squared with modern life. He was the first sitting pope to affirm that democracy and Catholicism could, and did, coexist. He was the first to encourage liberties like freedom of religion and freedom of press. He was the first to address the conditions of modern workers in industrial societies, condemning socialism but insisting that capitalism meet moral standards. Finally, and not incidentally, he forged a closer relationship with the most modern of countries—the country blazing a trail into the twentieth century—the United States of America.

Leo began his reign by writing letters to rulers around the world, including President Rutherford B. Hayes, in which he expressed his hope for amicable relations. His open and engaging tone met with a positive response. Otto von Bismarck, who had been waging war against the Catholic Church in Germany under the *Kulturkampf*, soon entered into secret negotiations with the Holy See and even sought its assistance in mediating a dispute with Russia. As a result, by 1880, just two years into Leo's pontificate, Bismarck began rescinding anticlerical laws in Germany and Pope Leo's letter to Tsar Alexander II brought a thaw in long frozen relations between Russia and Germany. From the United States, meanwhile, came an emissary in the form of Ulysses S. Grant, the Civil War hero and former president, who met with the pope in the Vatican.

Leo possessed a rare capacity to synthesize strength with accommodation, and he made clear that the latter in no way implied concession. He firmly held the line Pius had drawn: the Holy See was a sovereign, with land or without. In his 1885 encyclical *Immortale Dei*, he declared the church to be a distinct kind of society, spiritual rather than temporal, wanting no outside interference, sovereign in its practice and essence:

> It cannot be called in question that in the making of treaties, in the transaction of business matters, in the sending and receiving ambassadors, and in the interchange of other kinds of official dealings they have been wont to treat with the Church as with a supreme and legitimate power. And, assuredly, all ought to hold that it was not without a singular disposition of God's providence that this power of the Church was provided with a civil sovereignty as the surest safeguard of her independence.

The question of whether the Holy See is a sovereign entity is still raised today, and often distorted by the plot of real estate—the 109 acres of Vatican City State—that was added back to its domain by the 1929 Lateran Treaty. In accordance with the recognition theory of international law, the sovereignty of the Holy See derives from its role in the world, perceived and acknowledged as influential and important in dealing with the affairs of states and international political issues. It is a recognized sovereign under widely accepted international law principles, a status reinforced as recently as the Vienna Convention of 1961. Even Vatican detractors like author Geoffrey Robertson have admitted of the Holy See that "the fact remains that most states recognize it as sovereign, and state practice, however politically skewed, is a powerful formative influence on international law." One legal treatise cited by Robertson summarizes the predominant position among international law experts as maintaining that the Holy See "has an international legal personality of its own which permits it to take international actions such as the conclusion of treaties and the maintenance of diplomatic relations."

The Holy See was exercising sovereignty long before diplomatic relations and international law were initially codified around the year 1500. In fact, modern ideas of sovereignty—and diplomacy—evolved from the Holy See's relations with Europe since the fifteenth century. Even after the fall of Rome in 1870, when the Holy See had no temporal power whatsoever, civil states continued to make binding agreements, to accept diplomatic envoys, and to generally treat and respect the church as a sovereign power.

In his 1996 treatise on the international legal treatment of micro-states, Jorri C. Duursma succinctly summarizes the concept as it applies to Holy See:

> The distinct legal personality of the Holy See was a point of debate, especially during the Italian occupation between 1870 and 1929. Some international lawyers argued that the Holy See had continued to exist as a subject of international law, because it had not ceased to conclude concordats, receive and send diplomatic representations and settle certain disputes by arbitration. Others contended that the international legal status of the Holy See had only been established and recognized by the Lateran Agreements. However, according to the Lateran Treaty, Italy has recognized the sovereignty of the Holy See in the international law field as an inherent attribute of its nature. The most widely accepted view therefore is that the Holy See is an international legal person independent of any exercise of temporal sovereignty over a certain territory.

Although the Holy See remained sovereign after the loss of it temporal domains, its relationship to the rest of the world shifted considerably. As some Catholics and non-Catholics alike predicted, the pope gained in moral authority what he lost in terrestrial property. As noted earlier, Otto von Bismarck was among those who now saw the pope in a new impartial role as an international arbiter; he asked Pope Leo to negotiate an agreement between his country and Spain regarding ownership of the Caroline Islands in the western Pacific. (The pope decided for Spain.) Leo's name was later raised as a possible arbiter in other international matters, such as a dispute between Austria and Russia involving the Balkans and one between the United States and Canada over jurisdiction of the Bering Sea.

Non-Western nations, too, viewed the pope in a new light. From Constantinople, Sultan Abdul-Hamid II sent an envoy to Rome to meet Leo in 1888. A representative of the Chinese government had already approached the pope with a proposal to exchange diplomatic envoys between the Holy See and the Celestial Empire. "As the Pope has no troops and no territory, but is merely a kind of Dalai Lama," said the Empress Dowager, "there is no danger to China from opening direct relations with him."

The Sino-Vatican exchange never occurred. The government of France, concerned that direct papal relations with Peking would disturb its own privileged position at the Imperial Court of China, scuttled the deal. Nonetheless, the Empress Dowager's comment suggests how the church's loss of temporal power opened up new possibilities for the church as a diplomatic force.

★ ★ ★

Its meddling in the China exchange was just one way in which the nation of France proved to be a challenge for Leo's statecraft, one he met smartly and judiciously. The nation was undergoing another wave of anticlericalism at the same time that a reactionary—and mostly Catholic—pro-monarchy movement attacked the government from the right. Determined to make peace, Leo encouraged the monarchists to accept the republican constitutional government they despised. This represented a big step into the political future by the traditionally monarchist Catholic Church.

Leo's *Libertas* was another step. This 1888 encyclical outlined a kind of a *modus vivendi* for Catholics and modern forms of government. While critical of "unconditional freedom of thought, of speech, or writing, or of worship," the encyclical stated that liberty was permissible if observed "with such moderation as will prevent its degenerating into license and excess." Catholics could—and should—accept liberal government, so long as liberal governments accommodated Catholics.

Again, it is not of itself wrong to prefer a democratic form of government, if only the Catholic doctrine be maintained as to the origin and exercise of power. Of the various forms of government, the church does not reject any that are fitted to procure the welfare of the subject; she wishes only—and this nature itself requires—that they should be constituted without involving wrong to anyone, and especially without violating the rights of the church.

The audience for *Libertas* was the entire Catholic world, but it is impossible to read it without sensing a distinctly American influence. Leo was the first pope to embrace what America offered, albeit tentatively. His 1895 encyclical *Longinqua* chided the U.S. clergy for its drift to Americanism—an effort to tailor Catholicism to the democratic tastes of the American public—but this same encyclical acknowledged that America was fruitful for Catholicism. Leo genuinely seemed to admire the American system of government.

At the same time, through Leo's twenty-five-year reign, Americans increasingly looked to the pope as a friend. The chill that had descended over relations with the Holy See during the Risorgimento began to thaw. This is not to suggest that anti-Catholicism vanished from the public sphere in the United States. Regular outbursts continued from successors to the Know-Nothings, such as the American Protective Association and the Ku Klux Klan. Most Americans, though, no matter their beliefs, took seriously the principle of religious freedom. Perhaps this is what President Grover Cleveland was trying to communicate when he sent Leo a copy of the U.S. Constitution, printed on vellum, in 1887 (on the occasion of Leo's fiftieth anniversary as a priest).

America had already given an even finer gift to the pope a few years earlier, in 1884. The post–Risorgimento Italian government, in a wide-scale confiscation of church property, attempted to seize Casa Santa Maria, the building Pius IX obtained several decades earlier for the Pontifical North American College in Rome. When the archbishop of New York, Cardinal John McCloskey, took the matter to President Chester A. Arthur, encouraging him to "ask the King of Italy for a stay of proceedings, if it be not possible furthermore to exempt the institution as virtually American property from the operation of the law," President Arthur agreed to help. The U.S. government's intervention convinced the Italians to back off and leave Casa Santa Maria alone.

★ ★ ★

In addition to grappling with modern politics, Leo confronted the modern realities of industrialization. Railroads, steel mills, coalmines, factories, assembly lines, mass production, the explosive growth of cities—Leo's reign covered a period of phenomenal technological and demographic change in the western world.

In 1891, Leo issued what is commonly believed to be his most important encyclical, *Rerum Novarum*. It was "the Magna Carta of social Catholicism," as one church historian describes it, "the movement that more than any other within the church gradually forced Catholics out of their medievalism and state of siege mentality and inspired them to grapple realistically with the problems of the twentieth century." *Rerum Novarum* outlined a procapitalist position that affirmed the inherent right of the individual under natural law to enjoy the opportunities and benefits of his labor, including wealth and property—contra Karl Marx—but also stressed the obligation of employers to treat labor humanely. Later, the progressive movement in the United States would pick up this theme and give it a Protestant twist, but Leo was the first significant world leader to place democratic capitalism within a framework of moral acceptability.

The relationship between the modern, rapidly industrializing world and morality is a preoccupation the Holy See and the United States would share throughout the twentieth century. Slightly over a decade after Leo's death in 1903, the world would take the ugliest turn in modern history. Events in the first half of the twentieth century would strain both reason and faith, but they would also, eventually, draw the United States and the Holy See into a rapport that truly recognized, for the first time, the common ground these two great powers shared and cherished.

# 6

# THE WORLD AT WAR:
# PART ONE

Is this civilized world to be turned into a field of death?

—Benedict XV (1917)

## I.

St. Peter's Square on a warm spring day in the second decade of the twentieth century: a vibrant, happy sea of sightseers and pilgrims from around the world gathers before the grandeur of the St. Peter's Basilica. The scene here is a monumental one, but it's also comforting and inviting. Bernini's great curved colonnades reach out from the basilica and embrace all who approach, whether they come to pray or simply take a photograph.

It is difficult to imagine now, but there was a time, not so long ago—measuring time by Vatican standards, that is—when St. Peter's Square was an armed camp. Instead of tourists with cameras, soldiers with machine guns occupied the square. The year was 1943. German troops had invaded Rome and crossed the Tiber toward Vatican hill, rumbling over the bridges with motorized infantry, antitank guns, and mortars. They surrounded the Vatican, established check points and sentries, then painted a white line at the edge of St. Peter's Square to distinguish Vatican territory from Italian—or was it now Nazi?—soil. They were there to "protect" the pope, the Germans told the world, but their occupation appeared like a siege.

From the barbarians of the fifth century to the soldiers of Charles V in 1527 and Napoleon's army in 1809, there had been a long history of armed men descending on the Vatican to plunder its treasures. But this was something different. Here was a force that knew no scruples and possessed both the means and the will to destroy the Catholic Church. The Leonine walls, though thick and enduring, would crumble under German artillery. The Swiss Guard, though brave and able, was no match for German machine guns. The Germans promised to leave the Vatican alone, but their promises meant very little. They had broken nearly every one they had made since Adolf Hitler came to power.

Something fundamental changed in the world in the early years of the twentieth century. Progress itself had brought civilization face-to-face with a more destructive and dehumanizing ruthlessness than anything Attila the Hun could have devised. Here was the world of which the old popes had been warning since the Enlightenment—a world detached from its guiding principles, a future without faith—in which progress turned out to be a force not of creation and cooperation, but of destruction.

The causes of World Wars I and II are obviously complex and numerous, but both wars were responses to a secularization of Western culture that had been underway since the eighteenth century. As the influence and moral authority of religion waned, replaced by nationalism, the state replaced the church. The new secular states worshiped only their own power, and power led to the exercise of force. Long before the assassination of Archduke Ferdinand of Sarajevo in the summer of 1914, European nations were building up arsenals and preparing for battle to protect and enhance their hegemony. "War alone keeps up all human energies to their maximum tension," said Benito Mussolini, preaching the theology of the early twentieth-century nation-state.

The Catholic Church would never again exert the kind of influence it held over Europe in the Middle Ages, but in this environment it found a new role, a necessary and difficult one, as the buffer between nations that wished to eliminate each other. How well the Vatican performed during these critical years has been—and still is—a subject of great debate. The church has been criticized for intervening too much (especially in World War I) and too little (especially during World War II). War was a no-win situation for the church. As one diplomat prophetically (and sympathetically) wrote of the Holy See in 1915, "the role of the intermediary and of the mediator is nearly always an ungrateful one."

For a few decades prior to the wars much of civilized society, especially among those who considered themselves the most civilized, dismissed the papacy's role in international affairs as obsolete. Now, with the arrival of the twentieth century, the church was revealed as a bedrock of rationality and an urgently needed moral voice. What would Voltaire and his fellow *philosophes* make of this strange development? The only place on earth where reason seemed to endure was the bastion of ancient faith located around St. Peter's Square.

## II.

Madness descended on Europe at the end of July 1914. A month later, on August 21, Pius X, successor to Leo XIII, died suddenly; a death brought on, some said, by the commencement of World War I. On September 3, 1914, the College of Cardinals chose a new pope. The archbishop of Bologna, Giacomo Della Chiesa, was crowned as Benedict XV.

A tiny man with a raspy voice and a slight limp, possessing as one American journalist put it "neither spiritual or temporal majesty," Pope Benedict XV did not make a powerful first impression. When American Cardinal James Gibbons, arriving in Rome too late for the conclave, heard of Della Chiesa's election, he asked, "Who's he?" Benedict XV apparently did not make a long-lasting impression, either. He has faded into near oblivion in the years since his reign. The title of his biography by historian John Pollard says it all: *The Unknown Pope.*

But Benedict XV has not been entirely forgotten, certainly not by Benedict XVI, who honored him as his namesake. Benedict XV was a "prophet of peace," as Benedict XVI called him, a man who gave everything he had to stop a senseless war.

Benedict XV's humanitarian efforts alone—whether in providing relief for war refugees, care for battlefield casualties, or arranging the exchange of prisoners of war, were unparalleled—and they extended well beyond Catholics. Benedict used his bully pulpit to demand the protection of civilian populations—all populations—throughout Europe. When an American Jewish group sought help to ameliorate the suffering of European Jews caught in the war, it turned to the pope, asking him to exercise "the profound moral, ethical and religious influence with which the Roman Catholic Church is endowed." The Vatican handled an enormous correspondence during the war, tens of thousands of letters, as people of all nations wrote to inquire about missing loved ones or simply asked the church to forward mail to prisoners of war. Benedict XV spent so much on charity during the war that the Vatican was nearly bankrupt by the time the armistice came in 1918.

The humanitarian work was perhaps expected of the Catholic Church. More striking was Benedict's devotion to the achievement of a just and fair armistice among the belligerents before 1918. From the start of his papacy,

Benedict announced his intention to play an active, hands-on role in pursuing peace. "The Pope must actually place himself amidst the combatants," he declared, "instead of keeping away and preaching peace and concord from a distance." Two months after his election, with the nations of Europe already digging into trenches for a long and brutal stalemate, he issued an encyclical, *Ad Beatissimi*, in which he wrote movingly of the war and of the world's responsibility to bring it to a quick end:

> The combatants are the greatest and wealthiest nations of the earth; what wonder, then, if, well provided with the most awful weapons modern military science has devised, they strive to destroy one another with refinements of horror. There is no limit to the measure of ruin and slaughter; day by day the earth is drenched with the newly-shed blood, and is covered with the bodies of the wounded and the slain. . . .
>
> We implore those in whose hands are placed the fortunes of nations to hearken Our voice. Surely there are other ways and means whereby violated rights can be rectified. Let them be tried honestly and with good will, and let arms meanwhile be laid aside.

As the conflict continued unabated, Benedict offered a series of proposals, some made public, others kept secret. He was a graduate of the Vatican's Pontifical Ecclesiastical Academy, trained and experienced as a diplomat, and he put all his skills and energy to the peace effort. Working under him was Cardinal Secretary of State Pietro Gasparri, along with a brilliant young diplomat, already recognized as a rising star of the Curia, Eugenio Pacelli—the future Pope Pius XII.

The common theme in Benedict's peace proposals was their insistence on *status quo ante bellum*. In other words, peace required a return to conditions more or less as they were before the outbreak of hostilities, with no winners or losers. A punitive result, Benedict warned, would not sow a lasting peace but only plant the seeds of vengeance. "Remember, Nations do not die," he wrote with remarkable prescience on the first anniversary of the war's outbreak; "humiliated and oppressed, they bear the weight of the yoke imposed upon them, preparing themselves for their come-back and transmitting from one generation to the next a sad legacy of hatred and vendetta."

To excuse their deafness to the pope's entreaties, both the Allies (France, Britain, and Russia) and the Central Powers (Austria-Hungary, Germany, Bulgaria, and the Ottoman Empire) claimed that the Vatican favored the other side. To the French, he was *le pape boche* (the Kraut pope); to the Germans, *derfranzoesiche pape* (the French pope). The truth is that

Benedict worked hard to maintain strict neutrality. And the more complicated truth is that neither side really wanted peace, especially not in those early days. Having committed their nations to war, the belligerent nations' leaders required total victory. "Anyone suggesting peace now," said Jean-Jules Jusserand, French ambassador to Washington, as late as 1916, "would be considered by my people as a friend of Germany."

What Jusserand did not mention was the other reason his country would not—and could not—listen to the Vatican on the issue of peace. The Allies had made a deal with Italy in the 1915 Treaty of London, the secret agreement that brought Italy into the war on the Allies' side. The Italian government did not want to give the Vatican a chance to push for a restoration of its temporal property and worried that a peace conference would present a platform for the pope to do just that. With this in mind, Article 15 of the treaty prohibited the Holy See's participation in such talks if and when they occurred. The Allies were committed to ignoring Vatican peace efforts from the moment they signed on to Article 15.

The pope did have one presumptive ally in his quest for peace: Woodrow Wilson. During the first years of the war, when President Wilson vowed to keep the United States out of war, he presented himself, like Benedict, as a neutral and willing arbiter to end it. Indeed, Wilson's early peace initiatives could have been scripted by the pope himself: "I think that the chances of a just and lasting peace, and of the only possible peace that will be lasting," wrote Wilson, "will be happiest if no nation gets the decision by arms." The worst possible outcome would be if "one or a group of nations succeeds in enforcing its will upon the others." Wilson was still taking more or less the same line on January 22, 1917, when he delivered his famous "peace without victory" speech to the U.S. Congress, calling for an agreement "among equals, without humiliation, victors and vanquished."

Both the pope and the president based their proposals on a practical—and prophetic—assessment of human and national behavior. Both, too, took positions that were fundamentally moral. They sought a peace in Europe not from self-interest—the *raison d'être* and *modus operandi* of most nation-states—but on the conviction that peace and justice were valuable in their own right.

That Benedict's Vatican and the Wilson's America found themselves in alignment should have been no surprise, given the fundamental ideals shared by the Catholic Church and the United States (as explored in earlier chapters). In the past, much had come between them in the way of prejudice and suspicion which prevented each from recognizing its natural affinity with the other. At last, here was an opportunity for them to join forces to pursue a shared, symmetrical goal of ending the war and constructing a postwar peace which could endure, based upon universal moral principles and laws. It is one of history's great misfortunes that the opportunity was not taken.

The church attempted on several occasions to reach out and work with the United States, but these efforts were ignored by Wilson. The president and his advisors never warmed to collaboration with the pope. In part, their attitude reflected the administration's position, shared and shaped by the Allies, that the church's historic relationship with Catholic Austria-Hungary meant that the pope favored the Central Powers. Perhaps a less-than-noble desire among some of Wilson's advisors was to place their president in a position to claim sole credit for brokering peace. As one historian wrote of the president's attitude toward the Vatican's efforts, "he reserved for himself the exclusive right to make the proposals for peace."

No doubt reflexive American anti-Catholicism also played into the Wilson administration's reluctance to work with the Vatican. A number of prominent Protestant Americans urged Wilson to avoid dealing with the pope at any level, and any suggestion of Holy See–U.S. cooperation brought instant outrage from certain quarters. Wilson's personal feelings toward the Catholic Church are hard to decipher. He had many Catholic friends and political associates, but he had been schooled in the popular anti-Catholic prejudices of nineteenth-century America and seemed to share some of them. When Wilson was an undergraduate, one of his professors of "Civil Government" at Princeton had railed against papal influence as a danger "not only in European but also in American politics." As a law student at University of Virginia, he had engaged in a formal debate with another student on the question "Is the Roman Catholic element in the United States a menace to America institutions?" (virtually the same question John Adams posed to Thomas Jefferson in 1821). By lots, Wilson drew the negative in the debate and argued that the United States could easily assimilate Catholics without harm to its institutions. That he lost the debate is unimportant; that the "menace" of Catholicism was still a matter of debate is telling. Years later, Wilson unflatteringly portrayed Catholic immigrants—"multitudes of men of the lowest class from the south of Italy, and the men of the meaner sort out of Hungary and Poland"—in his 1901 book *History of the American People*. By the time he was president, his views seem to have become a bit more politic, but he remained snobbishly dismissive of Catholics.

Whatever the reason for the White House's reluctance to work with the Vatican, talk of peace was effectively tabled in February 1917. That is when Germany resumed unrestricted submarine warfare. The United States judged this a direct threat to its own shipping and broke off diplomatic relations with Germany. When the infamous Zimmerman telegram, in which Germany invited Mexico to join in future battle against the United States, became public on March 1, American neutrality ended. The United States declared war against Germany on April 6, 1917.

Benedict, now alone as peace broker, was more determined than ever to bring the war to a close. In mid-August 1917, he released the "Peace Note," his most detailed and ambitious proposal yet. Copies were prepared for the heads of belligerent states, placed in large engraved envelopes, then distributed. Because the United States did not have official diplomatic relations with the Holy See, President Wilson's envelope was delivered to him via the British government. The note was a remarkable document, both as a general indictment of war and as a brass tacks plan for resolving the conflict. After assuring the belligerents he strived to maintain "perfect impartiality," Benedict reminded them that he had already made previous efforts at peace:

> Unfortunately our appeal was not heeded and the war was fiercely carried on for two years more with all its horrors. It became even more cruel and spread over land and sea and even to the air, and desolation and death were seen to fall upon defenseless cities, peaceful villages and their innocent populations. And now no one can imagine how much the general suffering [will] increase and become worse. . . . Is this civilized world to be turned into a field of death? And is Europe, so glorious and flourishing, to rush, as carried by a universal folly, to the abyss and take a hand in its own suicide?

Ensuing from this aggressive introduction, the "Peace Note" stipulated seven conditions for peace, including simultaneous and reciprocal disarmament, an "institution of arbitration" that would settle international conflicts, restoration of all occupied territories to their prewar status, and a renunciation of indemnities—in other words, all belligerents would stand down, give back what they had taken, and forgo punitive measures. While none of these conditions was new, they were articulated more clearly than in previous papal writings. "He goes into details," praised the *Nation*, a liberal American magazine not known for praising popes. "He states terms."

Benedict's note was greeted with great public attention when it appeared. Newspapers around the world ran it in full as the warring nations paused to frame their responses. But the response everybody wanted to hear was that of the United States. As the French ambassador to Washington, Jean-Jules Jusserand, wrote to Secretary of State Robert Lansing on August

18, the Allies desired to know the president's opinion "so that a similar attitude be observed by those who fight on the same side of the trench."

In Jusserand's view, the note was written under "inimical influences," presumably meaning pressure from the Austrians and Germans. This opinion was shared by the other allies, who had perhaps greater reason than ever to deny Benedict's terms. With millions of their young now dead, and tens of thousands more causalities every week, how could they accept the pope's call for a nonpunitive peace? Such an end would imply that the war had been for nothing. The "Peace Note" was a dead letter before it was even delivered.

The one man who could have revived it was Woodrow Wilson. If he got behind the "Peace Note," it stood a chance of gaining ground. If not, it had no chance at all. Wilson consulted his advisors and met with a group of senators at White House on August 17 to discuss the pope's note. He appeared to be under a good deal of strain as he framed his response, though it's not clear that he ever gave serious consideration to answering other than as he did.

On August 28, he finally sent a letter to Pope Benedict XV. It was a courteous but devastating rejection, Benedict later told friends that receiving Wilson's response brought one of the bitterest moments of his life.

"Every heart that has not been blinded and hardened by this terrible war must be touched by this moving appeal of His Holiness, the Pope, must feel the dignity and force of the humane and generous motives which prompted it," wrote Wilson, "and must fervently wish that we might take the path of peace he so persuasively points out. But it would be folly to take it, if it does not in fact lead the goal he proposes."

Abandoning his own earlier concurrence with the pope that there should be "peace without victory," Wilson now insisted that the "stable and enduring peace" desired by the pope could not be achieved without total defeat of Germany, a country from which America suffered "intolerable wrongs." Wilson's tone managed to be both fulsome and patronizing at the same time.

President Wilson's response, soon made public, was praised in the press as a fine work of diplomacy. By turning down the pope, he was seen to have claimed the moral leadership for himself and the United States. When peace came, it would be the president, not the pope, who set the terms. In the short run, this was good for Wilson's image. In the long run, it was unfortunate for the world.

Four months after the pope's note, President Wilson came out with his own definitive proposal, the Fourteen Points, delivered in a speech to Congress on January 8, 1918. Among the terms were mutual disarmament and the creation of a league of nations to protect "mutual guarantees of political independence and territorial integrity to great and small states alike." Because of similarities to the pope's note, some historians have suggested that Wilson appropriated the pope's seven points for his own peace proposal, one scholar asserting that the president simply "rearranged them and proposed them more explicitly." Certainly, at a minimum, Wilson may have been influenced by Benedict. The similarities suggest how closely in alignment the president and pope were, and had been all along.

How might the future have turned out had the United States worked in greater coordination with the Holy See during the war? The president and the pope would have made a forceful alliance, the United States more closely tied to the Allies, the Vatican more closely tied to the Central Powers, and each adding depth and strength to the other's moral authority. Together, they might have brought the warring parties to the table before the United States even entered the war. But it was not to be.

After the war, the Holy See was excluded from the peace talks in Paris, as per Article 15 of the Treaty of London. As suggested by a letter, dated April 3, 1918, and preserved in the Vatican's archives, from the British foreign secretary Arthur James Balfour to Cardinal James Gibbons of Baltimore, some of the Allies regretted the Holy See's exclusion. "I can assure you that I personally would gladly see the clause eliminated or profoundly modified not only for the cogent reasons given by Your Eminence but also on the merits of the case. Your Eminence will, however, realize . . . that it is a matter of great delicacy for us to take further action in this direction at present."

Would the presence of the Holy See at Versailles have changed the outcome of that treaty? Might its voice have muted the vengeance of the Allies as they named their terms for the defeated Central Powers? All we know for certain is that when the Allies met in Paris, they went for Germany's jugular. They demanded onerous reparations of 132 goldmarks—the equivalent of $323 billion in present dollar value—while seizing $7 billion in foreign assets. Germany was forced to surrender 13 percent of the territory it possessed before the war and its army and navy were reduced to shadow forces. As Pope Benedict XV foresaw, such terms were a recipe for insolvency and bitterness, and Germany soon fell into ruin. When it rose again, the nation was a monster. The pope, it turned out, had been right.

An interesting and somewhat ironic coda: Wilson made a point of visiting Benedict when he came to Europe for the peace talks in January 1919. The second sitting American president to travel outside of country (President Theodore Roosevelt had visited the construction of the Panama Canal in 1906), he also became the first to meet a pope. There is no record that Wilson ever regretted missing the opportunity to work with the pope for peace or the pope's exclusion from Versailles. But Wilson took a political risk in going to the Vatican at a time when the United States was still fairly anti-Catholic. He must have believed that meeting Benedict was worth it.

Three years later, Benedict XV was dead and Woodrow Wilson was an invalid, felled by a massive stroke. Neither lived to see his predictions or admonitions come to pass. Wilson's dream for a league of nations remained unrealized, but his vision of America's role in the world as a moral force would guide American foreign policy for the next century. Benedict XV, after serving just seven years as pope, would quickly fade into history, but the papacy would continue to be more actively engaged with the world because of his work. The bar for future popes as peacemakers would be higher the next time war came.

It came far sooner, and brought far more devastation, than anyone in 1919 could have imagined.

# 7

# THE WORLD AT WAR:
# PART TWO

Gone are the proud illusions of limitless progress. Should any
still fail to grasp this fact, the tragic situation of today would
rouse them with the prophet's cry: "Hear, ye deaf and ye
blind, behold!"

—Pius XI (1939)

## I.

The crowd began gathering on the cold evening of February 11, 1922.
By the following morning, more than two hundred thousand people
stood under the warming sun in St. Peter's Square to await the appearance
of the new pope. At last, high above the square, the windows of the basilica's central loggia opened and onto the balcony stepped Pius XI. He raised
his hands and blessed the people below with the *Urbi et Orbi*. The crowd
burst into cheers. This was the first time a pope had given a postelection
blessing in front of St. Peter's since Pius IX in 1846. It was a sign that Pius
XI intended to engage the world beyond the Vatican's walls.

Pius XI shared an outward-looking vision of the papacy with Benedict
XV, but in personal appearance he was a distinct contrast to his predecessor.
Though a scholar and former prefect of the Vatican library, Pius XI—formerly known by his given name of Achille Ratti—was no egghead. He
was a robust, barrel-chested athlete. Earlier in life he had achieved renown
as an alpinist, having conquered some of the Alp's most challenging peaks,
including the Matterhorn and Mont Blanc. (Years later, another mountain
climber, John Paul II, would follow Pius XI's footsteps into the Vatican.)
He exuded strength, physical self-possession, and authority. After meeting

Pius XI, Hermann Goering, Hitler's infamous henchman, would remark, "For the first time in my life I believe I was afraid."

That February day, as Pius gave his blessing from above the square, another soon-to-be infamous fascist stood in the crowd below, impressed by the scene before him. "Look at this multitude of every nation; how is it that the politicians who govern the nations do not realize the immense value of this international force, this universal spiritual power?" The observer was Benito Mussolini. Later that year, Mussolini would lead a march of fascists into Rome and oversee a coup to install himself as prime minister of Italy.

An avowed atheist, Mussolini was no friend of the Catholic Church, but, like Napoleon, he understood its power and influence as the ultimate "soft power." He understood, too, how a personal relationship with the church could create the illusion, if only temporarily, that he was more than a dictator. And so it was Mussolini, at the height of his powers—the self-proclaimed *Il Duce*—who put an end to lingering issues of the 1870s, including the loss of the papal states and the fifty-nine-year "imprisonment" of popes in the Vatican.

The series of agreements between Mussolini's government and the church, signed on February 11, 1929—seven years after Pius XI's installation—is known collectively as the Lateran Treaty. The treaty granted the Holy See a small piece of land behind the Leonine walls that the church occupied for centuries. At 109 acres—approximately the size of an eighteen-hole golf course—the parcel bore little resemblance to the significant lands the church once held as the papal states. More important than the size, though, was the meaning: once again, the church held temporal property to accompany its recognized institutional sovereignty, ruled by the pope and legally independent from external powers. According to Article 24 of the Lateran Treaty, Vatican City was "always and in every case considered neutral and inviolable territory."

Other benefits were given to the church. A large cash restitution of $750 million lire—about $100 million in 1929 dollars—was to be paid out by Italy in exchange for the seized papal states. The treaty also included a provision for the pope to broadcast beyond its walls by radio. This may seem a minor point, but it went to the very crux of the Vatican's right to operate as an entity independent of Italy or any other foreign power. The pope could speak directly, without interference, to Catholics around the world. Vatican Radio was born on February 12, 1931, when Pius XI became the first pope to have his voice transmitted by radio. The microphone the pope used was later preserved—and still is—inside a glass case in the Vatican.

The argument was made in chapter 5 that the sovereignty of the church does not depend on territory, much less on money or radio. The church functioned as a sovereign entity in the years between 1870 and 1929, arguably with greater impact and authority than before 1870, having been relieved of the conflictive burden of administering the papal states. Nonetheless, the importance of the Lateran Treaty cannot be overstated. It served to define the physical independence of the Holy See, adding a valuable complement to its sovereignty. How much this mattered would become apparent when Rome fell under the control of Adolf Hitler in 1943.

★ ★ ★

But all that was still well in the future. First, in 1933, just months after becoming chancellor of Germany, Adolf Hitler pursued his own agreement with the pope. Privately, Hitler aspired to eradicate Christianity from Germany and replace it with National Socialism. Like his new best friend Mussolini, though, he also understood the benefits an arrangement with the church might offer him. A full third of the Reich's population, more than 20 million Germans, were Catholic. Hitler intended to use the church to consolidate his power over this Catholic constituency.

The 1933 Reich Concordat, negotiated for the church by Eugenio Pacelli (who had been promoted to cardinal secretary of state three years earlier) and for Germany by Vice-Chancellor Franz von Papen (himself a Catholic), was a compact under duress. Neither Pius XI nor Pacelli had any illusions that Hitler was a friend of the church. For exactly that reason, they wanted to make the best of a bad situation. The church entered into the concordat because it saw a choice, Pacelli explained later, "between an agreement on [Nazi] lines and the virtual elimination of the Catholic Church in the Reich."

According to the Concordat, signed July 20, 1933, the Holy See would gain full control over the German Catholic clergy—including the exclusive right to appoint bishops—along with the right to run schools for Catholic children. In exchange, the Catholic clergy would agree to stay out of German politics. In other words, the government would not interfere with the church, and the church would not interfere with the government.

That sounds like a better deal for the church than it was. A number of unsavory conditions were attached to the concordat. German bishops, for example, had to take an oath of loyalty to the Reich. More troubling, the German Center Party, an influential political base for Catholics, was to be dissolved, removing the last barrier to Hitler's complete domination of German politics. By agreeing to these measures, the church at least implicitly sent a message to Germany's Catholics that it accepted as a fact the rise of Adolf Hitler, a concession that arguably lent an aura of legitimacy to the Nazi regime. But the Reich Concordat was also the start of a hostile relationship between Nazi Germany and the Catholic Church that would haunt and challenge Pius XI, and later Pius XII (Pacelli), for years to come.

In the meantime, the church had to respond to the rise of another fascist leader in Europe, Francisco Franco in Spain. The church had dealt effectively with a variety of totalitarian and democratic regimes over its course. The initial inquiry the church would undertake about a ruler or government was not to discern whether he or it was fascist, but what environment was offered for treatment of Catholics and the church. In Spain, the answer was clear. The leftist opposition killed priests and closed churches. Franco's Falangists, in contrast, were friendly and cooperative. Like so many of the moves made by the Vatican in these anxious years, the support of Franco was intended to make the best of a bad situation. As far as the church was concerned, fascism had at least one quality to recommend it: it was not communism.

★ ★ ★

The best way to understand the response of the church to fascism in the 1930s is to appreciate its concerns about the rise of communism in Russia and elsewhere. Communism was *explicitly* atheistic and therefore viewed as an immediate, existential threat to the Catholic Church and to religion in general. While the fascists may have manipulated the church, they at least paid lip service to the idea that it had a right to exist. The communists did not. As Lenin so famously phrased the communist position, "Religion is opium for the people . . . in which the slaves of capital drown their human image." Lenin later exhorted the "proletariat of today" to take "the side of socialism" and enlist "science in the battle against the fog of religion."

In Russia, by one Vatican official's calculation, 50 percent of Catholic clergy had vanished in the five years following the Revolution. The church was later criticized for underestimating the threat of fascism, but it should also be credited for perceiving earlier than anyone the pernicious alternative that communism presented.

None of this suggests that the Reich Concordat was anything but a mistake. In hindsight, whether the church gave up too much or not, Hitler never seriously intended to honor the agreement. The Nazis interfered in ecclesiastical matters from the beginning. Meanwhile, they pursued increasingly hostile social policies. Five days after signing the concordat, the Nazis began enforcing sterilization of the mentally ill, the physically deformed, and all other Germans deemed unfit by the Nazis to pass on their genes. Hitler then turned on the Jews. As bad as Pius XI and Cardinal Pacelli knew Hitler to be, they would have been stunned by the brazen comment he made shortly after the concordat was signed. The Reich Concordat, said Hitler, would be "especially significant in the urgent struggle against international Jewry."

That it took time for the church to grasp the evil of Hitler owes to the fact that there had never been anyone quite like Hitler. It took time for the entire *world* to recognize the extent of his evil. As E. E. Y. Hales states, "nobody quite believed that any government, once in power, could really attempt to carry out the programme of *Mein Kampf.*"

Pius XI gradually wakened to the full horror of the man. In 1937, he angrily addressed the Nazi regime in an encyclical, *Mit Brennender Sorge* ("With Burning Anxiety"), smuggled into Germany to be read from bishops' pulpits on Palm Sunday. The encyclical excoriated the Germans for failing to live up to their end of the concordat. Its real focus was the graver crime of turning Nazism into a pagan religion which "certain leaders pretend to draw from the so-called myth of race and blood." Regarding Jewish persecution by the Nazis, Pius declared the sacredness of the Old Testament (and by implication the Jewish faith). In January 1939, the *National Jewish Monthly* commented that "the only bright spot in Italy has been the Vatican, where fine humanitarian statements by the Pope [Pius XI] have been issuing regularly."

*Mit Brennender Sorge* was a sequel to a similar denunciation by Pius XI of Mussolini's own brand of fascism and his suppression of Catholic youth and civil groups, including Catholic Action, in the 1931 encyclical *Non Abbiamo Bisogno*. Interestingly, since Mussolini had eliminated freedom of the press in Italy, the work was smuggled out of Italy to France by the American Monsignor—and future Cardinal—Francis Spellman so it could be printed in Paris. The pope may have been oblique in *Mit Brennender Sorge*, but his meaning was clear. For one thing, the encyclical was written in German, rather than the usual Latin—a good clue as to its intended audience. And the fact that Nazi troops confiscated the encyclical as quickly as it appeared suggests the message was heard loud and clear. But that was part of the problem. The pope's encyclical put Hitler in a fury. He threatened to "push them back," *them* being the Catholic Church. Rather than mend his ways, he became more antagonistic. Speaking out against Hitler seemed to make matters worse.

Worse was to come in any case. How much worse became clear only after Pius XI passed away in 1939. The man who succeeded him—Eugenio

Pacelli, Pius XII—would learn, along with the rest of the world, that Adolf Hitler meant every word of *Mein Kampf.*

II.

Never was a man better prepared for the papacy than Eugene Pacelli. Born into Rome's "black nobility," one of the city's aristocratic families that had served the Vatican for generations, Pacelli had been groomed in various roles over the previous four decades, as a nuncio and under secretary of state, and finally as cardinal secretary of state under Pius XI. He possessed the gifts of a great pope—a brilliant mind, a long resume of diplomatic experience, fluency in six languages—while also emanating an aura of holiness and moral rectitude. He seamlessly combined the worldliness of a seasoned diplomat with the otherworldliness of a mystic. He was, in short, a man born to be pope.

As it turned out, Pius XII, installed on March 12, 1939, served through one of the most difficult papacies in church history, and emerged as one of Catholicism's most controversial figures. He was, and still is, held in such esteem as to be declared Venerable in 2009, a big first step on the road to canonization. Numerous biographies of Pius affirm his life as extraordinary and heroic. Yet, at the same time, with his supposed failure to speak out forcefully against the Holocaust, he has been reviled by critics as an appeaser of Adolf Hitler. The titles of a few books about Pius XII that have hit the shelves over the past decade—*The Devil's Pope*; *Hitler's Pope*; *The Silence of Pius XII*—give a good indication of what Pius's critics think of him. Given that our interest here is to analyze and chronicle Pius's role in the context of the church as a diplomatic power during the war, particularly vis-à-vis the United States, there is no need to belabor the pros and cons of this debate here. But we cannot ignore them, either.

Sometimes lost in the controversy surrounding Pius XII and the Holocaust—we'll get to that in a moment—is the fact that the war years marked an important turning point in relations between the Holy See and the United States. Over the course of his papacy, Pius XII developed closer ties to America than any previous pope. Indeed, these ties were well established before he became pope. In the fall of 1936, then Cardinal Secretary of State Pacelli had become the highest ranking Vatican official to visit the United States. Pacelli's lengthy journey was covered with great fanfare in the American press, his every move detailed and dissected. He traveled eight thousand miles during his month-long stay, including a five-day, seven-city, coast-to-coast airplane excursion. The highlight of the trip was a meeting with Franklin Roosevelt at the president's family estate in Hyde Park, New York, on November 5, two days after Roosevelt was elected to his second term. Arranged with the assistance of prominent American Catholics such as Joseph P. Kennedy and Bishop Francis Spellman (a young auxiliary bishop of Boston at the time), the visit in itself was a challenge to diplomatic protocol. With no formal relations between the Holy See and the United States, no official meeting between a cardinal secretary of state and a sitting American president could occur. The ingenious solution was to have the president's mother invite the cardinal to an informal off-the-record luncheon with the president.

While the precise topics discussed by the future pope and the newly reelected president over lunch at Hyde Park were not revealed, it is generally supposed that the president solicited church backing to keep Italy out of any future war. He also wanted church support in muting the radio personality Father Charles Coughlin, whose 30 million listeners tuned in each week to hear anticommunist, anti-Semitic, and, increasingly, anti-Roosevelt tirades. For Pacelli, the meeting was an opportunity to warn Roosevelt about the dangers of communism, still a greater concern to the church than fascism. (Looking back at the lunch from the perspective of 1943, Roosevelt would recall with amusement that the cardinal secretary of state seemed obsessed with communism.) Pacelli and Roosevelt also apparently broached the possibility of establishing diplomatic relations. This was alluded to in a letter Pacelli sent to Joseph Kennedy in April 1938. "Ever in my personal judgment, [there is] no better opportunity than this for trying to carry on the plan that we had thought of while in America and that I know is amongst your aims," Pacelli cagily wrote. The "planned provision" would give the American government "a direct source of information from and a straight and intimate connection with the Vatican circles."

Less important than who said what at the lunch is that it occurred. An American president meeting with a high Vatican official gave a tangible and clear signal of a fundamental shift in relations between the United States and the Holy See. That shift was soon reflected in the diplomatic activity, albeit still unofficial, which picked up after Pacelli's visit. At first, the U.S. State Department looked to the Vatican as a possible peacekeeper in Europe, hoping that the church would influence the Italian government, which might in turn moderate the German government's aggression. When it became clear that no force or man could moderate Adolf Hitler, the United States came to prize the Vatican as a listening post. "I think it is unquestionable," wrote Under Secretary of State Sumner Welles in a 1939 memo to the president, "that the Vatican has many sources of information, particularly with regard to what is actually going on in Germany, Italy, and Spain." The intelligence coming out of those countries from the church prelates was useful. And while embassies were shutting down all around Europe, the Vatican remained one place where diplomats from belligerent countries—and many nonbelligerent—were still doing business.

By more covert methods, the U.S. State Department began collaborating with the official Vatican newspaper, *L'Osservatore Romano*, to air antifascist views. Speeches from the U.S. State Department officials or even the president himself found their way unedited into the paper. The conduit for these speeches was Fr. Joseph P. Hurley. An American monsignor from Cleveland, Hurley followed Cardinal Spellman as the second American prelate to work in a high position inside the Vatican. Hurley's passions, beyond his religious faith, were his love for America and his hatred of Nazis. With the apparent blessing of Vatican superiors, Hurley began secretly meeting with the U.S. ambassador to Italy, William A. Phillips, to receive news items of interest from the United States. Hurley would then pass these to the editors of *L'Osservatore Romano*, into which they would often go verbatim then circulate into Rome at large. This was a terrific feat of antifascist propaganda at a time when Italian papers were heavily censored and one-sided. Indeed, it was too good to last; circulation of the paper outside Vatican walls was banned by the Italian government in November 1940.

★ ★ ★

Holy See–U.S. relations took another momentous turn on October 2, 1939, five months after Pius XII's installation. Franklin Roosevelt wrote a memo to his secretary of state, Cordell Hull, suggesting "a special Minister or Ambassador on *Special Mission to the Vatican.*" Initially, Roosevelt saw the mission as being useful in dealing with the Catholic refugees he expected to flood out of war-torn areas of Europe, but the mission's scope soon became much broader.

Sending an American envoy to the Vatican was going to be politically difficult. The president would have to navigate around opposition from American Protestants, many of whom might view an envoy to the pope as an affront to their religion and an abridgment to the constitutional separation of church and state. This consideration recommended making as little fuss as possible about the envoy, slipping him into Rome without fanfare. But that strategy, too, carried risks. A quiet process lacking formality and publicity would diminish the envoy's stature and undermine his credibility in Europe and the Vatican. Caught between a political rock and a diplomatic hard place, Roosevelt resolved the situation by naming his envoy as a "personal representative" of the president. Though the envoy would not hold the formal title of U.S. ambassador, the president insisted he be given a rank equal to ambassador.

The man Roosevelt named as envoy, Myron C. Taylor, the sixty-six-year-old former president of U.S. Steel Corporation, made the appointment easier for the critics to accept. Taylor was one of the country's most highly regarded businessmen, a generous philanthropist, and a devout Episcopalian. He was also a man of sterling reputation who, despite his prominence, shunned the limelight, making him perfect for a discreet and sensitive assignment. All the better that he owned a villa in Tuscany, which put him close to Rome, and that his generous wealth meant that he required no pay, and hence no approval from Congress. Just in case, Roosevelt named him to the post on Christmas Eve, 1939, when Congress was absent from Washington and could not object.

## III.

By the time Myron Taylor arrived in Rome in late February 1940, World War II was well under way. The German army had invaded Poland on September 1, 1939, and France and England had immediately declared war on Germany. Though President Roosevelt originally directed Taylor to deal mainly with refugees, the envoy's task list expanded to encompass a broad range of issues. Most immediately, per Roosevelt's wishes, Taylor hoped to enlist the pope in keeping Italy from joining the war on Hitler's side. This goal met with disappointment in June 1940, when Italy joined Germany and declared war against France and England.

A second key task for Taylor was to persuade the pope to modify the church's position on the Soviet Union. The president wanted to extend the American lend-lease program to the Soviets but he knew the Catholic Church strongly objected to any dealings with the communist regime. In 1937, Pius XI had declared in his encyclical *Divini Redemptoris* that communism "is intrinsically wrong, and no one who would save Christian civilization may collaborate with it in any undertaking whatsoever." Those words put patriotic American Catholics in a moral bind—supporting lend-lease to the Soviets meant defying the pope. Roosevelt hoped the pope, with Taylor's encouragement, would soften the anti-Soviet sentiment of the encyclical. Here Taylor met with some success. The Vatican quietly sent out word to American clergy that *Divini Redemptoris*, while condemning communism and the Soviet system, was not meant as a condemnation of the Soviet people. A certain amount of cooperation with Russia, in other words, was permissible.

Even as the pope softened the church's stance on the Soviet Union, some Catholics, including some who worked inside the Vatican, such as Monsignor Joseph Hurley, grew frustrated that the pope did not more loudly voice opposition to the Nazi aggression. Some dismissed the reprimand the pope issued after Germany invaded Poland as too tepid. Privately, Pius was clearly angered by German acts of aggression as they occurred. "We would like to utter words of fire," he remarked after Hitler invaded Belgium, Holland, and Luxembourg, for example. But publicly he kept quiet. Why?

Contrary to some anti-Pius histories, Pope Pius XII clearly felt only distrust and disgust for Hitler, a sentiment that reached back beyond 1933 and the unfortunate Reich Concordat. He accurately gauged Hitler as "not only an untrustworthy scoundrel but as a fundamentally wicked person." Any doubt that Pius XII meant these words is erased by a remarkable but well-documented episode that occurred shortly after Pacelli became pope. In January 1940, he was brought into a secret plot, organized by anti-Nazi Germans, to assassinate Adolf Hitler. Though the plot never materialized, and though the pope's role was only supporting—his task was to use his diplomatic ties to the Western allies to secure the way for a post-Hitler Germany—his willingness to take part in an assassination plot, at enormous risk to himself and to the Catholic Church, is incontrovertible evidence of his anti-Nazi sympathies. Even so tough a critic of Pius XII as John Cornwell, author of the egregiously titled *Hitler's Pope*, acknowledges the pope's obvious "hatred of Hitler" and moral courage. "Pusillanimity and indecisiveness," writes Cornwell, "were hardly in his nature."

While it may be, as his critics maintain, that Pius XII did not speak up loudly enough in condemning Nazi atrocities, it is incorrect to suggest that he was "silent." A fairer appraisal of Pius XII might be that he, like his predecessor, was too indirect for today's parlance. "Pope-Speak" is how the scholar Fr. Gerald Fogarty, SJ, labels the tendency of papal encyclicals to speak in broad observations and articulate general principles rather than specific indictments. As another scholar, Fr. Thomas J. Reese, SJ, explains, "Vatican observers, including the press and bishops, must develop the ability to read between the lines of Vatican documents." This is not the place to dissect the nuances of papal rhetoric, but we must acknowledge the style of the pope's World War II writings and understand their context.

Pius XII's 1939 encyclical *Summi Pontificatus* is a good place to start. When Pius wrote in the encyclical that one of the "pernicious errors, widespread today, is the forgetfulness of that law of human solidarity and charity which is dictated and imposed by our common origin and by the equality of rational nature in all men," he did not specifically name the Nazi error of mistreating Jews, but the reader does not have to be a code breaker to figure out what he meant. When he stated that "the blood of countless human beings, even noncombatants, raises a piteous dirge over a nation such as Our dear Poland," he was clearly mourning the Nazi invasion of Poland. And when he stated that "the claim to absolute autonomy for the State stands in open opposition to this natural way that is inherent in man," he was condemning Nazi totalitarianism. Certainly the Nazis got the gist of what he was saying, which is why they tried to block the distribution of *Summi Pontificatus* in Germany, just as they had done in the case of *Mit Brennender Sorge*.

Of course, this does not fully answer the question of why Pius XII did not address himself to the Germans more forcefully, but the better we understand the motives and concerns—the context—behind Pius's encyclicals, the better we can understand why he chose the words he did.

\* \* \*

A final point of context might help us understand, if not excuse, Pius's actions. Several of Pius's critics have implied that he had a *special obligation* to speak out—an obligation greater, that is, than that of other world leaders. Recall that no leader said much of anything about Hitler's treatment of the Jews until late 1942, long after the Holocaust had begun, but Pius is singled out for criticism. Evidently this reflected the moral authority accrued to the papacy over the previous several decades. Leo XIII, Benedict XV, and Pius XI had all expanded this authority, and they had gained the respect not only of Catholics, but of Protestants and Jews as well. The greater the attribution of moral authority to the pope, the greater the expectation for him to take the lead in condemning evildoers.

Lost in this expectation, perhaps, was a recognition that the pope's first duty was to the church—to the Catholic community and to the survival of the institution itself. Putting his own before others may seem un-Christian for a pope, but protecting the Catholic flock was an essential component of papal duty. No pope since the French Revolution could escape the responsibility of defending the church against external threats.

"It should always be remembered that, as Supreme Head of the Universal Church, his first concern was the welfare of Roman Catholics throughout the world irrespective of what their nationality might be," wrote Harold H. Tittmann Jr., the career diplomat who served as Myron Taylor's assistant and eventually as *chargé d'affaires* to the Holy See.

With this concern in mind, and not yet knowing the outcome of the war, Pius worried that speaking too harshly or directly could be taken as a provocation by Hitler that would endanger the lives of Catholics. This was exactly the message he received from the antifascist underground, with evidence to fuel concern. After Dutch Bishops denounced the deportation of Jews from Holland, for example, Hitler had started deporting converted, baptized Jews, too. Revenge was a reflex for Hitler.

Pius XII's special obligation to Catholics did not mean he was indifferent to the rest of humanity. He genuinely wanted to bring peace to the world and to relieve the human suffering brought on by war. But he was a trained diplomat in a sovereign role, and he had the diplomat's habit of keeping options open, closing no doors, looking for wiggle room—of finding ways, as his longtime aide (and future cardinal secretary of state) Domenico Tardini once observed, to "sugar the pill."

Pius XII believed that to be useful to the cause of peace he had to maintain a neutral stance, as Benedict XV had during World War I, rather than advocate for one side or the other. What he may not have understood—and, in the beginning, who really did?—is how different the circumstances of this war would be from the last. World War I was a complicated tale of shifting and shared blame among the belligerents. The Second World War was far more straightforward: an evil power was attempting to dominate the world. "He was operating Benedict XV's policy," the papal historian Eamon Duffy writes, "but in a different war, and a different world."

In retrospect, it is easy to second-guess Pius's desire to maintain neutrality in the face of growing atrocities. Again, though, we must view it from Pius's vantage in the Vatican, without the benefit of hindsight. One important consideration for Pius was his belief that he could not condemn the Nazis without also condemning the Soviets. Yes, he had slightly moderated the church's stand on the communist Soviet Union in support of President Roosevelt, but he remained convinced—with good reason—that Joseph Stalin was as much of a threat to Western civilization as was Adolf Hitler. "[I]f I denounce the Nazis by name," Pius XII told Harold Tittmann, "I must in all justice do the same as regards the Bolsheviks whose principles are strikingly similar; you would not wish me to say such things about an ally of yours at whose side you are engaged today in a death struggle."

Making the moral distinction even blurrier, little direct proof existed early in the war that alleged atrocities were real and not wartime propaganda. As often as the Allies urged Pius to condemn the Axis, the Axis urged him to condemn the Allies. In both cases, the proof of alleged atrocities came to the Vatican second or thirdhand, more rumor than verifiable fact. It is true that Pius made no statement about the Jews until late 1942. Only then did evidence of Hitler's grisly scheme become clear—which explains why no *other* world leader issued a condemnation until late 1942. As Harold Tittmann wrote in September 1942, for the Holy See to confidently condemn one side or the other, would have required it "to develop into an organization whose major activity might well become the determination of the facts and the adjudging of the guilty."

IV.

I quote Harold Tittmann frequently here because no American had a better view of the papacy during the Second World War, for the simple reason that he spent much of the war inside the Vatican with the pope. Tittmann's memoir provides one of the most nuanced and empathetic views we have of Pope Pius XII.

A veteran of World War I, in which he lost a leg and use of one arm, Tittmann was a career diplomat. His previous appointment was in Geneva as consul general to the U.S. embassy there. In August 1939, he was transferred to Rome to serve under Myron Taylor in the U.S. mission to the pope. Operating from a suite of rooms in Rome's Excelsior Hotel on the Via Veneto, Tittmann was the permanent U.S. presence while Taylor traveled to and from the United States and Italy.

Tittmann's status changed markedly on December 7, 1941, when the Japanese bombed Pearl Harbor. The United States was suddenly at war against the Axis powers, including Italy. As the representative of an enemy nation, Tittmann could no longer legally or safely remain in the Excelsior, where previously friendly hotel staff and Italian acquaintances turned suddenly chilly. His choices were to return home to the United States, transfer back Switzerland, or move into the Vatican and continue the U.S. mission there. The last option was the riskiest, since the Vatican itself was vulnerable to Italian forces. Rumors lingered that Mussolini intended to defy the Lateran Treaty and enter Vatican City. Furthermore, the Italian government insisted that the American had no right to diplomatic immunity because the Taylor mission, due to the peculiar circumstances of its formation, was not on formal diplomatic footing.

Harold Tittmann may have been physically handicapped but he was not timid. On December 16, 1941, after his wife boarded a train for Switzerland, he loaded up his car and drove across the Tiber to the Vatican, expecting to be pulled over at any moment by fascist police. The Vatican took Tittmann in "without comment" and found him spacious accommodations on the second floor of a two-story "palazzino" next to Santa Marta. Just days after America declared war on Italy, Undersecretary of State Sumner Welles wrote to President Roosevelt on December 17, 1941 seeking *chargé d'affaires* status for Tittmann because "it is of very great importance that Tittmann remain in the Vatican City so that we may continue contact through him with the Holy See." This status was sufficient to gain Tittmann diplomatic immunity.

Thus began Harold Tittmann's two and one-half year "confinement" inside the peaceful, isolated 109-acre plot of land surrounded by a world at war. He quickly fell into a routine of work and socializing with Holy See personnel and the handful of other diplomats who had taken residence the Vatican. His closest friend was Sir D'Arcy Osborne, the British minister. On Fridays, he met with the Vatican undersecretaries, Domenico Tardini and Giovanni Montini (the future Pope Paul VI), to exchange views and information. To communicate with the U.S. State Department, he sent messages via a diplomatic pouch that left the Vatican twice a week, usually in the hands of a Swiss courier. The messages were dropped at the American embassy in Bern, Switzerland, where they were coded, then forwarded to the United States by cable or radio. The entire route, from Vatican City to Washington, could take as a long as a week. The lines of communication, extraordinary for wartime, went both ways, as Undersecretary Welles noted on May 8, 1941, to his European affairs Bureau chief, Ray Atherton:

> It is, in my opinion, much more useful sending Tittmann weekly summaries of the progress we are making here in rearmament and any salient features that develop from day to day indicating the strong policy which the Government is adopting, than to supply information of that character to our Embassy in Rome which cannot find any outlet for it under present conditions.

The issue that dominated Tittmann's early days at the Vatican was the pope's concern that the Allies might bomb Rome. Pius XII, as Bishop of Rome—and a native-born Roman—hoped for some sort of guarantee from the Allies that they would spare the city. The response from President Roosevelt was polite but firm. The Vatican itself would not be touched, he assured the pope through Tittmann; but Rome, as capital of an Axis power, was fair game.

As the Vatican continued to plead with the Allies to spare Rome, Tittmann pressed back on a very different issue: the relationship between the Holy See and Japan. No sooner had Tittmann moved into his Vatican apartments than Japan declared its intention to send its own ambassador to the pope. Tittmann was informed of this on February 4, 1942. Pius's cardinal secretary of state, Luigi Maglione, told Tittmann that the Holy See could not very well refuse the Japanese overture since Tokyo was already hosting a papal delegate. Tittmann urged the Vatican to reject it, but to no avail. On April 24, Ken Harada, the Japanese minister, arrived in Rome for accreditation with the Vatican.

The addition of the Japanese representative to a diplomatic corps which already included German and Italian representatives increased tension inside the Vatican. As matters turned out, however, this circumstance proved useful. The Vatican quickly became a channel of communication between Japan and the Allies. In 1945, working through Monsignor (later Cardinal) Alfredo Ottavani, Martin Quigley was sent by the head of the OSS, Colonel Bill Donovan, to make overtures for peace to Japanese Ambassador Ken Harada.

The Vatican's relationship with Japan may have been a vindication of its policy of neutrality, but the pope's apparently neutral stance toward Germany was ever more dismaying to some observers. In mid-June 1942, Tittmann reported to the State Department that even some Vatican insiders were commenting on the pope's "ostrich-like policy" regarding the Germans. In late July, the Brazilian ambassador to the Vatican approached Tittmann and asked if he would be willing to join a coordinated effort to urge the pope to make a strong statement against Nazi actions. Tittmann signed on, as did Minister Osborne from Britain and diplomats from Uruguay, Peru, and Cuba. Still the pope issued no statement. Rightly or wrongly, Vatican officials believed that had he done so, especially after the diplomats' *demarche*, he "would have laid himself open to the accusation of having yielded to Allied pressure." Furthermore, Pius XII remained concerned that a statement against Hitler might backfire by inciting the Nazis to greater acts of barbarism.

In late summer of 1942, Myron Taylor returned to the Vatican after travelling through the enemy territory of Italy. He met the pope privately several times during last weeks of September. His two most urgent goals now were, first, to convince Pius that the United States was going to win the war and, second, to present to him evidence that Nazi atrocities were real and encourage him to speak sharply against them. He carried with him a letter containing eyewitness reports of the Nazi's "liquidation" of the

Warsaw Ghetto, including accounts of corpses "utilized for making fats and their bones for the manufacture of fertilizer." Still, the pope hesitated to issue a direct condemnation. "The Holy See is still apparently convinced that a forthright denunciation by the Pope of Nazi atrocities, at least in so far as Poland is concerned, would result in the violent deaths of many more people," Harold Tittmann wrote to Secretary of State Cordell Hull on October 6. Ten days later, having received no further encouragement from the Vatican regarding a statement by the pope or other solutions to aid Poland's Jews, Tittmann wrote again to superiors in Washington in evident frustration. "I regret that the Holy See could not have been more helpful."

A statement from the pope finally came at the end of 1942. In a Christmas Eve radio broadcast, Pius XII mourned the killing of "hundreds of thousands, who, through no fault of their own, and sometimes only because of their nationality or race, have been consigned to death or slow decline." The pope, as in earlier statements, did not mention the Jews or the Nazis by name, but, as he told Tittmann a few days later, he believed he had been quite clear.

Indeed, as in previous cases, he was evidently clear enough for the Germans. After the broadcast, Joachim von Ribbentrop, Germany's foreign minister, sent a threatening message to the pope, informing him that "Germany does not lack physical means of retaliation." The warning, like the pope's message, may have been vague, but its meaning was unmistakable.

★ ★ ★

The bombs so dreaded by the pope began to fall on Rome in the summer of 1943. The first air raid came on July 19, when five hundred American planes roared over the city. Vatican Hill gave a good view of the action, and Harold Tittmann's fourteen-year-old—visiting on break from school in Switzerland—watched from the window of D'Arcy Osborne's apartment in Pallazzo Santa Marta. "Flying in perfect formations of three, they swept toward their objectives, gleaming in the bright sunlight," the boy recorded in his journal. "We had at first thought that they were bombing places around Rome, but when we saw huge clouds of smoke rising in the direction of the station, we knew that it was Rome's turn to suffer the horrors of war."

The bombers targeted rail and freight yards, sparing historic and residential sections of the city. Inevitably, in those days of imprecise bombing, civilians were killed, perhaps as many as fifteen hundred. Pius XII had not left the Vatican since Italy entered the war three years earlier, but now, accompanied only by Monsignor Montini, he sped in an automobile to the hard-hit neighborhood of San Lorenzo. The pope prayed tearfully over the wreckage as Montini handed out alms to the stricken populace.

Events moved very fast after that initial allied raid on Rome. On July 25, Mussolini was deposed by the Fascist Grand Council. The new government, under Marshal Pietro Badoglio, moved to have Rome declared an open city—to strip it of military assets in exchange for an agreement by the Allies to stop bombing it. The Vatican was the government's channel to the Allies to discuss terms; and Harold Tittmann, as chief American diplomat in Rome, became the chief conduit between the Vatican and the United States. The Badoglio government wished for peace, Tittmann reported, but was held back by the threat of a Nazi invasion.

Its fears were justified. The moment an armistice between Italy and the Allies was announced on September 8, the infuriated Germans attacked. Forty-eight hours later, Rome was in the hands of Nazis.

## V.

And so back to where we began this long chapter of war—to St. Peter's Square. It is the autumn of 1943 and Nazi troops surround the Vatican, armed with antitank artillery and machine guns. Motorcycle patrols speed along the edge of the square. A notice in front of St. Peter's Basilica warns away the curious and the devout: *Anyone attempting to enter will be shot.* The Germans announce they are offering "protection" to the pope.

"The German military authorities occupying Rome have the Vatican State lying almost helpless within their mailed fist," reports the *New York Times* on September 26. "The physical conquest of the Vatican would be only a matter of hours should the Germans decide to attack." As the *Times* notes, the pope did have a few hundred of his own soldiers inside, including men from the Swiss Guard, the Palatine Guard, and the Nobles Guard. These men could be "counted on to put up the stubborn resistance demanded by tradition and their high responsibility, but they would never have a chance."

The Germans had every reason to attack. They suspected—correctly—that enemy refugees, including Jews, escaped prisoners of war, and supporters of the resistance were hidden inside the Vatican, as well as in other church properties throughout Rome. Protection operations of this magnitude were ensconced in dioceses all over Italy, led by local bishops and clergy. Some of these underground operations were run by Vatican prelates, such as Monsignor Hugh O'Flaherty of Ireland (memorably portrayed by Gregory Peck in the film *The Scarlett and the Black*). Others were run by diplomats like Britain's D'Arcy Osborne. Harold Tittmann had himself been overseeing the shelter of 230 American prisoners of war who escaped before the Germans took over Rome. The Germans, aware of these operations, plotted retaliation. Heinrich Himmler, head of the German SS, talked of ridding the Vatican of its "nest of spies," while Adolf Hitler discussed plans to kidnap the pope and loot the church of its treasures.

It is important to revisit here, again, the stubborn refusal of Pope Pius IX, way back in 1870, to accept the conditions of Italy's Law of Guarantees and the reduction in legal status of Holy See concordats and other diplomatic exchanges. Had he capitulated, there would have been no such thing as the Vatican City State, nor in all likelihood would the historic role of the Holy See as a diplomatic presence throughout the world have been maintained.

Had Pope Pius allowed concordats to be reduced to non-treaty level agreements, as Prince von Metternich and others demanded, the Holy See might have lost its recognition and perception as an institutional sovereign. Then matters could have turned out very differently. The Vatican, as Italian soil, would have been subject to fascist rule when Mussolini came to power, and then subject to Nazi rule after the Germans took over Rome. The diplomats inside would have enjoyed no immunity. Refugees under the Vatican's protection would have been exposed. All of the Catholic Church's property in Rome would have come under Adolf Hitler's control.

The Holy See waited nearly sixty years to come to terms with the government of Italy, as it finally did in the Lateran Treaty, but the wait was worth it. The notice posted at entrances to the Vatican—"The Governor of Vatican City, on the orders of the Secretary of State, Cardinal Maglione, declares that this entrance to Vatican City, which is a sovereign and independent neutral State, enjoy the right of inviolability"—meant something, even to Hitler, who had respected the sovereignty of no one.

Of course, Hitler could have taken the Vatican had he chosen to do so, Lateran Treaty or not. That he did not suggests he feared the response such a violation would incite. Possibly he considered the reaction of his own 20 million or so Catholics, who had submitted to his rule thus far but might bridle at a German attack on the Vatican. All we know for certain is that *something* held Hitler back. The white line around the Vatican was one line he would not cross.

This raises again the old questions: could Pius XII have done more to deter Hitler from the start? Did he underestimate his own moral authority in confronting Hitler? Did he fear Hitler's power too much, failing to realize that Hitler feared his power, too?

These questions are especially pointed in regards to the Roman Jews, whose deportation was ordered by the Nazis starting on October 16, 1943. German troops raided Rome's Jewish ghetto, where about eight thousand Jews lived, and began transporting them by train to Auschwitz. Approximately two thousand of these Romans, including many children, would eventually be killed.

Some critics have asserted that Pius XII did not do enough to save the Roman Jews, even arguing that the pope complied with the capture and deportation of the city's Jewish citizens. Others who have studied the matter, however, strongly disagree with that assessment. Michael Tagliacozzo, an Italian—and Jewish—historian who is a leading expert on Nazi war crimes in Rome (and is himself a survivor of the Nazi roundup in Rome) concludes that Pius *did* protest on behalf of Rome's Jews and devoted Vatican resources to hiding thousands of Jews from the Nazis.

The controversy regarding Pius XII's behavior toward the Jews, either in Rome or elsewhere in Europe, is unlikely to die anytime soon, and certainly it will not end here. The argument that Pius could have used moral suasion to mobilize opposition to Hitler—that he failed to deploy his soft power as aggressively as he might have—will continue to be part of his legacy.

The fairest assessment of Pius XII probably belongs to Harold Tittmann, who had his own frustrations with the pope but came to the conclusion, after living through the war inside the Vatican, that Pius XII chose the best route *knowing what he knew at the time*; and that he really could not in good conscience have acted other than as he did. "If he had spoken out, would there have been fewer victims or more?" Tittmann asks. "Personally, I cannot help feel that the Holy Father chose the better path by not speaking out and thereby saved many lives."

In his 1997 book *The Myth of Rescue*, British historian William Rubenstein argues that it's a mistake to think that anyone could have stopped Hitler with mere words. Though not writing specifically about the pope, Rubenstein addresses a criticism directed against leaders of Allied nations, as well as against Jews who lived in the United States during the war, that they did too little to save the Jews in Europe. "Not one plan or proposal, made anywhere in the democracies by either Jews or non-Jewish champions of the Jews after the Nazi conquest of Europe could have rescued one single Jew who perished in the Holocaust." Blaming presidents and prime ministers—and popes—for the sins of a madman may give satisfaction at some level, but it is absurd.

★ ★ ★

The American army entered Rome on June 4, 1944. Two days later, on D-Day, Allied forces landed on the beaches of Normandy. The war still had another year to go, but Rome, at least, was free.

Shortly after American troops took control of the city, the head of the U.S. Office of Strategic Service, William Donovan, arrived to make changes in American spy operations in Italy. "Wild Bill" Donovan had created the American intelligence service during the war, and now that war was winding down, he looked forward to creating its postwar successor, the Central Intelligence Agency (CIA). Before leaving Rome, Donovan visited the Vatican and met with Pope Pius XII.

Donovan had realized during the war that the Catholic Church, with its own network of clergy and religious spread wide and deep around the world, was a valuable resource for the spy agency. He had written President Roosevelt back in 1942 about having met with Cardinal Cigognani about providing the United States all material the Vatican had obtained through its diplomatic channels. Furthermore, an extensive organization run by a Belgian priest named Felix Morlion, for example, had accumulated information and personal insights from priests and parishioners throughout Europe, a very good gauge of popular attitudes in warring nations. Donovan hoped for more of the same.

On his visit, as if to prime the pump, Donovan fed Pius XII a piece of information American intelligence agents had discovered: Japanese agents working within Japan's mission to the Holy See were about to install a radio transmitter in their embassy offices to secretly transmit information back to Tokyo. The pope thanked Donovan for the tip and vowed to deal with it. A small matter, but it was the start of an important alliance between the Vatican and American intelligence.

# III

## THE COLD WAR

# 8

# COMMON GROUND

Both religion and democracy are founded on one basic principle, the worth and dignity of the individual man and woman.

—Harry S. Truman (1946)

## I.

The war in Europe came to a quick and dramatic conclusion in the
spring of 1945. That April brought the deaths of three of the war's
main players. Franklin Roosevelt suffered a massive stroke on April 12;
Mussolini was found in hiding and executed on April 28; and Hitler
committed suicide on April 30. On May 7, Germany surrendered. Three
months later, President Truman ordered atomic bombs dropped on Hiro-
shima and Nagasaki.

The dust and ashes of the war had hardly settled when a new conflict
began, one that would be even more threatening to world peace—and
would last much longer—than the one just ended. The Cold War would
persist through nine American presidents and five popes, framing international relations during the decades between the World War II and the fall
of the Berlin Wall in 1989. Along the way, the Cold War drew the United
States and the Holy See into an extraordinary relationship, changing the
course of history.

Historians correctly credit President Roosevelt with opening modern
relations with the papacy during the Second World War. Less recognized are
the overtures made to the Vatican by President Truman in the early years
of the Cold War, as the Soviet Union grabbed land and power throughout

Eastern Europe. Almost from the day he entered office, Truman understood, perhaps better than Roosevelt, that the Soviets and their communist associates must be halted. The challenge of accomplishing this intensified through the course of his presidency, becoming dramatically more urgent in 1949, when the Soviets debuted their atomic bomb and the communist forces under Mao Tse Tung took control of China. Since direct confrontation with the Soviets risked nuclear conflagration, efforts to contain communism were asymmetrical in nature. The fight was waged at local levels, in covert operations and limited engagement proxy wars in the jungles of Asia and Central America, on the plains of Africa and the mountains of Afghanistan, on Caribbean islands and Arabian deserts—anywhere the communists hoped to gain a foothold and the United States intended to prevent that. The truth about the Cold War that Harry Truman instinctively grasped from the start, however, was that victory would ultimately owe less to the hard power of bullets and bombs than to the soft power of morals and principles grounded in faith. America and her allies, in other words, needed religion to prevail. Above all, they needed the Roman Catholic Church.

★ ★ ★

On March 6, 1946, a day after watching former British Prime Minister Winston Churchill deliver his famous "Iron Curtain" speech at Westminster College in Fulton, Missouri, President Truman gave his own important Cold War speech in nearby Columbus, Missouri, to a Protestant organization called the Federal Council of Churches. Truman did not mention the Cold War by name—the term was not yet coined—nor did he mention the Soviet Union, but his speech sounded themes that would define his approach to the Cold War.

> In our relations abroad and in our economy at home, forces of selfishness and greed and intolerance are again at work. They create situations which call for hard decisions, for forthrightness, for courage and determination. But above everything else, they call for one thing, without which we are lost. They call for a moral and spiritual awakening in the life of the individual and in the councils of the world. . . .
>
> If the civilized world as we know it today is to survive, the gigantic power which man has acquired through atomic energy must be matched by spiritual strength of greater magnitude. All mankind now stands in the doorway to destruction—or upon the threshold of the greatest age in history. And I prefer to face that great age. Only a high moral standard can master this new power of the universe, and develop it for the common good.

A devout Baptist, Truman saw religious faith, with its emphasis on "the worth and dignity of the individual man and woman," as the fundamental precondition for personal freedom and world order, and as the antidote to communist totalitarianism. This was not simply a spiritual epiphany for Truman; it was a mission statement.

> This is the supreme opportunity for the Church to continue to fulfill its mission on earth. The Protestant Church, the Catholic Church, and the Jewish Synagogue—bound together in the American unity of brotherhood—must provide the shock forces to accomplish this moral and spiritual awakening. No other agency can do it. Unless it is done we are headed for the disaster we would deserve.

As the Cold War scholar William Inboden wrote of this Columbus speech, "Truman was beginning to lay the theological foundation for opposing the Soviets."

His own Protestant roots notwithstanding, Truman envisioned a special role for the Roman Catholic Church in the struggle he foresaw against communism. Not only did the church possess the largest and broadest Christian constituency in the world (including, by the end of the war, a quarter of the American population), but it had also vocally led the charge against communism from the beginning, while the world focused on fascism. In his encyclical *Divini Redemptoris* (On Atheistic Communism) in 1937, Pope Pius XI had clearly and forcefully laid out the church's position. When Truman enlisted the Catholic Church in America's fight against the communists, America was really just joining a fight the church had been waging for years.

Not long after his speech in Columbus, President Truman conceived a grand, if not quixotic, plan to use the power of religion to combat Soviet communism, with Pope Pius XII out in front. Truman's idea was to bring together the religious sects of the world in a phalanx of the faithful—a unified force of godliness that would countervail the propagation of atheistic Marxism. As Truman wrote in his letter to the pope on November 21, 1946, America prayed "that all moral forces of the world will unite their strength and will create . . . well-being, peace, security, and freedom in an enduring world order." Communism was first and foremost an ideology; and the best way to defeat a bad set of ideas, believed Truman, was with a better set of ideas.

Pius XII welcomed Truman's letter. The pope was eager for closer ties to the United States. This was one reason, in 1944, that he had offered the job of secretary of state to his old friend Cardinal Spellman, archbishop of New

York, an appointment which would have made Spellman the first American cardinal secretary in history. (There has yet to be one.) Spellman turned down the pope on the grounds that he could do more good for the church in his position in the United States than in Rome. As we'll see, he continued to be a vital channel between the Vatican and important American institutions during a critical time in the history of both.

Another continuing channel of communication in the postwar years was Myron Taylor, still filling the role he had been appointed to under Roosevelt. On November 23, 1946, two days after writing the pope, Truman announced the reappointment of Taylor as personal representative of the president to the Vatican.

The pope was just one of several religious leaders Myron Taylor consulted over the next several years. He shuttled among Anglicans in Canterbury, Lutherans in Berlin, Calvinists in Geneva, Orthodox Christians in Istanbul, and Catholics in Rome, attempting to forge the kind of alliance President Truman envisioned. Taylor reported on his progress directly to Truman, mostly in secret. The president was initially very hopeful. "Looks as if he and I may get the morals of the world on our side," Truman wrote to his wife, Bess, in 1947, after consulting with Taylor. "I may send him to see the top Buddhist and the Grand Lama of Tibet. If I can mobilize the people who believe in a moral world against the Bolshevik materialists . . . we can win this fight."

Perhaps bolstering his optimistic view, and certainly corroborating it, President Truman had seen the soft power of the Holy See at work in June 1946, when he sent former President Herbert Hoover to urge the newly elected Juan Peron, bitterly opposed by the United States, to donate grains to Europe to help alleviate the hunger there. Truman was informed that Peron would see Hoover, despite the Argentinian's feelings toward America, because the pope had already requested this humanitarian aid. Hoover's personal diary notes that he "had his friend Hugh Gibson use a Vatican connection to get his first interview with Peron."

Myron Taylor at first met with a positive reception on his travels to religious leaders. Before long, though, his mission was hindered by differences dating back to the schism between the Roman Catholic and Orthodox churches in the eleventh century and between Roman Catholics and Protestants in the sixteenth. Along with theological disputes, the old animosities and resentments still simmered. To some Protestants, Catholicism was little better than communism; to some Catholics, the Eastern Orthodox sects were in league with the Communists, to the point of being a state church in Russia and other Communist countries.

Ties between state and church remain tight in Russia even today. President Vladimir Putin is reported to confer frequently with Archimandrite Tikhon Shevkunov, a high-level Orthodox prelate. In July 2012, when a Moscow musical group staged a protest in an Orthodox church over the unseemly links between the Putin regime and the church, its members were promptly arrested. The episode only fueled more speculation of church-state collaboration.

## II.

While Taylor's mission of peace was dissolving into internecine Christian quarrels, a more pragmatic U.S. effort was meeting success in Rome. The CIA, the postwar successor of William Donovan's Office of Strategic Services (OSS), was attempting to block the communist party from gaining power in the Italian elections of 1948. The agency found a willing and able ally in the Vatican.

Of course, this was not the first time American intelligence operations and the Vatican worked together. During the war, the OSS took great interest in the intelligence resources of the Vatican—one reason William Donovan had met the pope in the spring of 1944—and found the church to be a provident, if occasionally unwitting, source of information. Copies of reports filed by the Vatican's nuncio to Japan, for example, were mined for valuable information about Allied bombing targets. As noted earlier, Harold Tittmann made valuable use of the Vatican diplomatic pouch to get his communiqués transported out of Italy.

Along with such OSS successes had come some glaring embarrassments. The most infamous was the "Vessel" case. In the fall of 1944, the OSS had begun purchasing reports that appeared to come directly from inside the Vatican's Secretariat of State. The supplier, known to OSS officials as Vessel, was someone who evidently had access to sensitive materials, including verbatim transcripts and detailed descriptions of conversations between the pope and other heads of state. So valued were these materials that they were promptly distributed to the top levels of the American government, including President Roosevelt. Not until February 1945 was the truth discovered: Vessel was a fraud. The tip-off came from Myron Taylor, after one of the reports carried a transcript of a purported conversation between Taylor and Japanese Ambassador Ken Harada. This conversation, Taylor told OSS, never occurred. Nor had any of the other dialogue in purported transcripts purchased by OSS from

Vessel. Every report was fabricated by an Italian scam artist, Virgilio Scattolini, who had once briefly worked inside the Vatican.

Following the OSS's wins and losses with the Vatican during the war, Rome was where, in 1948, the recently organized CIA undertook its first major covert operation. That spring, the Italian Communist Party (PCI) and the Italian Socialist Party (PSI) were joining forces in an effort to wrest power from the Christian Democrats, the moderate party supported by the Vatican. The pope was deeply concerned that the "Socialist-Communist bloc could very easily win a plurality," according to a CIA intelligence report in January 1948, and "emphatically agrees that all anti-Communists should form a bloc in order to give the electorate a clear choice between Communism and anti-Communism."

Another CIA report, dated March 5, methodically outlined what a Communist victory would mean to Italy and the world. "There would follow a discreet, but rapid Communist infiltration of the armed forces, the police, and the national administration" which would eventually lead to Italy becoming a "fully developed police state under open and exclusive Communist control." According to CIA analysts, the Soviet Union would then use Italian territory for air and naval bases, giving it control over Mediterranean shipping lanes. To avoid upsetting Catholics and courting civil war, the incoming communists would initially attempt to be "more Catholic than the Vatican." But eventually, CIA analysts warned, the Communists would impose a police state over "the most ancient of seat of Western Culture" while "devout Catholics everywhere would be gravely concerned regarding the safety of the Holy See."

The CIA descended on Rome and went to work. With the help of the Vatican's network of priests and other religious, and filtering resources through Catholic Action (a political front closely associated with the Vatican), the agency used propaganda and millions of lira to influence and ultimately orchestrate the outcome of the election. "We had bags of money that we delivered to selected politicians, to defray their political expenses, their campaign expenses, for posters, for pamphlets," recalled CIA officer Mark Wyatt who worked on the project. Suitcases stuffed with cash were handed off in the lobby of a four-star Rome hotel. While perhaps rudimentary as far as covert operations go, the tactics worked well. The Vatican-backed Christian Democrats carried the day with 48 percent of the vote and kept the Communists at bay.

★ ★ ★

Circumstances in Eastern Europe offered less reason to cheer. Events there confirmed every concern the church had ever voiced about communism.

Soviet-backed governments confiscated church lands, nationalized Catholic schools, claimed the right of investiture, and, in a number of cases, persecuted Catholic clergy. Such abuses were notably widespread in Catholic minority countries such as Yugoslavia, Albania, and Romania. In countries with large Catholic populations, such as Poland, Czechoslovakia, and Hungary, the Communists moved more slowly, but the result was much the same. The local church hierarchy either submitted to government authority or faced retribution. A few cases of Communist authorities cracking down on church officials became international incidents in the early Cold War years. None of these was more infamous than the arrest of Cardinal Mindszenty near the end of 1948.

Joseph Mindszenty was the fifty-six-year-old primate of Hungary and archbishop of Estergom, the traditional seat of Catholic power in predominantly Catholic Hungary. He was powerful, popular, and brash, all qualities he had demonstrated during the war in standing up to the fascists. Once the Communists came to power after the war, Mindszenty turned his wrath on them. He dismissed the government-run press as a "bitter disgrace," becoming ever more tendentious as the regime moved to take over Catholic schools in Hungary. By November 1948, the regime had enough of Mindszenty and his rebellious fellow Catholics. A government official publicly threatened "liquidation of clerical reaction" should protests continue. But Mindszenty refused to be quiet. On December 26, 1948, he was arrested by the Communist government.

The following February, as the Vatican and Western nations watched in disgust, Cardinal Mindszenty was subjected to a three-day show trial. The government presented forged documents to frame the cardinal for treason and conspiracy to overthrow the government. He was sentenced to life in prison. The whole charade was an act of "wanton persecution," in the words of U.S. Secretary of State Dean Acheson, leaving the American people "sickened and horrified."

III.

The Myron Taylor mission ended in 1950. Taylor was now seventy-seven and in poor health, and his efforts to form a coalition among the world's religions had achieved little. Taylor's retirement raised the question of what form future U.S. relations with the Holy See should take. In January 1950, President Truman's State Department prepared a memo outlining a few options. One of these was to appoint another personal representative, in the model of Myron Taylor, who would require no congressional approval.

Other options included turning all Holy See matters over to the American embassy in Italy or letting the relationship lapse entirely. The last option was to establish full and formal diplomatic relations with the Holy See.

The State Department favored this last option. The church would be "of some assistance in securing the influence of the Holy See on 300,000,000 Catholics throughout the world in support of our objectives, and, to some extent, on the thirty-eight governments who now maintain diplomatic relations with the Holy See." As for what those objectives might be, "It is well known that the Holy See is vigorously engaged in the growing fight against Communism, and direct relations would assist in coordinating efforts to combat it, particularly in the ideological field." The State Department had been skeptical of FDR's effort to appoint a high-level representative to the Holy See before World War II, but it now saw value in expanding and formalizing the relationship.

President Truman concurred. He instructed the State Department to move ahead with the nomination of an ambassador. "The President feels that the time has now come to bring this matter to a conclusion and would like to proceed expeditiously with this appointment," reads another State Department memo, this one filed in May 1950. The name Truman had in mind at the time—a surprise to me when I read about it—was Allen W. Dulles, formerly William Donovan's right-hand man at the OSS and the future director of the CIA. The Dulles appointment did not go forward—perhaps Dulles was already focusing on CIA—but the memo suggests that Truman's desire to have a high-level diplomatic representative to the pope was serious and sustained.

In October 1951, President Truman raised the issue again. Secretary of State Dean Acheson tried to talk him out of it, but Truman was determined. On October 20, the White House announced the nomination of U.S. Army General Mark Clark to the post of full ambassador to the Holy See, "to maintain diplomatic representation at the Vatican" and "assist in coordinating the effort to combat the Communist menace." General Clark had been Allied commander in Italy during the war, one of General Eisenhower's favorites; it was Clark who had led American troops in the liberation of Rome (and later accompanied Eisenhower to meet the pope). Had the nomination gone through, Clark would have become the first full American ambassador to the Holy See.

What happened, instead, was a political firestorm. Indignant letters poured in from Protestant congregations and clergy around the country, criticizing the nomination as incompatible with the U.S. Constitution. Telegrams to the White House ran six to one against the appointment.

The National Council of Churches, among other Protestant organizations, mobilized in force, and Protestant clergy staged demonstrations in front of the White House. Meanwhile, in Congress, the Chairman of the Committee on Foreign Relations made clear that he was "violently opposed" to the nomination and would not even bring it before the committee.

Not everybody thought the appointment was a bad idea. A number of newspaper editorial pages came out in favor of it. "The fuss over the appointment continued to seem a spectacular case of much ado about nothing," wrote the young Harvard historian—and future John F. Kennedy advisor—Arthur M. Schlesinger Jr. in the *Atlantic Monthly*. "The Vatican is constantly in process of making political decisions. These decisions influence great masses of people. It is the injunction of elementary good sense that we should do what we can to make sure that these decisions support rather than obstruct our own foreign policy."

But even some people who approved the idea in theory criticized the nomination of Clark as a cynical move on Truman's part to draw Catholic voters into the Democratic tent before the 1952 election. His critics asserted that Truman never seriously thought Clark would survive the process and was simply playing politics at the general's expense. Evidence suggests, however, that Truman was indeed sincere in wanting an ambassador to the Holy See, and it was far from clear that he stood to gain more in Catholic votes than he would lose in Protestant ones. Truman's error was that, despite impassioned Protestants speaking up against a perceived special treatment for the Catholic Church, he caved too quickly when the pressure rose. "When any president begins to flinch from making wise decisions because they will enrage a section of the population," wrote Arthur Schlesinger, "he might as well resign."

Unfortunately for Clark, the process became personal. As protests against his appointment grew in volume and vitriol, the general found himself under personal attack. He finally withdrew his name in January 1952. President Truman wrote a long regretful letter to Pius XII in May 1952 to explain what had happened. Describing the "perfect furore [*sic*] of opposition" that led Clark to withdraw, he told the pope that "Under these several circumstances I feel, to my deep regret, that it would be unwise for me to pursue my intention with respect to the naming of a Minister or Ambassador to the Vatican." The pope's response was gracious but perplexed. Why would Americans be so opposed to diplomatic relations when there was much to gain and nothing to lose? "If opposition of such a nature cannot but be deplored, nevertheless it is difficult to believe that it represents the feelings of the majority of the American people, whose open-mindedness is disposed to much broader and more serene views."

While the Clark nomination was an obvious setback, too much had been achieved in the relationship between the United States and the Holy See to allow it to regress to its prewar state. After this, American presidents would never again ignore the Vatican. Only one president prior to Truman—Wilson—had met a pope; no president after Truman would fail to visit the Vatican at least once while in office. The political and diplomatic value of the papacy would rise and fall in the estimation of Washington, but on the whole its value increased during the Cold War. Official diplomatic recognition was only a matter of time in coming.

"The Vatican is fated to be a continual object of United States interest," Robert Graham would write with characteristic prescience in 1959. "International life is no respecter of national susceptibilities or customs. . . . [I]t is unrealistic to expect that real important issues can be solved short of direct and avowed diplomatic relations."

IV.

Following the Mark Clark fiasco, President Dwight Eisenhower understandably had little interest in pursuing formal relations with the Holy See when he entered the White House in 1953. Public diplomacy between the Washington and the Holy See remained understated throughout the eight years Ike served as president. It would be inaccurate to assume from this, however, that relations were absent or static in the 1950s, just as it would be wrong to infer from the rejection of General Clark's ambassadorship that anti-Catholic bias was unyielding in the country. The standing of the church, and of Catholics, grew dramatically in America during the 1950s. One obvious proof of this was the election in 1960 of a Catholic as president, something quite unthinkable just a short while earlier.

To understand how this came about—how America changed between Clark's nomination in 1951 and John Kennedy's election in 1960—we might begin with U.S. foreign policy under Eisenhower which, to an even greater extent than under Truman, was influenced and shaped by deeply rooted religious undertones. The 1950s were a time of spiritual revival in the United States. New churches of all denominations sprang up as fast as the suburbs they were located in, and pews were full on Sundays. The Eisenhower administration reflected the new American religiosity by inaugurating the National Prayer Breakfast and adding the motto "In God

We Trust" to American currency. God had seldom been so much a part of American public discourse. The reasons for this are no doubt complex, but one significant factor was the rise of communism. The atheism and dialectical materialism of Marx and Mao elicited a robust religious response throughout the United States.

Other than Eisenhower, who came to embrace religion as a necessary component of American life—and was himself baptized at a Washington church while in office—the two men most responsible for the religious tone of the administration were the brothers John Foster Dulles and Allen Dulles. With John Foster serving as secretary of state and Allen as director of CIA, the brothers oversaw the overt and covert aspects of an American foreign policy that focused squarely on halting communism. The Dulles brothers came from a long a line of American statesmen; their maternal grandfather was secretary of state under President Benjamin Harrison and their uncle, Robert Lansing, was Woodrow Wilson's secretary of state. Equally important, though, they came from a line of Presbyterian missionaries and ministers, including their own father. They undertook public service with a missionaries' devotion. Defeating communism was not just a matter of *realpolitik*; it was a moral imperative. "There is a moral or natural law not made by man which determines right and wrong," John Foster Dulles declared in 1952, in language that could have been written by Thomas Jefferson or Thomas Aquinas—or spoken by Pope Benedict XVI in 2011—"and conformity with this law is in the long run indispensable to human welfare."

Though the Dulleses epitomized Protestant America, their view of the world made them natural allies of the Catholic Church. The alliance became personal in 1956 when Avery Dulles, the son of John Foster and nephew of Allen, was ordained as a Jesuit priest. While it would be unduly conjectural to speculate on the religious formation of this young priest, it is possible to see in Avery's conversion a link between the old Protestant world of his forefathers and the modern American Catholic Church, including a popular recognition that a Catholic could be just as American as a Protestant.

★ ★ ★

The changing attitude about Catholicism in the 1950s was driven by at least two engines in American life: the demographic shift of the postwar baby boom and anticommunism.

Like their Protestant compatriots, young American Catholic men returned from war (where they had made up more than a quarter of the armed forces), married and had children, and moved to suburbs. As James

O'Toole points out in his history of American Catholicism, the mass migration of young families to the suburbs meant that ethnic and religious groups left behind old communities and prejudices, mingling and assimilating as never before: Methodists lived next to Lutherans, who lived next to Catholics, who lived next to Jews. Even if they attended separate churches and synagogues, their children played in each other's backyards. The uniquely American experiences of the First Amendment and the "melting pot" continued to stimulate religious pluralism, on the one hand, and cultural cohesion, on the other.

Beginning with the early responses of Pius XI and Pius XII to communist ideology and teaching, the position of the Catholic Church was clear. By the late 1950s, Catholics were widely perceived as one of the most vocally pro-American, anticommunist groups in the country. Catholicism was now "prima facie evidence of loyalty," as Daniel Patrick Moynihan put it at the time. When it came to questioning patriotism in the 1950s, joked the future New York senator, "Harvard men were to be checked; Fordham men would do the checking."

In the absence of official diplomatic relations, Archbishop Francis Spellman of New York, himself an ardent and vocal anticommunist (and a Fordham man), was America's primary liaison to the Vatican. He was correct in believing he could achieve more for the church from his post in New York than he could have done in Rome, and he became the face of the Catholic Church to most Americans. Spellman played an important behind-the-scenes role in virtually every major U.S. foreign policy decision of the time, particularly decisions regarding the containment of communism. He was a member of the National Committee for a Free Europe, an organization headed by CIA Director Allen Dulles, which promoted anticommunist ideals, and he lent his support to a broad array of American efforts to curb communism. In 1954, for example, the CIA approached Spellman to assist in its efforts to overthrow the left-leaning regime of Jacobo Arbenz in Guatemala. The agency asked him to arrange a "clandestine contact" for a CIA agent in Guatemala with Archbishop Mariano Rosselli Arellano "so we could coordinate our parallel efforts there." Soon afterward, the Guatemalan church released a pastoral letter denouncing communism. This was read in churches throughout Guatemala, airdropped by CIA planes over the country, and generally added to the impression that Jacobo Arbenz had to go.

Following the Guatemala episode, the Catholic Church would be involved in a number of similar efforts to keep unsavory characters out of power in Latin America. Some occurred during my tenure in Rome, as I will describe in part 5 of this book. Even more recently, in the summer of 2009—following my ambassadorship—the church intervened when Honduran President Manuel Zelaya usurped his country's constitutional process to seek an additional term in office. After being dispatched from the country by the military, Zelaya ended up in Nicaragua, where the Sandinista regime of Daniel Ortega was glad to host him. On July 4, 2009, Honduran Cardinal Oscar Rodriguez Maradiaga called publicly for Zelaya to abandon any attempt to return to Honduras. Along with more discreet actions, the Cardinal's strong words served to arouse the populace, nurture several days of anti-Zelaya demonstrations, and ultimately prevent his return.

★ ★ ★

CIA operations continued in Italy through the 1950s with the cooperation of the Vatican. The young, devoutly Catholic CIA officer William Colby, former agent of the OSS—and future director of CIA—took over the Rome operation in 1953, arriving in the Eternal City excited for "an unparalleled opportunity to demonstrate that secret aid could help our friends and frustrate our foes without the use of force or violence." As in 1948, the CIA was determined to keep the Communists out of power in the election of 1958, no small challenge after leftist gains in June 1953 and with Moscow contributing as much as $50 million a year. The CIA poured in its own funds, much of this funneled through the Vatican.

Eastern Europe was the specter that gave continuous urgency to the fight against Communists. Life under Soviet-dominated dictatorships became only grimmer as the years wore on. Stalin's death in 1953 raised the hopes for reform behind the Iron Curtain, but these turned out to be false. In 1956, following student demonstrations and the overthrow of the Hungarian government, the Soviet army invaded Hungary to crush the revolution and impose its own puppet regime, even more repressive than the preceding one.

One glimmer of good news for freedom in 1956 was Cardinal Mindszenty's escape from imprisonment amidst Hungary's chaos. Another man might have taken the opportunity to leave the country entirely but not Mindszenty. He hurried to Budapest to assist the revolution. As Soviet tanks rolled into the city in early November 1956, he took asylum in the American Embassy, where he was welcomed on orders from Washington. The cardinal would remain inside the embassy, a guest of the U.S. government, for the next fifteen years.

By the time he came out, the world would be a very different place.

# 9

# WAR AND *PACEM*

Peace on Earth—which man throughout the ages has so
longed for and sought after—can never be established, never
guaranteed, except by the diligent observance of the divinely
established order.

—John XXIII (April 11, 1963)

## I.

It would take an entire book, and then some, to adequately address the
changes in the lives of American Catholics in the five years between the
death of Pius XII in the autumn of 1958 and the death of President John
Kennedy in the autumn of 1963. The themes that emerged from this period
reshaped the Catholic Church and its role in the modern world, setting the
stage for the future relations between the United States and the Holy See,
and between the Holy See and the world.

The new era began with the death of Pius XII on October 9, 1958.
Within the wider church, the end of Pius's papacy was both mourned and
welcomed. He had been pope for nineteen years and a dominant force in
the church for almost forty years. The Italians have a saying, *Un papa grasso,
ne seguiva uno magro,* which translates as "always follow a fat pope with a
skinny pope." In other words, the church is ready for a change after a long
papal reign. Change is exactly what it got in 1958.

John XXIII was everything the austere, aristocratic Pius XII was not.
Born in a rural village in the northern Italy, the third of thirteen children
of a poor farmer, Angelo Roncalli was gregarious and seemingly unsophis-
ticated, despite his considerable erudition. He was also, at seventy-seven,

already advanced in age. The consensus was that he would be a transitional pope, a congenial caretaker whom both the reformers and the conservatives in the church could accept at the time.

Almost at once, though, John XXIII shocked the Vatican by proposing an ecumenical council, the first since Pius IX called for one in 1869. That council, Vatican I, had reinforced orthodoxy and shored up papal power within the church. This council, Vatican II, would do almost exactly the opposite.

While the Second Vatican Council was being prepared in Rome, Senator John F. Kennedy launched a run for the presidency of the United States. Kennedy was young, telegenic, and wealthy—all to his benefit. But he was also Catholic, heretofore an insurmountable obstacle for a presidential candidate. The only Catholic ever to become a serious contender for the presidency was Governor Al Smith of New York, who had been pilloried for his religious beliefs when he ran against Herbert Hoover in 1928. He lost badly, largely due to anti-Catholicism and fears that Smith would be a puppet of the pope if he were elected president. Thirty-two years later, John Kennedy would have to overcome what remained of anti-Catholic sentiment in the United States; not just in the general election, but in his own party's nomination process. "Catholic-baiting," as one conservative stated, "is the anti-Semitism of liberals."

According to a 1959 Gallup poll, 24 percent of Americans would not vote for a Catholic. The old suspicion that a Catholic leader would be beholden to the pope resurfaced. Kennedy once joked that, if elected, he would appoint G. Bromley Oxnam, an anti-Catholic Methodist bishop, as his personal envoy to the Vatican to immediately "open negotiations for that Trans-Atlantic Tunnel" from Washington to Rome. More seriously, he expressed frustration that his religion was an issue. "I'm getting tired of these people who think I want to replace the gold at Fort Knox with holy water," he complained. In September 1960, he tried to put the matter to rest in a speech before a group of Protestant ministers in Houston, Texas. "I do not speak for my church on public matters," he declared, "and the church does not speak for me." Appealing to basic American values of fairness, he asked his audience to consider what it would mean if "40,000,000 Americans lost their chance to being President on the day they were baptized."

One possibility historians overlook is that Kennedy's religion may have *helped* him politically in his campaign against Vice President Richard Nixon. For reasons mentioned earlier, his Catholicism boosted his anti-communist credentials. And if there was one creed nearly every American observed at the time of the 1960 election, no matter what his religion, it was anticommunism. John Kennedy may have been a Massachusetts democrat, but he was also, like many American Catholics, an anticommunist hawk, a credential particularly important after Fidel Castro came to power in neighboring Cuba. Richard Nixon, himself a fervent anticommunist, believed that Kennedy's success in outflanking him on Castro and communism was the deciding factor in the election. In this case, at least, Kennedy probably had his Catholicism to thank.

John Kennedy's election in November 1960 was a mixed blessing for the Vatican. The last thing President Kennedy wanted was to appear to take orders from the Holy See, and so he was careful to minimize overt contact. Nonetheless, Kennedy's election counted as a net gain for Catholic Americans. President Kennedy put away forever doubts about the ability of a Catholic to hold the highest office in America without interference from Rome. "Above all," wrote Arthur Schlesinger Jr., the historian who served under Kennedy in the White House, "he showed that there need be no conflict between Catholicism and modernity, no bar to full Catholic participation in American society."

That comment has special resonance when we recall that Schlesinger's father, the renowned historian Arthur Schlesinger Sr., once described anti-Catholicism as the most enduring prejudice in American society. Times changed. And a major hurdle in relations between the United States and the Holy See was removed.

II.

The Second Vatican Council commenced on the sunny autumn morning of October 11, 1962. St. Peter's Basilica was specially decorated for the occasion with wall-sized sixteenth-century Belgian tapestries. The pope entered grandly, in accord with tradition, on a gilded throne carried by attendants. Were it not for the television and film cameras and the state-of-the-art computer installed in the basilica to tabulate the votes of the bishops, the scene could have been straight out of Renaissance Rome. The Catholic Church council had evolved, as one newspaper headline put it, "From Nicaea to the Space Age."

Beyond expressing a general aspiration for Christian unity and "renewal," Pope John XXIII announced no set agenda for the council. Merely by calling 2,300 bishops to Rome, though, he guaranteed a lively debate about the future of the church. This pope was not afraid of debate. Nor was he unwilling, after decades of popes pushing for more and more power in the hands of Rome, to relinquish some of his authority to the bishops and decentralize the power of the church. Years earlier, the Italians pursued the *Risorgimento* at the expense of the church. Now the church was embracing its own *aggiornamento*—modernization. Before the council closed in 1965, the bishops would consider a new liturgy to allow for greater lay participation, greater inclusion of local vernacular and customs in mass, and greater openness to—along with explicit recognition of—other faiths.

For the moment, the *aggiornamento* was best observed in the faces of bishops who sat on either side of the central nave. The Catholic Church was much larger and more expansive than it had been in 1869, when seven hundred bishops traveled to Rome, most of them from Europe. More than three times that number came for this new council, some 2,300 bishops from fifty-five countries on six continents. Among these were 240 from the United States, 250 from Africa, another 250 from Asia, and 600 from Latin America. The most notable contingent, though, was the small group from the Soviet Bloc. A few came to Rome from Hungary and Yugoslavia. About two dozen came from Poland. This group was led by Cardinal Wyszynski, the Polish primate who spent three years in Polish prison for his opposition to the Communist regime, and included an up-and-coming young prelate named Karol Wojtyla—the future John Paul II. (An even younger future leader and pope, Fr. Joseph Ratzinger, attended the council as a "peritus," or theological consultant, to Cardinal Frings of Cologne.) As we will see in later pages, the presence of these Iron Curtain prelates, who had lived for years deprived of liberty and freedom, would deliver crucial support to efforts by Americans, notably John Courtney Murray, to move the church toward greater acceptance of religious liberty for all faiths.

Also to Rome came a delegation of Russian Orthodox clergy who would sit in on the council as observers. Their arrival was a personal triumph for the John XXIII, since one of his goals for the council was to bridge the nine-hundred-year schism between the Roman Catholic and the Eastern Orthodox churches. That same spirit of ecumenism prompted the pope to invite a number of Protestant clergy to join the Catholic bishops in St. Peter's. The broad array of bishops and observers was proof that the Catholic Church was more catholic (small c) and more global than ever.

Pope John's appeal to "separated brethren"—as the pope referred to other Christian denominations—carried important implications in the context of the Cold War. The church had negotiated with Soviet Bloc countries to arrange for Eastern bishops, Catholic and Orthodox alike, to visit Rome. If negotiating with communists seemed to go against the spirit of the Pius XI's *Divini Redemptoris*, it was very much in keeping with the new spirit of Vatican II. This was effectively the start of Ostpolitik, the policy of greater papal engagement with Communist countries. Ostpolitik did not imply that the pope now approved of communism. On the contrary, as John XXIII made clear when he excommunicated Fidel Castro at the start of the year, the church still adamantly opposed communist ideology. But Pope John also believed that his obligation to tend to Catholics in the Soviet Bloc required him to treat with leaders of those countries. Ostpolitik followed naturally from a long tradition in Holy See diplomacy of making the best of a bad situation. More broadly, it put the pope in a position to work for peace, which was exactly what the world needed in the fall of 1962.

In moving toward dialogue and broader engagement with the communist world, Pope John XXIII shifted the Holy See's diplomacy away from the rigid, unbending opposition to communism of Pope Pius XII. Years later, as we'll see, the pendulum would swing the other way, as Pope John Paul II moved from the Ostpolitik of Popes John XXII and Paul VI to assert a policy of confrontation with communist-led states.

### III.

The day after the Second Vatican Council opened, October 12, 1962, the pope gave a speech in the Sistine Chapel in which he linked the council's aspirations to peace in a nuclear age. Pointing to Michelangelo's Last Judgment, he admonished that the heads of state must ultimately "render an account to God" and be "ready to make the sacrifices that are necessary to save the world's peace." The alternative, the pope said, "would mean the destruction of humanity."

At that very moment, the Soviet Union was installing silos in Cuba for missiles aimed at the United States. Ten days later, on the evening of Monday, October 22, President Kennedy appeared on American television to announce "unmistakable evidence" of the missile sites in Cuba, "an explicit threat to the peace and security of all the Americas." Kennedy announced a quarantine on all Soviet ships approaching Cuba and warned that any missiles launched from Cuba would be met with retaliation. The most dangerous international standoff in world history commenced.

In the midst of this, at noon on Thursday, October 25, the pope was on Vatican Radio. Speaking in an emotion-charged voice from his private library in the Apostolic Palace, he urged the "world's leaders" (i.e., Kennedy and Khrushchev) to step back from the "horrors of a war that would have tragic consequences such as nobody can foresee." The broadcast was unscheduled, but the Vatican had already secretly sent the pope's message to Washington and Moscow, where it met with approval from the president and the premier. The day after his radio broadcast, the pope's message was printed on the front page of *Pravda*, an indication that even within the Soviet Union, a Communist country with a relatively small Catholic population, John XXIII's words were taken very seriously. Certainly they were important—and welcome—to Khrushchev. The following day, the Soviet Premier wrote to Kennedy to suggest a deal, the first real move in deescalating the crisis.

It is impossible to gauge the precise impact of the pope's message on Khrushchev's actions, but evidently it helped create a space for the Soviet premier to back down from confrontation while limiting his political liabilities within the Kremlin. He could look like a peacemaker in consort with the pope, rather than a weakling who conceded to the Americans. Pope John XXIII is seldom linked to the Cuban Missile Crisis, but his role was important and may well have been decisive. Indeed, it could be argued that his message, and the exchanges that followed, sowed the seeds of détente with the Soviet Union, later successfully exploited by Henry Kissinger during the Nixon administration.

★  ★  ★

Much to the consternation of the Kennedy administration, John XXIII continued to seek dialogue with the Soviets after the missile crisis. Nikita Khrushchev, in turn, seemed to develop a genuine if grudging admiration for the pope, in contradistinction to Joseph Stalin's contempt. Near the end of 1962, the Soviet premiere would tell Norman Cousins—the editor of the *Saturday Review* who became, for a time in the 1960s, an unlikely liaison among the Vatican, Moscow, and Washington—that he would never convert the pope to communism and the pope would never convert him to Catholicism. "But stranger things have happened," added Khrushchev.

Five months after the missile crisis, on March 7, 1963, Pope John stunned the world by welcoming Khrushchev's daughter and son-in-law, Alexei Adzhubei, who was the editor of a major Soviet propaganda machine, *Izvestiya*, to the Vatican. The meeting was the first between a high level Soviet Communist and the pope. It lasted a mere eighteen minutes, but to some in the Kennedy administration this was enough to suggest further papal appeasement with the enemy.

Pope John XXIII soon surprised the world again, with *Pacem in Terris*. Issued on April 11, 1963, the encyclical was a call for "peace in the atomic age," as the *New York Times* described it, but that was just one of many notions it encompassed. Addressed to "all men of goodwill" (rather than Catholics alone), *Pacem* opened with a paean to inalienable rights. "The world's Creator has stamped man's inmost being with an order revealed to man by his conscience; and his conscience insists on his preserving it." The pope went on to list numerous rights that naturally belong to all humans, from the "right of bodily integrity" to the rights of free speech and freedom of worship.

If these rights bear an uncanny resemblance to those enumerated by America's Founding Fathers it is because, as discussed in earlier chapters, they are derived from a similar understanding of humans' capacity for moral reason. Reason allows humans to recognize certain absolute and inviolable truths; and recognition of these truths compels the rational person to follow their accords and to behave morally. The same goes for the governments composed of, and for, rational humans: they are compelled by reason to recognize and observe the dictates of natural law.

As Fr. Drew Christiansen, SJ, former editor of *America*, told me, *Pacem in Terris* is a lynchpin of modern Vatican diplomacy. "It is *the* document for the church's political reality," said Christiansen. "It established political theology on a cosmopolitan basis. Now the root of everything is the person, which the state is responsible to protect. . . . *Pacem in Terris* really launched the church's involvement in the human rights movement."

Before April 1963, President Kennedy steadfastly avoided giving any hint that he listened to the pope. But *Pacem in Terris* moved him to speak. "As a Catholic I am proud of it," said Kennedy, "and as an American, I have learned from it."

★ ★ ★

John Kennedy and John XXII never met. The pope died on June 3, 1963, after a long fight with stomach cancer. President Kennedy died the following November, killed by an assassin's bullet. These like-named leaders served in their respective offices only briefly, but the world saw remarkable change in those years. Nowhere was the change more obvious than in the relationship between the United States and the Catholic Church. America finally discarded the anti-Catholic prejudices that had infected it from the start. The church at last moved beyond the monarchical, antidemocratic tendencies that had kept it from embracing the very rights its history and theology supported. For the first time, each was in a position to recognize what was best in the other.

The theology of Catholicism and the ideals of America were most brilliantly reconciled in the person and writings of a third man named John: Fr. John Courtney Murray, SJ, the most influential American Catholic writer of his day. Murray, a Jesuit priest, was best known for his book, *We Hold These Truths: Catholic Reflections on the American Proposition*, published on the eve of John F. Kennedy's presidency in 1960. Murray's argument that Catholic faith and American convictions were compatible put him on the December cover of *Time* magazine.

Within the church, Murray made his greatest mark in the waning days of Vatican II, during which he acted as a powerful, if somewhat controversial, voice for religious liberty. Murray was part of group of Americans who pressed church leaders to accept two documents that forever changed the Holy See's attitude toward other religious faiths. The first of these, *Nostra Aetate*, was promulgated in late October 1965. This document explicitly acknowledged that non-Catholic religions, both Christian and non-Christian, might contain truth and value in their worship of the divine.

> The Catholic Church rejects nothing that is true and holy in these religions. She regards with sincere reverence those ways of conduct and of life, those precepts and teachings which, though differing in many aspects from the ones she holds and sets forth, nonetheless often reflect a ray of that Truth which enlightens all men.

The second document was the landmark *Declaration on Religious Freedom*, known as *Dignitatis Humanae*. Largely written by John Courtney Murray, and promulgated on the last day of the Council, December 7, 1965, *Dignitatis Humanae* was a broader and more philosophical work than *Nostra Aetate*. It not only acknowledged the validity of other religions, it set out a formal argument for why all humans have a right to worship as their conscience dictates. The Catholic Church remained "the one true religion," according to *Dignitatis Humanae*, but this did not mean other religions should not be equally free in the eyes of civic law.

> This Vatican Council declares that the human person has a right to religious freedom. This freedom means that all men are to be immune from coercion on the part of individuals or of social groups and of any human power, in such wise that no one is to be forced to act in a manner contrary to his own beliefs, whether privately or publicly, whether alone or in association with others, within due limits.
>
>   The council further declares that the right to religious freedom has its foundation in the very dignity of the human person as this dignity

is known through the revealed word of God and by reason itself. This right of the human person to religious freedom is to be recognized in the constitutional law whereby society is governed and thus it is to become a civil right.

Not surprisingly, this new view was resisted by numerous traditionalist European prelates, especially Italian and Spanish cardinals, who maintained, as the church had for centuries, that religious teaching other than Roman Catholicism was in error. To Catholic critics of religious freedom doctrine, *Dignitatis* came dangerously close to relativism. They believed that American ideas of democracy and tolerance had no place in the Catholic Church. Murray's counterargument was that American ideals did not limit or weaken Catholic faith; in fact, the former had been born of the latter. "The question is sometimes raised, whether Catholicism is compatible with American democracy," wrote Murray. "The question is invalid as well as impertinent; for the manner of its position inverts the order of values. It must, of course, be turned round to read, whether American democracy is compatible with Catholicism."

In a 1966 speech, Murray further squared freedom of religion with Catholic doctrine, insisting, again, that the right of free worship was not simply compatible with Christianity; it was inspired by Christianity:

(1) The human person's right to religious freedom cannot be proven from Holy Scripture, nor from Christian revelation. (2) Yet the foundation of this right, the dignity of the human person, has ampler and more brilliant confirmation in Holy Scripture than can be drawn from human reason alone. (3) By a long historical evolution society has finally reached the notion of religious freedom as a human right.

The most American part of Murray's doctrine may have been its implications regarding the power of government. His conception of religious freedom was greater than a mere acknowledgment that people should be free to pray as they wish; it was also a check on the power of government to impose restrictions on its people, by insisting on a sphere of human life that belongs solely to the conscience of the individual.

For exactly this reason the religious freedom doctrines gained key support from the Easter European prelates at Vatican II, men who knew firsthand the horrors of unrestricted government power. The Soviet Bloc contingent, in fact, became a key faction of the coalition that ultimately passed both *Nostra Aetate* and *Dignitatis Humanae*, for its members understood, as the historian Owen Chadwick states, "that you can only truly claim religious freedom for yourself if you concede it on principle to every-one else." *Dignitatis Humanae* was ultimately passed by a significant margin, 1954 votes in favor to 249 opposed.

The same day the church promulgated *Dignitatis Humanae*, December 7, 1965, it also released *Gaudium et Spes*, one of four "Constitutions" of the council. *Gaudium et Spes* is perhaps the defining document of the modern international church. It outlined a broad range of rights and obligations for both Catholics and non-Catholics. More generally, it defined the church's mission to improve the lives of all humans, not just Catholics.

The progress of the early 1960s did not mean that the Holy See and United States were now in constant agreement about everything; that has never been the case and never will be. Nor was all the change positive. Pope John's successor, Pope Paul VI, formerly Cardinal Giovanni Battista Montini, would struggle to steer the church through the aftermath of Vati-can II, walking the fine line between reform and tradition. "No pope since the time of Gregory the Great," writes papal historian Eamon Duffy "has had so daunting a task."

In short, Vatican II brought the Holy See into the modern era of diplomacy and relations with states. It was a milestone in a tradition of engagement lasting more than 1,500 years, including Pope Pius VII's con-frontation with Napoleon, Pius IX's refusal to yield the diplomatic stature and sovereignty of the Holy See upon the loss of the papal states, and Pope Pius XII's defense of the church and the Holy See from fascist Hitler and communist Stalin.

IV.

The United States underwent its own tumult in the 1960s, fueled by an intractable war in Southeast Asia. This early experience with asymmetrical warfare consumed the presidency of Lyndon Johnson. On the surface, the besieged Johnson administration seemed to revert to a Wilsonian position vis-à-vis the Vatican, dismissing papal intervention as a distraction in a time of crisis. No overt or public effort was made to establish diplomatic ties, ei-ther formal or informal. However, a review of State Department documents reveals that the pope was a constant factor in the calculations of the Johnson administration. Few major American foreign policy initiatives seem to have been undertaken without consideration of, or consultation with, the Vatican.

Vietnam was naturally the overarching topic and concern in dialogue between the U.S. government and the Holy See. The protracted violence of the conflict profoundly disturbed the pope. The conflict was a particular concern to the church because South Vietnam had a Catholic population of approximately 1.6 million people, many of whom had migrated south after the Communist Viet Minh took over North Vietnam.

The United States was already enmeshed in the war when Pope Paul VI arrived there for a brief but historic visit in the autumn of 1965. Touching down at New York's Kennedy Airport on the chilly morning of October 4, 1965, Paul became the first pope ever to visit America (not including Pius IX's awkward boarding of the USS *Constitution* at anchor in Gaeta, Italy, in 1849). New York City virtually bowed in his honor. Many schools and stores closed for the day, and millions of New Yorkers lined the streets to catch a glimpse of the papal motorcade. City road crews had spent the previous week patching streets along the entire route of the pope's journey to ensure him a ride undisturbed by a single pothole.

The centerpiece of Pope Paul's visit was a speech at the United Nations that afternoon. "No more war!" he declared when he took the podium in the hall of the General Assembly. "War never again. Peace, it is peace which must guide the destinies of people and of all mankind." He also met with President Johnson for forty-five minutes in a suite at the Waldorf Astoria. That evening, the Pope said a mass at Yankee Stadium to ninety thousand people. He was back in the air before midnight, less than fourteen hours after landing, leaving behind a city breathless and amazed.

Not only was New York deeply affected by the visit. James Reston of the *New York Times*, a hardened veteran journalist, reflected a few days later that the pope had given Washington's politicians "a vision of the common human pilgrimage," shaking the city, for at least a few moments, out of its usual cynicism. "It was not that he said anything new . . . but simply that he said a lot of old fundamental things that have been overwhelmed for so long that they sound new again." After so much talk of war, the pope's simple call for peace, wrote Reston, was "almost startling."

Pope Paul VI's visit to the United Nations did not prevent the escalation of the Vietnam War, which developed a momentum of its own. The pope responded by stepping up his pursuit for peace. In 1966, he tried to get Ho Chi Minh, president of North Vietnam, to agree to peace talks with the United States, and even offered the Vatican as the venue. At his urging, the United States suspended bombing of North Vietnam for more than a month, a good faith effort that backfired. Hanoi used the break to mobilize troops and equipment for further assaults.

These were darkening days in the Johnson administration, as American casualties mounted and antiwar rallies grew in size and vituperation.

President Johnson and his advisors were desperate to end the war, but do so without humiliation to the United States or calamity in South Vietnam. With options few and dwindling, they turned to the pope for help.

On December 23, 1967, flying home from Australia and a quick visit to American troops in Vietnam, Johnson landed, unannounced, in Rome. A meeting with Pope Paul had been hastily arranged. Many of Johnson's own advisors, including Johnson's chief logistical aid, were not informed until they were in the air.

It was well into the evening when Air Force One touched down at Rome's Ciampino Naval Airport. After a quick formal call on the Italian president and prime minister, the president flew by helicopter to the Vatican. The helicopter saved time—and embarrassment—by allowing Johnson to leapfrog war protestors flooding the streets of Rome. As if things weren't difficult enough for the Johnson presidency, the president's helicopter began to sink in a patch of soft ground the moment it landed in the Vatican gardens. While the president met inside the Apostolic Palace with the pope, the helicopter was extracted and flown to higher elevation.

Johnson's visit to Paul VI has been characterized in one history as "disastrous." A contemporary account in *Time* described the pope slamming his hand down in anger at Johnson. If such dramatics took place, they are missing from the transcript drafted by the president's aid, Jack Valenti, who was present at the meeting. Johnson is described as considerate but pushy, while Pope Paul VI is sympathetic but firm.

Unlike many visits between presidents and popes, which usually include a measure of ceremony and publicity, this one was all business from the start. Sitting down just before 9:00 p.m., Johnson started by assuring the pope that he wanted peace in Vietnam. He had two specific requests for the pope. One was for the Vatican to send a representative to American prisoners in North Vietnam, in hopes of obtaining more humane treatment for American POWs. The other—clearly the main reason for the visit—was to enlist the pope's help in getting the South Vietnamese government and the Communist Viet Cong to sit for informal talks, without the interference of North Vietnam and the United States.

The pope had his own agenda in the meeting. He wanted Johnson to halt the bombing of North Vietnam. "The Church cannot give its approval to bombing as a means of defending liberty." He offered to help. "Can I be an intermediary for you? I could say that I know that what the U.S. says is true—that it truly wants peace. Can you give me your assurances of this?"

Johnson reminded the pope that every time he had halted bombing in the past, North Vietnam used the pause to its tactical advantage. "We have stopped bombing five times but this only increases the murder."

"I believe it important for you to give new aspects to this war—to make it a more defensive war instead of an offensive war," said the pope. "It will strengthen your moral position in the world."

Johnson returned, again—and again—to his hope that Paul VI could intervene in South Vietnam. He worked the pope with a persistence familiar to Washington politicians who had been subjected to the "Johnson treatment," as it was known in the halls of Congress. "I hope the Pope will encourage them to talk, just as the Pope encouraged me to pass my education bills. We are now spending $9 billion more on education. And the Pope can claim some responsibility for this."

"I think I can do something," said the pope with a smile.

"I don't want to press the point," said Johnson once more before the meeting ended, "but I did want to know if I can assume that the Pope will try to bring the South Vietnamese to informal talks—and will immediately help out the prisoner problem."

"I will do whatever is possible," said the pope. "This is a cause which is close to my heart."

Before they parted, the two men exchanged gifts. The pope gave Johnson a fifteenth-century painting. Johnson gave the pope a package, which he then proceeded to open with a pen knife. Inside the package was a bust—of himself.

★ ★ ★

I have not seen any records to indicate what the pope did to encourage peace talks in South Vietnam. Without question, though, he was very helpful several months later, in the spring of 1968, in nudging the North Vietnamese toward negotiations with the United States in Paris. President Johnson, embittered and exhausted, had recently told the American people he did not intend to seek the Democratic nomination for the presidency. But he still wanted to end the war, and Pope Paul VI still wanted to help him do so.

In late April 1968, President Johnson directed his aide, Joseph A. Califano Jr., a Catholic, to contact the Apostolic Delegate to the United States, Archbishop Luigi Raimondi, to ask if the pope would be willing to propose the Vatican as a site for peace talks, as he had done in the past. On April 27, the Vatican responded to Califano: the pope would be pleased to issue an invitation to both the United States and North Vietnamese.

"This is a beautiful message," said Johnson after reading the pope's invitation. The invitation was also a clever diplomatic ploy, leveraging the "soft power" of the Holy See, as the president no doubt intended and the pope surely understood. Either North Vietnam agreed to participate in peace talks or Washington could show the world that it was more willing than Hanoi to come to table, giving the United States the moral high ground in the court of world opinion.

Less than a week later, on May 3, Hanoi agreed to negotiate. Predictably, the North Vietnamese preferred to hold talks in a secular location instead of the Vatican, and so the site was changed to Paris. Nevertheless, the pope's invitation served its purpose. The Paris peace talks were long in coming, and would be even longer in producing a truce, but they were a start—a start that would have been delayed without the pope.

## V.

Neither the pope nor anyone else could seemingly save the United States from the malaise that settled over the country in the late 1960s and persisted through the administrations of the three presidents who came after Johnson. From Vietnam to Richard Nixon's Watergate scandal, followed by a prolonged recession under Gerald Ford and the ill-fated Jimmy Carter, whose term culminated with the failed attempt to rescue American hostages in Iran, the office of the presidency was diminished and the prestige of the United States reached a low point around the world.

These were years when Holy See–U.S. diplomacy became quietly normalized, if not formalized. Following in the footsteps of Roosevelt and Truman, Nixon appointed a personal representative to the pope. As with FDR's appointment of Myron Taylor in 1939, his choice was a distinguished, important American leader, Henry Cabot Lodge, the former senator who was Nixon's running mate in 1960 and served under Kennedy and Johnson as ambassador to South Vietnam. Lodge, like Taylor, visited Rome regularly as Nixon's envoy, taking rooms in the Grand Hotel and working with a small staff. Among other accomplishments, he helped negotiate the departure of Cardinal Mindszenty—at last—from the American embassy in Budapest. The United States cooperated with the Holy See to secure Catholic holy sites in Jerusalem, while the Vatican worked to obtain better communications with American POWs. Presidents Ford and Carter both continued the practice of sending envoys to the Vatican. Holy See–U.S. relations covered a wide variety of issues, but the context of *all* U.S. diplomacy, as it had been since 1945, was the Cold War.

The Communists were more aggressive during the post–Vietnam era of American vulnerability. The Soviet Union built up its military and pushed its influence into ever wider spheres. Under Nixon, *detente* brought a short respite in the Cold War, but what followed was even more alarming than what had come before. "The Soviet collapse in 1991 should not obscure the reality of their challenge in the 1970s," writes Robert Gates, who worked in high-level positions in both CIA and the White House during the 1970s (and would later serve as both director of CIA and secretary of defense). Henry Kissinger describes the shift in communism's fortunes this way: "At one moment, at the beginning of the 1980s, it was as if communist momentum might sweep all before it; at the next, as history measures time, communism was self-destructing."

What happened to bring about this change is a story that begins with two men who shared a bold idea: a president and a pope.

*Painting of John Carroll by Gilbert Stuart. Courtesy of Georgetown University.*

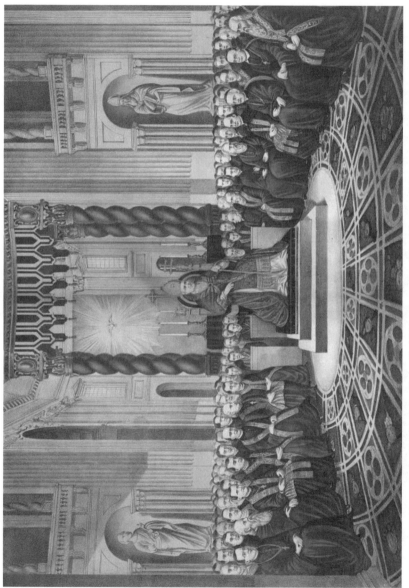

First Vatican Council, 1869. Courtesy of the Library of Congress.

Signing of the Lateran Treaty, February 11, 1929, at the Lateran Palace in Rome. Seated left, Cardinal Secretary of State Pietro Gasparri signing for Pope Pius IX and seated right, Prime Minister Benito Mussolini signing for King Victor Emmanuel III. Courtesy of the Institute on Vatican Diplomacy.

*Myron Taylor, the personal representative of President Roosevelt with Pope Pius XII. Courtesy Fotografia Felici.*

*Allied troops under the command of U.S. General Mark Clark in St. Peter's Square, June 1944. Courtesy of Corbis Images.*

*Second Vatican Council in St. Peter's Basilica, 1962. Courtesy Fotografia Felici. Source: Rev. John Courtney Murray, S. J. Papers, Box 25, Folder 1222, Georgetown University Library Special Collections Research Center, Washington, D.C.*

*John Courtney Murray and Francis Cardinal Spellman at the Second Vatican Council. Source: Rev. John Courtney Murray, S. J. Papers, Box 25, Folder 1222, Georgetown University Library Special Collections Research Center, Washington, D.C.*

*Pope John XXIII and Mrs. John F. Kennedy, March 1962. Courtesy of Corbis Images.*

*Pope Paul VI in Yankee Stadium, the first visit of a pope to the United States, October 4, 1965. Courtesy of the Associated Press.*

*Pope Paul VI and President Richard Nixon. White House Photo Office Collection, Nixon Administration.*

*President Ronald Reagan and Pope John Paul II, May 2, 1984, at the Fairbanks International Airport, Fairbanks, Alaska. This was the first meeting of President Reagan and Pope John Paul II after the establishment of formal diplomatic relations between the United States and the Holy See. Courtesy of Corbis Images.*

*Pope Benedict XVI in Cuba, March 2012. Courtesy of Thomson Reuters.*

*Ambassador Rooney and Archbishop (now Cardinal) Harvey in the Apostolic Palace. Courtesy of Photographic Service L'Osservatore Romano.*

*Ambassador Rooney and Pope Benedict XVI. Courtesy of Photographic Service L'Osservatore Romano.*

*President George W. Bush giving a gift of a walking stick carved by Roosevelt Wilkerson, a homeless man in Dallas, to Pope Benedict XVI, June 2007. Courtesy of Photographic Service L'Osservatore Romano.*

*President George W. Bush and Ambassador Rooney meeting with the Community of Sant'Egidio, June 2007. Courtesy of Photographic Service L'Osservatore Romano.*

*Ambassador Rooney and family with Pope Benedict XVI. Courtesy of Photographic Service L'Osservatore Romano.*

The Holy See Diplomatic Corps, January 2006, in the Sala Regia, Apostolic Palace, following the annual meeting of the diplomatic corps with the Pope. Courtesy of Photographic Service L'Osservatore Romano.

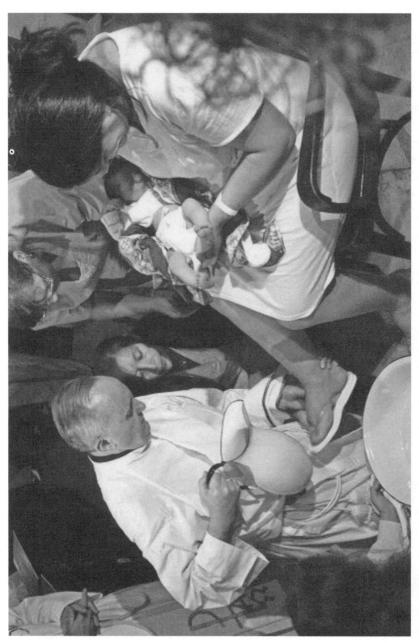

*Cardinal Bergoglio, now Pope Francis, washing feet at the Sarda Maternity hospital in Buenos Aires, Argentina, in 2005. Courtesy of Photographic Service L'Osservatore Romano.*

# 10

## PARALLEL INTERESTS

Overwhelmingly Catholic Poland . . . with its intense loyalty to
the Holy See, will sooner or later edge closer to normal relations
with the Vatican. In this eventuality the Communist government will find itself carried by forces which it cannot control.

—Fr. Robert A. Graham, SJ (1959)

### I.

One was a Polish priest from behind the Iron Curtain. The other was a
movie star from Hollywood. Despite geography and vocation, Pope
John Paul II and President Ronald Reagan shared a great deal in common.
Both had been dark horse candidates for the positions they held. Both
possessed streaks of disarming humor, as well as a serenity rare in men of
high achievement. Both were charismatic performers and former actors
(John Paul briefly considered a life in the theater as a young man). Most
importantly, both came to power following years of tumult and confusion
in their respective domains, and then quickly set clear paths toward the
future—paths that led them, at first separately and then together, down a
road that ended in the rubble of the Berlin Wall. Many people contributed
to the collapse of the Soviet empire, but no two were as indispensable as
the president and the pope.

The end of communism began during a remarkable year in Vatican
history: 1978, the year of the three popes. In early August, Paul VI died,
leaving behind a church revitalized but still preoccupied by the changes
brought by Vatican II. The following month, Paul's successor, John Paul
I, died of an apparent heart attack after just thirty-four days as pope. Then,

on October 16, 1978, the white smoke rose again from the chimney above the Sistine Chapel: a new pope had been chosen.

Karol Wojtyla, former archbishop of Krakow, was the first non-Italian pope elected by the College of Cardinals in nearly five centuries, and the first Polish pope. Where he came from was just the start of what made this man remarkable. At a time when many people were, once again, predicting the decline of the Catholic Church, John Paul II quickly established himself as one of the most important popes in history, and one of the most significant world leaders in the twentieth century.

That John Paul II was destined to be an important historical figure was immediately evident to those whose job it was to know such things. Analysts at the CIA issued a report on October 19, 1978, just three days after Wojtyla's election, which turned out to be largely accurate. The report, "The Impact of a Polish Pope on the USSR," calculated that John Paul II's election spelled trouble for the Soviets. "In the near term . . . there should be no crisis in Soviet-Polish relations," the report stated; the long-term effect was a different story. "A Polish pope will reinvigorate the Catholic faith in these areas and may embolden Catholic dissidents to engage in more vigorous protest activities." The report concluded that "the Soviet leadership is probably already anxious about how to cope with the ultimate impact of a Polish papacy on East European nationalism as well as such derivative issues as Eurocommunism and Soviet dissidence."

The CIA was on the mark about Soviet anxiety. Leaders in the Politburo began worrying about John Paul at once. The KGB, which had pegged Karol Wojtyla as an anticommunist as early as 1971, produced a conspiratorial analysis that framed his installation as a conspiracy to destabilize Poland. Should this destabilization succeed, Soviet leaders adduced, it could lead to further destabilization in other parts of the empire, such as the Ukraine and Lithuania, where Catholics made up a large portion of the population. Declaring the pope "our enemy," the Polish Communist Party concluded that "all means are allowed and we cannot afford any sentiments."

The Communists' worries reached a head when the pope began planning a visit home to Poland in 1979. Soviet Premiere Leonid Brezhnev warned Polish Communist Party leader Edward Gierek to keep the pope out of Poland, but Gierek was in a bind. "How can I not receive a Polish pope when the majority of my countrymen are Catholic?" he asked Khrushchev. "They view his election as a great achievement. Furthermore, how could I justify why we are closing the border to the pope?" Gierek was probably right that he had no choice but to allow the pope to visit. Brezhnev was right to worry.

Even before he departed for this much anticipated homecoming in Poland, John Paul II was establishing himself as a force of practical diplomacy to be reckoned with. In late 1978, for example, he offered to mediate a dispute between Argentina and Chile regarding territories in the Beagle Chanel, a signal that he intended to engage the world actively in the tradition of popes like Leo XIII and Benedict XV. Indeed, he was continuing a tradition of papal activism in territorial dispute resolution that reached back even further, to ratification of the well-known Treaty of Tordesillas in 1494, which gave most of South America (except Brazil) to Spain.

John Paul II would prove to be the most active pope in history, a man in near perpetual motion. Over the course of his 9,665 days as pope—the longest term in the papacy with the exception of Pius IX—he would visit 129 countries, 1,022 cities, and log more than 750,000 miles of travel, according to his biographer George Weigel. None of his trips would be as important as that first nine-day return to Poland—"nine days," as Weigel states, "during which the history of the twentieth century turned in a fundamental way."

John Paul II landed in Warsaw on Saturday, June 2, 1979. In a brief speech at the airport, the pope stated that his visit was "dictated by strictly religious motives" to allay suspicions in the government that he was here to stir up trouble. He never directly criticized the communist regime during his visit. Yet the mere fact of his presence, from the moment he knelt down and kissed the airport tarmac in Warsaw, was freighted with political import. Simply exhorting his fellow Poles to renew their Catholic faith was an act charged with subversive implications. "Christ cannot be kept out of history in any part of the globe," he told a crowd in Warsaw's Victory Square. "The exclusion of Christ from the history of man is an act against man." Already, the Polish people were bridling under communist rule, and now the pope reminded them of their Polish—and still very Catholic—identity beyond the crumbling facade of communism.

Wherever John Paul II went in Poland, from urban cathedrals to rural shrines or the grisly ruins of Auschwitz, he spoke to enormous crowds. They sang and cheered and wept. As much as a third of the entire population of Poland saw him in person over the course of his nine-day visit. When he flew back to Rome on June 9, he left behind a country energized for change. He set the Holy See on a new course, beyond Ostpolitik and into an active engagement against repression.

Not long thereafter, the new energy in Poland was channeled into political action. When the Polish government raised food prices in late summer of 1980, a thirty-six-year-old electrician in the Polish city of Gdansk, Lech Walesa, helped organize a strike which led to the formation of a movement called Solidarnosc (Solidarity). This was the first nongovernment union in all of communist Eastern Europe, and it owed its birth, in large part, to the pope. "The Holy Father told us: 'Don't be afraid, change the face of the Earth, be strong believers,'" Lech Walesa later recalled. "Then all of a sudden people thought about his words and woke up." Just over a year after the pope's visit, the power of Solidarity was already so great that the Polish government had little choice but to authorize an agreement recognizing the trade union's legality. Lech Walesa signed his name to the agreement with a souvenir pen from the pope's 1979 visit.

## II.

As Solidarity was taking root in Poland, Ronald Reagan entered the White House to become the fortieth president of the United States. The Cold War was now in its thirty-fifth year. The Soviet Union and its satellite Communist dictatorships were an accepted, albeit detested, fact among the Washington foreign policy community. Containment, articulated by George Kennan in 1946 and implemented by Secretary of State Dean Acheson in 1949, had been the policy of every president since Truman. Now Ronald Reagan came along and asked a simple question that some people found impertinent: why should America contain Soviet communism; why not *abolish* it? "My theory of the Cold War," Reagan told his future National Security Advisor, Richard Allen, "is that we win and they lose."

Allen later paraphrased Reagan's position as follows:

> The United States would no longer be content merely to shape and influence Soviet behavior, but would set out to change the Soviet system itself, and literally "roll back" Soviet advances and conquests outside its borders. The objective was to find weak points in the Soviet structure, to aggravate the weaknesses, and to undermine the system. This represented a sea change in U.S. policy.

Robert Gates, who served as deputy director of intelligence at CIA in the early 1980s, writes that "Reagan, nearly alone, truly believed in 1981 that the Soviet system was vulnerable, not in some vague, long-range historical sense, but right then." After years of *detente* and *mutually assured destruction* and a raft of other jargon, Reagan's view was disarmingly straightforward, but his method was a sophisticated application of several levers of coercion at once. The most obvious and controversial of these was increased defense spending. To his critics, Reagan seemed a warmonger, wantonly adding new military systems to an already overloaded nuclear stock. Richard Allen insists that Reagan was "in fact, fundamentally a disarmer." He believed the way to end the Cold War was to take the upper hand—to go on offense and put the Soviets on defense—and show them that their own expensive military buildup was futile. Henry Kissinger, an outside observer of the Reagan White House, agrees with Allen's assessment that Reagan, far from welcoming war with the Soviets, feared it intensely and yet was convinced that confrontation was the best strategy, in the long run, to make the Politburo stand down. As Kissinger writes, "Reagan believed that relations with the Soviet Union would improve if he could make it share his fear of nuclear Armageddon."

Adding to the Soviets' woes, the Reagan administration also deployed a number of economic tools, including embargoes, to challenge their already feeble economy. Yet Reagan, like Truman, knew that military and economic tools were only part of the equation. Ultimately this was a fight for the souls of humans, for there was no better way to defeat the Communists than to give hope of a better life to those living under Communist rule. And there was no greater messenger for delivering this hope than Pope John Paul II.

★ ★ ★

In the spring of 1981, the president and the pope shared something else in common: each narrowly survived an assassination attempt. Reagan's near-death encounter came on March 30, 1981, when John Hinckley shot him in front of the Hilton Hotel in Washington, D.C. Reagan recovered fully, and emerged from the shooting more spiritually alive. Specifically, his brush with death seems to have awoken a latent interest in Catholicism. Though raised as a Protestant, Reagan (whose father was Catholic) already displayed an affinity for Catholics. He surrounded himself with a notable number of Catholics in his administration, including William Casey at CIA, Alexander Haig at the Department of State, Richard Allen as national security advisor, and Vernon Walters as his roving ambassador. Shortly after returning to the White House from the hospital, he invited Cardinal Terence Cooke of New York to visit. "I have decided that whatever time I have left is for

Him," he told the Cardinal. What He wanted the president to do, Reagan believed, was to bring communism to its knees.

Six weeks after Reagan's scrape with death, John Paul II had an even closer call. On May 13, 1981, the pope was shot several times from nearly pointblank range in St. Peter's Square. Unlike the attempt on Reagan's life, which was the work of a disturbed individual, the assassination attempt on John Paul II gave every indication of conspiracy and spawned a mystery that remains unsolved to this day. The question at the center of the mystery was—and still is—whether the shooter, Mehmet Ali Agca, acted on behalf of the Soviet Union, either directly or indirectly.

The circumstantial evidence for Soviet involvement in the pope's shooting is intriguing but inconclusive. The leading theory is that Agca was hired as a hit man by the Bulgarian secret service, which operated under the orders of—or at least as a proxy for—the Soviet government. The first person to advance this theory publicly was the author Clair Sterling in a *Reader's Digest* article in 1982. Other authors, including Paul Henze, John Kohler, and Nigel West, have written similar accounts. Gordon Thomas, in his book about the Israeli intelligence service Mossad, proposes that Ayatollah Khomeini was behind the attempt, but this theory is an outlier. Agca himself has given so many conflicting statements over the years as to render his testimony useless, but his travel itinerary and standard of living in the months before he shot the pope suggest that he was being financed and supported by someone with deep pockets. He also had frequent contact with Bulgarians, including a fifty-day visit to Sofia shortly before he went to Rome.

If the Bulgarians were behind the assassination attempt, Soviet complicity would be a given. The Bulgarians were unlikely to carry out such an operation without Soviet sponsorship. The Soviets were not lacking in motives to offer this, for the pope had brought them nothing but grief since his visit to Poland in 1979.

Solidarity had grown steadily into a resistance movement against the Polish government. At the start of 1981, Lech Walesa visited Rome and met the pope, telling him that nothing could have happened in Poland "without the church." By the spring of 1981, Solidarity had four times the membership of the Communist Party and was continuing to expand, with the pope's encouragement. Brezhnev saw the unrest in Poland spreading across the Soviet empire, much as American officials once pictured communism spreading—like falling dominoes. "All of us are deeply alarmed by the further course of events in Poland," Brezhnev told the Politburo on April 8, 1981, a month before the assassination attempt. "In the meantime the counterrevolution is on the march all over." In their efforts to stop the counterrevolution, might the Soviets have found reason to kill the man who was one of its chief inspirations?

CIA Director William Casey was convinced the Soviets were the prime movers behind the papal assassination plot, a view shared by some members of congress, but the CIA's investigation revealed little hard evidence to support this conclusion. A final CIA report, issued in 1987, reviewed an investigation into the matter by the government of Italy. This investigation raised more questions than it answered.

According to at least one source, the pope himself believed the Soviets were behind the attack. But he never publicly said so; and, in any case, he seemed more interested in moving forward—even going so far as to forgive Agca in person—than in wondering who had tried to kill him.


### III.


Whether or not the Soviets had anything to do with the attempt on the pope's life, they were squarely and blatantly behind efforts to block John Paul II's influence in Poland. With the antigovernment demonstrations, strikes and threats of more strikes, calls for free elections and demands for civil rights, the Soviets could see Poland slipping from their iron grip. They pressured the Polish government to take action. That action finally came in late 1981.

It began late on the evening of December 12. As phone lines in much of the country went dead, shutting off communication with the outside world, army tanks rumbled into downtown Warsaw. Thousands of Solidarity activists, including Lech Walesa, were rounded up within hours, many of them charged with treason. Martial law was in effect, and would remain so for as long as it took to restore order in Poland. At least that is what the Polish military and their Soviet masters thought. In fact, martial law was the beginning of the end of the totalitarian grip that had held Eastern Europe tight for the last four decades.

For the United States, the developments in Poland may have been a shock, but they were not entirely a surprise. The CIA had a highly placed mole in the Polish general staff's office, the remarkably courageous Colonel Ryszard Kuklinski, who had provided thousands of documents to the CIA in the 1970s and 1980s. Not only was Kuklinski aware of the preparations for martial law that were under way in Poland over the previous year—he wrote some of the plans himself. Within a few days of the plan's approval in September, he delivered it to his CIA contact in Warsaw. Unfortunately, Kuklinski was no longer in Poland when the hammer came down because he had been exfiltrated from the country. The Kuklinski saga is a sideshow to the larger drama of Poland in the early 1980s, but it offers an intriguing insight into the breadth and depth of espionage activities among the CIA, KGB, and Vatican at the time.

Prior to the imposition of martial law in Poland, at least two high level American officials had met with the pope to share some of what they knew about Poland. One of the pope's visitors was CIA director William Casey. Another was General Vernon Walters, former deputy director of CIA and now a roving ambassador for Ronald Reagan, who arrived in Rome in September 1981. Walters shared intelligence with the pope, including satellite reconnaissance shots of Polish troops. He may also have also shared Col. Kuklinski's information about martial law planning in Poland. In any case, soon after Walter's visit to the Vatican, the KGB informed the Polish military that they had a mole within their general staff. The possibility exists that Kuklinski was betrayed by a Soviet Bloc spy inside the Vatican. In interviews with Polish media years after the fact, Kuklinski revealed that he had been told by Polish military intelligence officials that the Vatican was indeed the source of the leak.

As John Kohler details in his book *Spies in the Vatican*, the KGB and other Eastern Bloc intelligence services were spying on the Vatican for years before John Paul II came to power. Communist spies managed to tap Vatican telephone lines and intercept Vatican telegraphs. At one point, as I have been told by a senior Holy See diplomat, the Vatican discovered that the Soviets were remotely eavesdropping on the pope's conversations from their residence, Villa Abamelek, on Janiculum Hill, using a detection method—laser beam eavesdropping—to monitor the voice-generated vibrations in the windows of the Apostolic Palace. If this was an invasion of the pope's privacy, it was also a kind of backhanded compliment. Stalin had dismissed the importance of the pope ("How many divisions . . . ?"), but Stalin's successors knew better.

By 1980, the KGB was making a concerted effort to step up its spying efforts. One plot involved sending a group of Ukrainian priests, who had been recruited and trained by the KGB, to Rome for infiltration into the Vatican. These spies were soon rooted out by the Vatican's resident counterintelligence expert, Fr. Robert Graham, SJ—the same Fr. Graham whose 1959 book on Vatican diplomacy I have quoted liberally in these pages, and who, along with his work as a church scholar, developed a sideline expertise as a spy catcher for the Vatican.

Despite the counterintelligence efforts of Graham and the Vatican, Communist spies did manage to infiltrate the pope's inner circle. John Koehler identifies three priests, two Germans and one Pole, as possible KGB plants who may have learned about some of the information provided by the CIA to the pope. Whoever the source, there was evidently a channel—or several—from the Apostolic Palace to the Kremlin, and that channel may have betrayed Kuklinski. The unfortunate result was that Col. Kuklinski could no longer stay in Poland and send intelligence to the CIA. In November, aware that their best Polish spy was in danger, the agency exfiltrated him and his family from the country and into hiding.

It may seem to follow that American officials held their cards closer to their vests when visiting the Vatican after the Kuklinski affair, and perhaps they did, but William Casey and Vernon Walters made many more visits to the pope in the months and years ahead. One of the first calls William Casey placed after learning that martial law was imposed on Poland was to Cardinal Secretary of State Casaroli to set up a meeting. As for Casey's boss, Ronald Reagan, the imposition of martial law in Poland only served to remind him of how much he despised Communist dictatorships—and how much he wanted to reach out to the Vatican "and make them an ally."

## IV.

The term Holy Alliance was coined by journalist Carl Bernstein (of Woodward and Bernstein fame), who first wrote of U.S.-Vatican relations for *Time* magazine in 1992, then later coauthored a book with that term as its title. As described by Bernstein, the president and the pope undertook an extraordinary coordinated campaign in the early 1980s to defeat the Communist government in Poland. There had been high-level contacts before martial law was imposed in Poland (as mentioned earlier), including a correspondence of a dozen letters between Reagan and John Paul II. According to Bernstein, however, the true start for the alliance was June 7, 1982. That was the day Reagan visited the pope at the Vatican. Reagan and John Paul discussed a number of topics in their forty-five-minute private chat, including the assassination attempts both of them survived. Reagan told the pope that he believed they had been spared for a purpose—which brought them to the main topic, their shared concerns and aspirations regarding Poland and communism in the Soviet Bloc. "In that meeting," according to Bernstein, "Reagan and the Pope agreed to undertake a clandestine campaign to hasten the dissolution of the communist empire." Bernstein goes on to quote Richard Allen: "This was one of the great secret alliances of all time."

In actuality, the collaboration was never quite as dramatic or defined as Bernstein's article described. Perhaps it would be more accurate to call it a symmetry of goals and actions so strong and clear as to make overt coordination unnecessary. In an interview for the University of Virginia's Miller Center, Richard Allen acknowledged that the phrase he used with Bernstein—"secret alliance"—may have given the wrong impression. "I went to great pains to let him know there was nothing formal about it, that it happened that the Vatican was moving on one track and we on another track, our tracks were parallel. . . . It wasn't secret by agreement, it was just a secret alliance. Maybe a "silent alliance" would have been better."

The fact that it was not a formal alliance in no way diminishes the remarkable relationship between the United States and the Vatican in the 1980s. Both shared a very real interest in assisting the downfall of the Communist regime in Poland—and then elsewhere—and collaborated, if informally, in their efforts.

Those efforts were carried out on the American side mainly by the man who initiated them, William Casey, director of CIA. Casey had come to CIA directly from his position as Ronald Reagan's campaign manager, but he was no novice in spy craft, having worked under William Donovan in the OSS during World War II. He approached his job as director with the same can-do zeal he exhibited as a young man, when he earned a bronze star as head the Secret Intelligence Branch in Europe. Now approaching seventy, he flew around the globe in the CIA's black C-141 Starlifter, aggressively pursuing the mission which President Reagan entrusted to him, to destroy communism. Bill Casey often made the Vatican his first stop when he visited Europe.

Again, CIA-Vatican contacts were not formal or extensive, but at the very least the church seems to have put the agency in contact with members of Solidarity. The CIA then channeled funds and equipment to support the group during martial law. In revolutionary movements, the quintessential currency is communication, and so, as in Italy back in 1948, the CIA focused on cultivating this within Poland. Money went to funding underground antigovernment publishing ventures and to supplying radio transmitters, among other basic items. The equipment allowed Solidarity members to talk to each other and to broadcast from their own moveable radio station, located in the back of a van. All the while, the CIA used its own sophisticated electronic surveillance equipment to eavesdrop on army communications, which were then passed on to Solidarity and, very likely, to the Vatican.

In keeping with Richard Allen's description of the "silent alliance," Robert Gates, deputy director of intelligence at the time, acknowledges that "there was considerable sharing of information" and a "modicum of coordination" between the CIA and Vatican, but reinforces the point that "each of these institutions, for important reasons of its own, maintained a clear separation from the other in its activities." The Vatican would have been extremely reluctant to abridge its neutral and independent status by entering into clandestine activity with the United States or any other country. At the same time, any evidence that the CIA was colluding with either the Vatican or the Solidarity would only have undermined antigovernment efforts within Poland.

Like Casey, Vernon Walters continued to make Rome a frequent destination in his capacity as Reagan's ambassador-at-large, visiting two or three times a year. Walters was no intelligence novice himself, having served as deputy director of CIA under Richard Nixon. Walter's portfolio under Reagan included the task of tightening ties with the pope. After that first visit—described previously—in which he brought the satellite reconnaissance photos, Walters met the pope one-on-one. "He always received me alone and whenever anyone attempted to interrupt the briefing he would wave them out of the room," Walters later wrote. Possibly this gesture was the pope's way of making sure no more leaks of American intelligence came from the Vatican.

For all the care both men took to keep their meetings private, the KGB formed the definite idea that the Vatican was involved in helping Solidarity with American collaboration. A 1984 KGB report claimed that the pope's natural anticommunist leanings were amplified by "reactionary political figures, especially of the USA," and that the Vatican was planning "an international alliance to combat communist ideology." The pope rankled the Soviets by dealing firmly with the communists, and by aggressively deploying his moral authority as he traveled the world.

★ ★ ★

In the early spring of 1983, John Paul II took a historic trip to Central America that included a visit to Nicaragua, then under the control of the leftist Sandinistas. Some advisors in the Curia worried that the pope would be courting disaster in Managua, where the Sandinistas had shown open contempt for the Catholic Church and where he was sure to encounter anti-Vatican demonstrators. To make matters a bit more complicated, a number of Catholic priests in Nicaragua openly supported the Sandinista government; several even held positions within it despite orders from their religious superiors to step down. Altogether, Nicaragua presented a hornet's nest of potential embarrassments for the pope. Canceling the trip would have been the easiest option, as some in the Curia advised.

John Paul II decided to go to Nicaragua.

He began his visit at Managua's airport on March 4, 1983, by openly reprimanding Fr. Ernesto Cardenal, the Sandinista's culture minister, on the tarmac. "Regularize your position with the Church," he instructed Fr. Cardenal. A photograph of this encounter, showing the stern-looking pope wagging his finger at the kneeling priest, was published in newspapers around the world.

Later that day, as the pope said mass before seven hundred thousand people at a Managua park, a group of Sandinistas tried to shout him down with slogans and jeers. "Silencio!" the pope finally commanded with a flash of temper—then twice more, until the rabble rousers quieted. It was a small gesture but a sign that this pope would brook no interruption, nor any attempts to turn his pastoral visits into a political sideshow. It might have been the Sandinistas' stage, but it was the pope's script.

Three months after Managua, in June 1983, the pope showed his mettle again. He returned to Poland in a far less conciliatory mood than in 1979. Meeting General Jaruzelski, head of military government, John Paul bluntly described his homeland as having become "one great concentration camp" under martial law. He made it clear that he intended to meet with Lech Walesa, under house arrest in a remote hunting lodge, but the Polish government balked. According to George Weigel, the pope's own advisors, including Secretary of State Casaroli, counseled John Paul to drop the matter, but the pope was insistent. "If I can't see him, then I'm going back to Rome." Confronted with this ultimatum, the Polish government gave in. The pope met with Walesa in a cabin in the Polish countryside. One month later, martial law was lifted in Poland.

No one would ever characterize John Paul II of the 1980s as a rash or irascible man, but he had a firm resolve and great way of moving past the usual diplomatic parlance to say exactly what he meant, while motivating his diplomatic corps to follow. The world is a better place for it.

V.

The 1980s were dangerous years around the world, more dangerous than most people knew at the time. In the Able Archer affair of 1983, for example, the United States and the Soviet Union came closer to nuclear war than at any time since the Cuban missile crisis. The Reagan administration, with the help of the Vatican and other allies, had the Soviets against the wall. But would they submit or would they strike back?

The world would need some luck, or maybe that same divine intervention that saved the president and the pope from assassins' bullets earlier in the decade, for communism to go away peacefully. In the meantime, Ronald Reagan was not one to sit by and watch events unfold. Three years into his presidency, he made a decision to ensure that, no matter how this all worked out, the United States and the Vatican would face it together.

On January 10, 1984, the Reagan administration announced its intention to "restore" full diplomatic relations with the Vatican after a pause of 117 years. Restore was the operative verb, since relations were never formally broken; back in 1867, Congress merely voted to stop funding the mission. The administration only needed Congress to retract that decision.

I have heard many explanations for why Reagan restored diplomatic relations with the Holy See. In one version it is asserted that Margaret Thatcher influenced Reagan. Her own country, Great Britain, had recently elevated the status of its representative to the Holy See to that of an ambassador, and Prime Minister Thatcher convinced President Reagan that her country gained much by doing so. It has also been written that William Wilson, Reagan's personal envoy to the pope at the time, made the case to the president that the U.S. representative to the Holy See should acquire the status of a full ambassador. The simplest explanation is that Reagan understood, as had Robert Graham back in 1959, that formal relations between the United States and the Holy See were inevitable, "a sensible and long overdue move," as the *Washington Post* put it.

That Reagan awarded the Vatican embassy post to Wilson was no surprise; Wilson was an old friend of Reagan's from California, a businessman, a fellow horseman, and a converted Catholic. The real surprise, given all the history that had come before, was the public reaction to the White House's announcement—which was almost no reaction at all. Muted expressions of discontent came from some evangelical groups, and a few legal scholars took issue on constitutional grounds, but polls showed that a majority of Americans supported diplomatic relations with the Holy See. Congress approved Wilson's appointment with a landslide vote. Most Americans seemed to agree that the status of the Holy See as a sovereign power and—thanks to the 1929 Lateran Treaty—temporal power, duly qualified it as a legitimate diplomatic partner for the United States.

"We respect the great moral and political influence which he and the Vatican exercise throughout the world," said the president's spokesman of

Pope John Paul II, announcing diplomatic relations on January 10, 1984. "We admire the courageous stand he takes in defense of Western values." At the same time that Wilson was nominated to be ambassador, Cardinal Pio Laghi, who had been serving as the papal envoy to the United States, was immediately elevated to the status of nuncio, or ambassador, in Washington. The process in the United States took a little longer, requiring the confirmation of Congress. This was not long in coming. On March 7, 1984, 205 years after John Adams predicted the United States would never have diplomatic relations with Rome, something occurred that was both remarkable and natural: the United States named its first full ambassador to the Holy See.

# IV

## ACROSS THE TIBER

# 11

## TO THE VATICAN

If diplomacy is the art of persuading others to act as we would wish, effective foreign policy requires that we comprehend why others act as they do.

—Madeleine Albright

### I.

The first hint that President George W. Bush might have a role for me in his second administration, or even, more incredibly, that he was considering me as his ambassador to the Holy See, came on the evening before the president's second inauguration, in January 2005. Kathleen and I were attending a dinner organized by the inaugural committee at the Washington Hilton Hotel. As dinner was breaking up, I spoke briefly with a high-ranking White House official seated nearby. "How about the Vatican?" he asked. I don't recall my response, other than surprise. I certainly expected nothing. If I were on a list of candidates for the ambassadorship to the Holy See, I figured it would be a long and distinguished list. Putting the possibility out of my mind, I returned to enjoying the inaugural activities and celebrating the reelection of President George W. Bush.

I was in Tulsa a few weeks later when the phone rang. Dina Powell was calling from the White House, asking if I might be available to visit Washington soon. Dina was head of presidential personnel, responsible for filling positions in the executive branch, so I knew something was up. I assumed that they might be considering me for a post in Latin America since I had done business there and speak Spanish. The previous September the president had named me to join Secretary of State Colin Powell in the delegation to represent him at the inauguration of the new president of the Republic of Panama, Martin Torrijos.

A few days later I went to the West Wing to meet Dina. After chatting briefly about some common friends, Dina came to the point. "President Bush wants you to go to the Vatican."

"Really?" My jaw must have dropped. "Are you sure about that?"

She looked surprised. "What? Don't you want to go there? Do you want to me to tell the president you don't want to do that?"

"Of course I want to go!"

I had a lot to learn about the Vatican. But I already knew enough to understand that the Holy See, by virtue of what it does and how far it reaches, and given the alignment of its values with the president's, would be a fascinating and satisfying place to work. I also knew that 2005 was likely to be a pivotal year for the Catholic Church. Pope John Paul II was eighty-four-years-old and in poor health; at the very moment that I was meeting with Dina Powell in Washington, he was in a hospital in Rome with influenza. His papacy was ebbing. A new pope would soon be installed in the Vatican, and when this occurred it would present an important opportunity to institutionalize the U.S. mission to the Holy See—to go beyond the personal charisma of Pope John Paul II, which had been so important to the mission's founding, and to pursue values and goals shared by the Bush administration and the church.

Perhaps most importantly, I understood, contrary to conventional wisdom, that organized religion was becoming *more* important, not less important, in international relations. Among those who had come to this same conclusion was Madeleine Albright, who had served as secretary of state under President Clinton and later wrote a book—*The Mighty and the Almighty*—about her epiphany on the role of religion. "The star most of us navigated by in those years was modernization," Albright reflected on her earlier views, "which many of us took as a synonym for secularization." Her generation of diplomats had seen religious rivalries as vanishing "echoes of earlier, less enlightened times." But then came 9/11: "Since the terror attacks, I have come to realize that it may have been I who was stuck in an earlier time." What humans believe in their souls, Albright and many others came to realize, matters as much to world affairs as economics, political alliances, or weapons.

While I lacked Secretary Albright's experience in foreign policy, and came from a different end of the political spectrum, her perspective certainly made sense in 2005, and it was reinforced and deepened by the reading materials given to me by the State Department. There was no better place to confront the new religious reality than the Holy See.

★ ★ ★

About a month after meeting Dina Powell, I returned to Washington and stopped by the State Department, where I was handed a stack of forms to begin the presidential appointment process. The forms contained detailed questions concerning financial assets, foreign travel, political contributions, and personal relations. The White House had its own questionnaire, as did the Senate. In the meantime, personnel from the diplomatic security section of the State Department conducted a thorough background check, calling on neighbors and friends.

Along with completing the paperwork, I dove into the intellectual preparation for serving at the mission to the Holy See. The process began with a large stack of books suggested by the State Department and church leaders, supplemented by conversations with an ad hoc group of friends and advisors. In early April 2005, I had a series of consultations in the State Department with other ambassadors and officials who had expertise in the issues I would encounter at the Holy See mission. Additionally, Kathleen and I attended the ambassadors' seminar, held at the main State Department building on Virginia Avenue and at the George P. Shultz National Foreign Affairs Training Center in Arlington. This two-week session was a valuable introduction to the internal State Department processes and procedures, and gave us information on a broad range of issues pertinent to service as a U.S. ambassador.

We were still attending the State Department course in early April when John Paul II passed away. The death of a pope is always an extraordinary event, but the death of this pope was especially moving. Hundreds of thousands of pilgrims poured into the Borgo neighborhood around Vatican City in the days after John Paul's death to pay their respects and pray. Among these were tens of thousands of Poles who traveled across the continent to Italy to mourn the man who had freed their homeland. The city of Rome could barely accommodate the flood of pilgrims, whose numbers were soon swelled by an influx of foreign dignitaries arriving to attend the pope's funeral.

The delegation from United States was unprecedented. Led by President Bush, and including former presidents George H. W. Bush and Bill Clinton, the American presence in Rome spoke to the important place Pope John Paul II held in the hearts of the American people.

Kathleen and I watched the television coverage of the funeral mass from our hotel room in Washington, along with an estimated 2 billion people around the world, many of whose lives were touched and transformed by Karol Wojtyla.

On April 19, Cardinal Joseph Ratzinger of Germany was elected by the College of Cardinals to become the 265th pope of the Catholic Church. Cardinal Ratzinger was already well known in Catholic circles and beyond. He had served under John Paul II as prefect of the Sacred Congregation for the Doctrine of the Faith, the overseer of church doctrine. As the chief spokesman for Catholic dogma, he developed a reputation as a fierce conservative—"God's Rottweiler," as the American press often called him. My own limited experience with media had taught me to take such characterizations with a grain of salt, and I looked forward to meeting Pope Benedict XVI and having a chance to draw my own conclusions. Undoubtedly, the papal transition would be a challenge on many fronts, but it would also be a chance to deepen and broaden the relationship between the United States and the Holy See.

But first we had to complete the process and get to Rome. Kathleen and I were back in Washington, this time with our children, for my confirmation hearings in September before the Senate's Foreign Relations Committee. Presided over by Senator George Allen of Virginia, the hearing was fairly straightforward. My wife sat behind me in the gallery with our sons, Larry and Michael, and our daughter, Kathleen. "For the record," joked Senator Allen after I introduced my children, "you don't have to send three kids to Notre Dame to get this job. Georgetown or any of the Loyola's are OK, too."

As Senator Allen humorously acknowledged, every ambassador since Wilson has been a Catholic. While being a Catholic is not necessarily a prerequisite for capable representation of the United States at the Holy See, it definitely enriches the personal experience. A great many official diplomatic events occur at Mass, usually in St. Peter's. Furthermore, a diplomat's success depends largely on rapport and understanding, including an appreciation of the traditions, culture, and core beliefs observed by his interlocutors. As described earlier, the broad principles and values the Holy See projects in world affairs are derived and grounded in Catholic teaching, the scriptures and the Gospel. Of course many non-Catholic and non-Christian ambassadors from other countries serve at the Vatican with distinction. Some of these, wisely, retain priests as advisors to their missions to guide them in dealing with the Holy See. "You must always remember that we are men of faith before we are anything else," Monsignor Peter Wells, the most highly placed American in the Vatican's Secretariat of State, once told me. It's an important point: at the end of the day, the Holy See is the home of a religion; to understand the Holy See, one must first understand the essential doctrines of Catholic teaching and faith.

★ ★ ★

I was sworn in by Secretary Andrew Card, the White House chief of staff, at his office in the West Wing. Kathleen and our children could not attend, but Monsignor Girelli from the Holy See's Washington nunciature (embassy) and my assistant, Michael Napolitano, were there. "We have a surprise for you," said Secretary Card after swearing me in. He walked us to the Oval Office. President Bush was at his desk, and he stood to greet us with a warm grin. I told the president that I would represent him to the very best of my abilities. "I know you will," he said. "That's why I picked you."

I first met President George W. Bush in the early 1990s, when our construction company built the Texas Rangers' ballpark for him. The job was a huge opportunity for the company and we made sure to justify the confidence the future president and his team had placed in us. Now, as his ambassador-designate to the Holy See, I had every intention of justifying his confidence again. No president since Ronald Reagan had so truly appreciated, nor been so aligned with, the values of the Holy See as President Bush. Accordingly, I knew that I would have an important advantage in my work—some degree of understanding of what the president would want to accomplish with the mission to the Holy See.

A few days after the swearing in, a package arrived at my office in Tulsa. Inside were my official instructions from President Bush. The letter outlined the duties of an ambassador of the United States in the year 2005:

> Our commitment to freedom is America's tradition. The advance of freedom is also the surest way to undermine terror and tyranny, and to promote peace and prosperity. Your task is to help in advancing this great cause by:
>
> - waging a relentless global war, to defeat those who seek to harm us and our friends;
> - overcoming the faceless enemies of human dignity, including disease, starvation, and poverty; and
> - assisting American citizens, institutions, and businesses as they pursue their charitable and commercial interests.

Not long thereafter, instructions in hand, Kathleen and I were on a plane to Rome.

## II.

I began this book with a description of the credentialing day, the climax of which was a private meeting with Benedict XVI in his library. After those first moments, when nerves briefly froze my tongue, I began to speak about the areas in which I hoped the Holy See and United States could cooperate successfully. I had been given a series of topics to discuss in our meeting. These ranged from human trafficking to immigration to religious freedom, all concerns in which the United States and Holy See shared parallel interests and goals. Though our mutual principles remained fundamentally the same as they had been when William Wilson sat down with Pope John Paul II, much in the world had changed since 1984. The Cold War was over, and the United States was now engaged in a new high-stakes struggle against terrorist organizations. As the president's instructions indicated, the Global War on Terror would be the focus during much of my tenure in Rome.

The Holy See was as concerned as we Americans were about terrorism. But if we agreed on the threat, we did not entirely agree on how to deal with it. John Paul II's Vatican had vigorously protested America's invasion of Iraq in 2003. Cardinal Pio Laghi, the former nuncio to the United States, had been dispatched on a special papal mission to Washington, where he met with President Bush to deliver the pope's message opposing an intervention in Iraq. My immediate predecessor, Ambassador Jim Nicholson, engaged in a series of intense disagreements with various elements of the Holy See on account of the war. Now, three years into the conflict, sitting before the new pope, I was prepared to defend our actions in Iraq, what we were trying to accomplish there and what success would mean for the cause of freedom in the world. I was surprised, then, by the pope's response when I raised the issue. He waved his hand with a gentle sweeping motion. "Let us speak no more of Iraq," he said. "Iraq is past history. Let's talk of the future." The Vatican had spoken with conviction against the war, but the war was three years old. The pope intended to focus the Vatican's energies now on ways to work constructively to bring stability and reduce conflict in the country.

The Vatican was deeply engaged and informed on all aspects of Islamic fundamentalism. Indeed, the dynamic between the Christian West and Muslim East had been occupying the Holy See since the Crusades, when the church's commitment to peace—and to understanding other religions—was not quite as evolved as it later became. Interestingly, an early occurrence of schism between the Shiite Muslim and Sunni Muslim sects benefitted the Holy See during the First Crusade in 1099, when Christian warriors tried to take Jerusalem from the Fatimid Shiites of Egypt. The Crusaders were successful because the rival Seljuk Turks, Sunnis from Aleppo, refused to go help their fellow Muslims in Jerusalem. Absent this rivalry, the Christians might never have taken Jerusalem and held it for eighty-eight years, until Saladin and a more cohesive and united Muslim force would take it back in 1187, defeating a Christian coalition that sank into its own internal rivalries.

Pope Benedict himself had thought a great deal about the question of Islam, both as pope and in his earlier life as a scholar. "You know, there are two Mohammeds," he said to me now as we sat in his library. "The Mohammed of the early Koran, who is tolerant, and the Mohammed of the later Koran, who is aggressive." This was a distinction he would come back to again in public, most dramatically and controversially in a speech the following year in Regensburg, Germany. Looking back, I realize I was seeing a preview of Regensburg and an important glimpse into the new pope's worldview.

The pope's concerns were hardly limited to the Muslim world. He also spoke at some length about the troubling trends of relativism and secularism creeping into Western culture. The church was bigger than ever, but its growth was in the third world, and especially in Africa. Although Benedict did not make the connection explicit at the time, the two major threats were conjoined in his mind—on the one hand, religious fundamentalism growing in the east; on the other hand, faith collapsing in the west. He believed he had a special role in mediating between these fundamentally opposed worldviews.

Over the eight years he served as pope, Benedict XVI's critics tended to categorize him as a kind of Manichean fundamentalist, but that was a simplistic and flawed reading of the man. Certainly he took seriously the church's obligation to clarify and defend the articles of the Catholic faith, but Benedict also demonstrated strong support for the clear separation of church and state, providing, of course, that the state made due accommodation for the free practice of religion. As noted earlier, Benedict was a great admirer of our First Amendment. "Where the Church itself becomes the state freedom becomes lost," he once wrote. "But also when the Church is done away with as a public and publicly relevant authority, then too freedom is extinguished, because there the state once again claims completely for itself the justification of morality." His words are worth considering especially at a time when an alternative, more restrictive interpretation of the religious freedom language in the amendment is being advanced in the United States.

Benedict once noted that his childhood in Germany during the Nazi reign stood as a lifelong example to him of what happens when nations expel God and worship only themselves and their leaders. "Politics must be a striving for justice," he declared to the German Bundestag on September 22, 2011, quoting Saint Augustine, "'Without justice, what else is the State but a great band of robbers?'" Linking belief in God to the concept of human rights, Benedict argued that faith is a fundamental precondition of human decency. "The conviction that there is a Creator God is what gave rise to the idea of human rights, the idea of the equality of all people before the law, the recognition of the inviolability of human dignity in every single person and the awareness of people's responsibility for their actions."

These concepts resonate with the founding principles of the United States as stated in the Declaration of Independence and the Preamble to the Constitution, and have been expressed by popes and moral leaders for centuries. Benedict often amplified their importance as necessary truths, cautioning against the marginalization of religion and the pitfalls of a "dictatorship of relativism," the phrase he'd used in an address to the College of Cardinals on April 18, 2005, the day before the cardinals elected him pope.

In a sense, Benedict's model for the proper relationship between religion and civil society was the United States of America. In our conversation in his library, his eyes lit up as he extolled the "great experiment" of the First Amendment of the U.S. Constitution. Perhaps more than any pope in history, he had a genuine and abiding fondness for America, a country he had visited and enjoyed. Such was his degree of contact with the United States that Fr. Theodore Hesburgh, CSC, the president of the University of Notre Dame, once offered the future pope a teaching position. Benedict admired America's civic institutions and its capacity to absorb and assimilate people of many different ethnicities and religious beliefs, as he told me in the credentials visit. America at its best, he understood, is a place where faith and freedom coexist in mutual accommodation and understanding.

## III.

By the time I met the pope, I had already been in Rome long enough to establish normal working procedures at the embassy. Generally, the day began with a short drive from the residence, Villa Richardson, down the Janiculum Hill and across the Tiber to the chancery near the bottom of the Aventine Hill. The chancery, too, had a name—Villa Domiziana—making it sound more ornate than it was. A sturdy-looking 1950s structure attractively set in a grove of umbrella pines, it had once been the residence of the Soviet ambassador to Italy. The best feature was the view from the office. The large picture window looked out over the ruins of the Circus Maximus. Not much is left of the Circus now, but in its heyday tens of thousands of Romans gathered at a time to watch chariot races or gladiators battle with live beasts—or early Christians getting devoured by lions. It struck me as ironic to have the mission to the Holy See look out on the site where many of the Christian martyrdoms took place.

Our offices were modest. The embassy to the Holy See is small partly because it does not handle the type of trade development and business promotion, as well as consular activities—processing visas and hosting trade delegations—that consume secular embassies. The size made the embassy a highly interactive and team-oriented culture. I had the interesting challenge of leading and managing a staff which, for the most part, had been in place when I arrived and would be in place after I left. I had spent much of my life running businesses, hiring, incentivizing, and managing employees, but this was a management task of a very different sort. These were not my employees; they worked for the U.S. State Department. I did not have the power to hire or fire them, nor offer much in the way of incentives. I had to learn to build a team and manage differently. Fortunately, we had a talented staff of dedicated professionals who were glad to be there, who believed in the mission, and were eager to help me do the best job possible for President Bush.

At my first staff meeting, I asked everybody to arrive at work a half hour earlier than they had been accustomed to doing, so as to get a jump on the Roman morning. To set a tone of teamwork and efficiency, one of my first instructions was to request that the staff not stand up when I entered the room, an unnecessary formality. But I also made clear that punctuality was a priority. Early in my tenure, Kathleen and I once arrived a couple of minutes late for a papal mass to find everyone already seated. This was a concern to me because I knew it might reflect negatively on the United States. Some people would think we did not know enough to be on time, while others might say we did not feel the need. Either way, we lose. After this, we made sure to arrive at least three to five minutes early wherever we went.

I soon figured out that the best hours to accomplish anything outside the embassy, at the Vatican or other embassies, was in the morning or late afternoon. We also took advantage of the Italian lunch tradition to entertain and build relationships. Nowhere do personal relationships matter more than in the Vatican, a closed world that does not unfold easily to strangers.

In my experience, the only one way to foster relationships is to go out and meet people, talk to them, and let them know you are genuinely interested in what they have to say.

I had a good idea of who I needed to know based on information provided by the State Department and the embassy staff, but I had some outside help as well. Cardinal Pio Laghi, the former nuncio to the United States (who had also been the pope's envoy to Bush just before the Iraq War), knew everybody in Rome and was particularly helpful in steering me to people who would be important to our mission. Since deceased, Cardinal Laghi was a robust eighty-three when I met him. "Mr. Ambassador, you may know how to swim in the waters of the Potomac," he told me. "Now I will show you how to swim in the Tiber." He gave me a list of people to visit. With the cardinal's help, I got a quick start.

Most of my visits were friendly, but not all. One of my first stops was at the home of an ambassador from the tiny principality of San Marino. This gentleman, by virtue of simple seniority—he had been representing his country to the Vatican for twenty-five years, as I recall—held the title of Dean of Vatican diplomatic corps. His role was ceremonial, but it did give him the privilege of speaking on behalf of the diplomatic corps at the annual New Year meeting with the pope. In light of some prior comments he had made about the Iraq War, we were concerned he intended to use his next opportunity, in January 2006, to berate the United States. I figured it was within my job description to neutralize this, so I went out to visit the ambassador in his house on the outskirts of the city. "Listen, don't say anything about Iraq," I told him. "If you do, we'll speak up openly against what you say."

Iraq came up again a few evenings after my credentialing, when I visited the Patriarch of Babylon, leader of the Catholic Church inside Iraq. Emmanuel III Delly was an elderly man, tall and frail, who seemed to materialize out of the New Testament, as ancient as the long line of Chaldean Catholics he represented. Under his white beard and hair, though, worked a keen and forward-looking mind. His Beatitude (as the patriarch was called) asked to meet me to express his great concern about the future of Christians in Iraq. Saddam Hussein had possessed many faults but he generally left Christians alone, so long as they did not challenge his power. Now, with Saddam gone, the Patriarch feared the rise of an Iranian-backed Shiite government that would be far less accommodating to Christians. Already persecution of Iraqi Christians, who made up just 3 percent of the population, was on rise, and many had fled; by August 2006, half of all Christians would be gone from Iraq. The new constitution, calling for Islamic Law, only added to Patriarch Delly's concerns. How would this affect Catholics and other Christians? I tried to assure the Patriarch that the United States would do everything in its power to protect Christians inside the country. I left that meeting moved by his yearning for religious freedom.

I heard similar concerns when I met Iraq's ambassador to the Holy See, Albert Yelda, a few months later. Ambassador Yelda was an Assyrian Christian, descended from ancient inhabitants of the Euphrates valley. Like Chaldean Catholics, who were themselves ethnic Assyrians, his people had lived in Mesopotamia almost since the time of Christ. The ambassador was concerned that they would not last there much longer.

Conditions for Christians did indeed deteriorate through the rest of 2005 and into 2006. On January 29, 2006, car bombs were detonated in front of four Christian Churches in Baghdad and Mosul, and another in front of the residence of the Vatican's nuncio to Iraq. Unfortunately this violence continues unabated to the present—on October 31, 2010, bombs went off in the Baghdad Cathedral killing more than fifty Syriac Christians—and has spread throughout the Middle East. On January 1, 2011, twenty-three Coptic Christians were murdered while attending services in Alexandria. Similar attacks have continued to occur throughout the region.


## IV.


Mornings often meant going to the Vatican to meet Curia officials. Visiting the Vatican is a unique and memorable experience, but in those early days I was often too preoccupied with the task at hand to fully take in the surroundings. I would return from a visit at the secretary of state's office and try to make notes of what I had seen there, but with little success at first. Even the most observant visitor would be likely to find the Apostolic Palace a complicated maze.

I usually entered the palace the same way I had come for the credentialing, through the Cortile San Damaso, or else by the large Belvedere courtyard at the back of the Apostolic Palace. The entire conjoined complex of Vatican buildings extends north from St. Peter's Basilica and includes the archives, library, and museum, along with miles of corridor and thousands of rooms, but the Apostolic Palace is the heart of the operation. In addition to the pope's private residence and the numerous marbled "salas" and frescoed loggias, the palace houses the key administrative offices of the Vatican.

Small mahogany-paneled elevators carried me to these offices on the third floor. I would be met by one of the staff of the secretary of state, who would escort me through the loggias that surround the Cortile St. Damaso, then down a hall to one of several small meeting rooms. No matter which meeting room I was taken to, the custom never varied. The door was closed behind me, I waited a few minutes, and then the door opened again and the official I had come to meet entered and greeted me, and we sat and got down to business.

In those early days, as I learned the decorum and habits of the Vatican, a lot of my effort went into figuring out its organizational structure. As one Vatican insider recently states, "the Vatican is a ball of wool that's almost impossible to untangle—even by a pope." One simple fact is that all power in the Vatican emanates from the pope. He is head of state of Vatican City—that tiny territory with its own post office, bank, and police force, and a population of about one thousand—and of the sovereign institution of the Holy See. He is also the chief priest of a worldwide religion. His domain is far greater than the territory he rules; it is the entire Catholic Church, governed under the auspices of the Holy See.

As discussed earlier in these pages, the possession of Vatican City embellishes the Holy See's sovereignty, but its sovereignty does not depend of its territory. The Holy See, as the governing body of the universal Catholic Church, would survive even if it had no land to call its own. It *did* survive without land for nearly sixty years, between the fall of the papal states in 1870 and the Lateran Treaty in 1929.

In any case, the pope holds a position of huge symbolic and ceremonial importance. From nuts and bolts bureaucratic decisions to great theological disputes, from setting the general direction of the church to performing specific religious functions, the pope is the person in whom final authority is vested. There is no separation of powers in the Vatican. Every chain of command leads ultimately to him.

To perform his many duties, the pope depends on a staff, called the Curia. The Curia is composed of approximately six hundred employees, including clergy of all ranks and levels and lay people, many of whom both work and live inside the Vatican. These officials are dispersed among the numerous congregations, councils, and tribunals—collectively known as "dicasteries"—that oversee various responsibilities and jurisdictions. One of the nine congregations, for example, is the Sacred Congregation for the Doctrine of the Faith, formerly under the direction of then Cardinal Joseph Ratzinger. Others include the Congregation for the Evangelization of Peoples and the Congregation for Catholic Education. The tribunals deal with excommunications, annulments, and similar matters. Unlike the American judiciary, which operates as a separate branch of government, the tribunals answer to the pope.

The dicastery that works most closely with the pope in his administration of the church is the Secretariat of State. Through this "dicastery of dicasteries," as it is sometimes called, the Holy See communicates with the larger Catholic Church and the world at large. The highest ranking member of the Curia, the man second only to the pope, is the cardinal secretary of state. Centuries ago, when nepotism was the rule inside the Vatican, this position was known as the cardinal-nephew. In fact, the word nepotism is derived from the Italian word for nephew, *nepote*, to capture the once-common familial relationship between popes and their advisers.

The cardinal secretary really runs the day-to-day operations of the church, functioning as a combination of prime minister and foreign secretary, and leaving the pope to set broad strategy and tend to his important spiritual role as head of the church. When I became ambassador in 2005, the man in this job was the long-serving Cardinal Angelo Sodano.

The Secretariat of State is divided into two divisions. The General Section, also called the section for "ordinary" affairs, or the "first section," accounts for matters that are intrachurch, which is to say matters of administration of the worldwide Catholic Church. The head of the first section, known as the *Sostituto*—the substitute—is generally the third most powerful figure inside the Vatican, after the pope and secretary of state. He essentially acts as chief of staff, the channel between the Curia and the pope, deciding which issues and problems are brought to the attention of the pope. Archbishop Leonardo Sandri, an Argentinean, held this position when I was in Rome. Much of the world got its first glimpse of Archbishop Sandri on the evening of April 2, 2005, when he stepped out of the front entry of St. Peter's onto the Piazza to announce the death of John Paul II.

For my purposes as ambassador, the more relevant branch of the Secretariat of State was generally the Second Section, that is, the Section for Relations between States, or "extraordinary" affairs. The Second Section, like the U.S. State Department, handles relations with other governments. Under the secretary for relations with states—a position held by Archbishop Giovanni Lajolo in 2005—the Second Section is subdivided into geographical concentrations, each headed by a desk officer, much like our state department. They are quite efficient. The entire diplomatic arm of the Vatican, covering 179 countries, employs no more than eighty people, about thirty of these support staff.

To handle both civil government and church affairs around the world, the staffs of the first and second sections rely heavily on nuncios, the Holy See's ambassadors. Posted in most of the countries with which the Vatican maintains diplomatic relations, the nuncios are the pope's eyes and ears, and sometimes his voice. Serving in a dual capacity as the Vatican's channel to the local church and to the civil government of the nation where they are posted, the nuncios are a highly trained, well-educated, and diverse group. Most are graduates of the Pontifical Ecclesiastical Academy in Rome, the world's first and longest standing school of diplomacy, and are experienced in diplomatic affairs, having served on the staff of nunciatures around the world. Given limited Vatican manpower, young would-be diplomats are taught the important communication skill of boiling down complicated situations into several good pages—"to take 100 pages and turn it into three," in the words of Monsignor Peter Wells. "I tell them that if they can't make it short, no one will read it."

★  ★  ★

The pope is the last remaining absolute leader in Europe, his power is hardly without limits. He is constrained both by the conventions and precedents of the church and by the practical exigencies of the institution's administration. Although the church is hierarchical, much of its day-to-day business is delegated to dioceses around the world. Popes paint the broad strokes, but details are left to the discretion of local bishops. When combined in national conferences, such as the U.S. Conference of Catholic Bishops, the bishops wield enormous influence within the church. All decisions and pronouncements are meant to be coordinated with the Vatican—which is to say, with the pope—but the conferences act with a significant degree of independence.

Complicating matters further are the dozens of orders of priests and nuns, from Jesuits to Dominicans to Carmelites, all with their own structures and perspectives, each forming a satellite of power outside the Vatican. Like local bishops, these orders fall nominally under the domain of the pope, but only in general terms; for the most part, they operate under their own jurisdictions and authority. Finally, of course, there are individual priests and nuns whose daily behavior the Vatican cannot possibly supervise closely. A large part of the Vatican's task is to attempt to unify these various factions and personalities under a single and consistent message.

Even if it were possible to draw a flow chart of the circuits of power within the Catholic Church, it would fail to capture the human aspect. As in any bureaucracy, the personalities who occupy the positions define them more completely than any job description. The Curia is populated by men of God, but they are human nonetheless, and they bring strengths and weakness to their offices. This is true at all levels. Pope Benedict XVI, for instance, obviously had a very different style than Pope John Paul II, and used his authority differently. Whereas Pope John Paul II was an extrovert, a powerful stage presence, and his own best spokesman, Pope Benedict XVI was an academic and an intense intellectual. Neither type is necessarily better than the other, but the pope's personality and predilections will inevitably affect the office he holds and the entire tenor of the Vatican.

# 12

## NEW FRIENDS

Everything that happened in Eastern Europe would have been impossible without the pope.

—Mikhail Gorbachev

## I.

During spare moments in Rome, I often thought about the great wealth of history that had passed through the Vatican. Not just the distant history, but also the more recent past. The previous twenty years alone had furnished an abundance of dramatic episodes, starting with those great days in the late 1980s, when communism gradually crumbled throughout Eastern Europe.

The end came pretty much as the KGB's gloomiest prognosticators had predicted. Following the pope's visit to Poland in 1979, the spirit of freedom spread into other Catholic countries of the Soviet Empire, then, in a kind of reverse domino effect, into the Catholic provinces of Russia itself. The Soviets did everything in their power to stop it, but they could not.

Many forces combined to end communism in Eastern Europe, the most obvious being the failure of communism itself as an ideology and system of government. The efforts of the United States and its allies, especially Margaret Thatcher's Britain, did much to accelerate the process. But the role of the Catholic Church must not be overlooked. What the Holy See lacked in guns, money, and economic leverage, it supplied in moral authority, the uniquely effective exercise of soft power. Much of this power emanated from the fact that the church, unlike the communist governments, could be trusted. In his biography of John Paul II, George Weigel quotes a Polish priest: "People came to church to find out what the hell was going on in the rest of Poland." The church provided not just sanctuary from the morally bankrupt totalitarian regimes of Eastern Europe, but a flag under which the faithful could gather.

The events in Eastern Europe in the 1980s are a valuable model for the application of this recurrent idea of soft power. Soft power is most effective when it reaffirms what people already believe, then provides those people a community and platform to cultivate and exercise their beliefs. Consider the Arab spring of 2011, when certain social networking sites (such as Facebook) and certain physical locations (such as Tahrir Square) became places where antigovernment protestors convened and organized. No international institution, nor any social network, brings people together more effectively than the Catholic Church. As the veteran Vatican diplomat and current nuncio to Poland, Archbishop Celestino Migliore, once expressed to me, the power of the church is its potential force of cohesion. "We have a theological concept of 'communion' or 'community,'" said Archbishop Migliore, "but in political terms this cohesive community can threaten governments. Politicians fear that cohesion." A precondition of the cohesion is a critical mass of Catholics, of course, but where such exists, as it did in Poland in the 1980s, the church can be a formidable agent of social change.

One reason for this is that the church is a universal sovereign. As a sovereign entity, the Catholic Church can speak for people within a nation yet not be subject to the politics of that nation. Compared, for example, to the orthodox churches of Eastern Europe, which have longstanding ties to the state, the Catholic Church is supranational and subject to no authority other than its own. Even if individual Catholic priests and bishops could be bullied or threatened or murdered—as some were in Eastern Europe in the 1980s—the church itself persists and endures. Not even an assassination attempt on a pope can change this; not even a *successful* assassination could change it. The authority of the church may be temporally located in a particular place (Vatican City) and invested in certain individuals (the pope and his bishops), but it exists independently of any place or person. The church is a set of beliefs and ideas combined with a tradition and structure, and no bullet or bomb or despot can destroy these.

★ ★ ★

In 1986, Soviet Premier Mikhail Gorbachev began instituting reforms within the Soviet Union. Three years later, the Revolutions of 1989 broke out across Eastern Europe, first in Poland, then in Hungary, then East Germany. The Berlin Wall fell in November 1989. By the end, the outlook turned around so completely in Poland that the government of General Jaruzelski was relying on the Polish Church to help pacify its people, effectively admitting that the moral authority of church carried more real power—the power, that is, to sway people—than all the threats and arms of the government.

Diplomatic relations and routine communication between the United States and the Holy See through those hopeful but anxious days proved quite useful. Open channels of communication via the American ambassadors to the Holy See—first William Wilson, then Frank Shakespeare, and later Thomas Melady—ensured, at the very least, that the Holy See and White House avoided working at cross-purposes.

John Paul II's gratitude for Ronald Reagan is evident in a letter he wrote to Nancy Reagan upon the former president's death in 2004, shortly before his own death. "I recall with deep gratitude the late president's unwavering commitment to the service of the nation and to the cause of freedom as well as his abiding faith in the human and spiritual values which ensure a future of solidarity, justice, and peace in our world."

## II.

The level of Holy See–U.S. cooperation has varied since Ronald Reagan's presidency, depending on the priorities and values of individual presidents and the particular strategic interests of the United States and the Holy See at each point along the way. Predictably, as the Cold War ended, George H. W. Bush's administration was not as openly engaged with the Vatican as Ronald Reagan's had been. Bill Clinton's engagement was even more attenuated due both to other administration priorities and some sharp disagreements in principle with the Holy See. The current administration of Barack Obama appears to have little interest in the Holy See. I was fortunate to work for a president who, due to an alignment of his principles and values with those of the Catholic Church, as well as the nature the post-9/11 world, had a very close relationship with the Holy See. The six visits George W. Bush made during his eight years to see John Paul II (including the pope's funeral) and Benedict XVI set a record for U.S. presidential visits. But even in moments of tension and discord, our mutually beneficial diplomatic ties have allowed the United States and the Holy See to manage differences reasonably and effectively, and to move quickly together to leverage and advance shared goals and objectives.

One of the first post-Reagan tests of Holy See–U.S. relations arose in 1989 during Operation Just Cause, the American invasion of Panama, when General Manual Noriega sought and was granted asylum in the Vatican's nunciature in Panama City. Noriega was trying to avoid the grasp of the American military, which intended to extradite him to the United States and put him on trial for drug trafficking, among other serious charges. Like other embassies, the nunciature enjoyed diplomatic immunity and was therefore off-limits to U.S. troops. The nuncio to Panama, a Spanish monsignor named Jose Sebastian Laboa, had no time to consult the Vatican in the tumult of events, so he alone made the controversial decision to admit Noriega and several of his cohorts into the nunciature. Monsignor Laboa had no affection for Noriega, who had become a corrupt quasi-dictator and had never been a friend of the Catholic Church—nor of human rights—but the nuncio believed that allowing the Panamanian strongman into the nunciature might prevent further bloodshed in the streets of Panama. Furthermore, granting asylum was in keeping with church policy and international norms. As Fr. Robert Graham, SJ, explained to newspaper reporters, granting asylum, especially in Latin America, was in no way equivalent to granting residence to a refugee. "It is a question of Latin American diplomatic norms, not of Vatican policies or procedure. This is simply a device to grant temporary haven while a person's status is negotiated." Fr. Graham's assurances notwithstanding, the U.S. government's reaction was very negative when Noriega and henchmen entered the nunciature on Christmas Eve 1989.

Thomas Melady was the U.S. ambassador to the Holy See at the time. He learned of Noriega's entry into the nunciature that Christmas Eve in a phone call from the U.S. State Department operations center. "My instructions were clear," he writes of that phone call. "The United States government did not want the Holy See to grant asylum in the nunciature to Noriega." Later in the evening, dressed in his formal best, Ambassador Melady made his way to St. Peter's Basilica to attend the pope's midnight mass. He sent a note across the nave to Cardinal Secretary of State Casaroli, requesting a meeting directly after mass.

As the audience filed out of St. Peter's that Christmas morning at about 2:00 a.m., the two men conferred in the basilica. Ambassador Melady spelled out the American position, which was that Noriega was a criminal and not worthy of asylum. Later, to support the American case, he gave the Vatican a full copy of the U.S. indictment against Noriega, which may have brought the pope and his advisors into closer sympathy with American objectives. Also, he had recently discussed the global drug menace with the Holy See, ensuring that officials in the secretary of state's office knew just how serious and harmful were Noriega's activities. There is nothing like prior cooperation to lay the foundation for new cooperation.

Though he followed State Department orders and worked to convince the Vatican to expel Noriega, Ambassador Melady warned the State Department not to expect immediate action. The pope, he explained, would go slow and do nothing that might create an impression that the Vatican had caved under American pressure.

The Noriega episode unfolded with a number of awkward twists and turns. In an attempt to hasten the general's exit, the U.S. military, under advisement from its psych-ops unit, surrounded the nunciature and blasted round-the-clock heavy metal rock music at ear-splitting volume. Among the victims of this cacophony, of course, were the papal nuncio and his staff. A Vatican spokesman complained that an "occupying force" had no right to demand that the Vatican turn over Noriega. American clergy joined in the defense. Cardinal John O'Conner of New York was "appalled by the attacks against the Church and Holy See." At least one prominent official in the G. H. W. Bush White House, National Security Advisor Brent Scowcroft, seemed to agree. He later publicly expressed regret for inflicting heavy metal music on the nuncio.

Even with the deafening noise, Monsignor Laboa managed to keep his wits. He composed a letter to the U.S. military command on December 26 (still displayed on a wall in a conference room at Fort Bragg), in which he calmly and carefully outlined the conditions under which he would release the "hostages" to the care and custody of the United States. He refused to be pressured by the American military, but neither did he appease Noriega. Laboa spent many hours talking with the general during the ten days Noriega was in residence. He later explained that he intentionally created a "psychological environment" to lead Noriega to accept the inevitable outcome—his voluntary surrender to the United States. The nuncio hinted that if Noriega refused to leave, then he (Laboa) would himself depart and set up the nunciature elsewhere, taking the Vatican's immunity with him.

Ultimately, Laboa's persuasiveness evidently swayed Noriega. The nuncio's performance was applauded by some diplomats in Washington as a masterpiece of their art. "He closed all the doors one by one," said one, "until Noriega himself concluded that his only alternative was to surrender to the United States." This outcome probably saved a lot of trouble and bloodshed for all. On January 3, 1990, Noriega donned on a military uniform and walked out the embassy, turning himself over without one shot fired.

★ ★ ★

Ambassador Melady confronted a more difficult challenge a year later, when the United States and a UN-backed coalition launched Operation Desert Storm to push Saddam Hussein out of Kuwait. The Vatican deplored Saddam's ruthless aggression but likewise opposed military action against him. The pope took pains to declare that the Catholic Church was *not* "pacifist at any cost" and still subscribed to "just war theory"—the proposition advanced by Saint Thomas Aquinas that war can be morally justified under certain conditions. In fact, though, the church had become increasingly antiwar after the promulgation of *Pacem in Terris* in 1965. Certainly in the case of this first Iraq war the pope made repeated efforts to encourage a peaceful resolution, pressing Hussein to leave Kuwait while urging President Bush to hold his fire. John Paul's last effort to stop the war came on January 15, 1991, when the pope sent letters to Saddam Hussein through the Iraqi ambassador to the Holy See and to President Bush through Ambassador Melady.

In his memoir Ambassador Melady describes his own concerns about the coming war but makes clear that his job was to serve his country and president, and so he did. He personally delivered a letter from President Bush to the Pope John Paul II on January 16, alerting the Vatican that the bombing would soon commence. Arriving at the papal apartments, he found Monsignor Claudio Celli, the Holy See's deputy foreign minister at the time, waiting for him on the steps of the papal apartments to receive it.

The war started a few hours later, on the morning of January 17, 1991, with a heavy air campaign. The first Iraq War lasted six weeks, until February 27, when Saddam finally agreed to withdraw his forces from Kuwait.

Though the pope's pleas to avoid war had been ignored, the Vatican quickly moved to support U.S.–initiated postwar peace efforts. To allay any suspicion of hard feelings, the pope greeted President G. H. W. Bush warmly when he visited the Vatican in November 1991. The pope and president met alone for an hour, even longer than John Paul's meeting with Reagan in 1982. The pope then spontaneously insisted on escorting Bush to the president's meeting with several hundred Americans who worked at the Vatican or attended the North American College as seminarians. This was a small courtesy, but an important gesture of continuing warmth toward the American people. As Melady states, "The United States (the world's only real superpower) and the Holy See (the world's only sovereign moral power) had a disagreement on how to resolve the crisis caused by Saddam Hussein. But there were no hurt feelings as each power appreciated the other's overall commitment to a just and peaceful world order."

★ ★ ★

One of the most difficult moments in Holy See–U.S. diplomatic relations occurred in 1994 and concerned the United Nations International Conference on Population and Development in Cairo. Ambassador Ray Flynn, a former mayor of Boston, found himself representing a U.S. government that had staked out differences with the Holy See over many of the issues to be addressed at the conference. Many of President Clinton's policies were not aligned with the Holy See's, and his then-ambassador to the United Nations (and future secretary of state), Madeleine Albright, had not yet experienced her epiphany about the critical role of religion in international relations.

Prior to the Cairo conference, an early draft of the "program of action" had circulated among the attending delegates. Included in this document's articles was a guarantee of the right of "pregnancy termination." The Clinton administration not only supported this; it was one of the draft's key sponsors.

Ambassador Flynn was himself offended by the measure. A devout Catholic, he was faced with a personal quandary: his duty to the president versus his personal convictions as a Catholic. "I found myself between a rock and a hard place," Flynn would later write, "representing the Clinton administration on the one hand but agreeing with John Paul II on the other." As ambassador, Flynn had little choice but to do as instructed by the Clinton administration. Still, he tried to warn the administration that the abortion clause was bad policy and bad politics. He also tried to arrange meetings of top Clinton officials, including Ambassador Albright, with leading Catholic Clergy, hoping the administration might hear the Catholics' concerns. The Clinton White House was not interested.

Five months before the Cairo conference, Ambassador Flynn was contacted by Archbishop (now Cardinal) Jean-Louis Tauran, then serving as secretary of relations between states at the Vatican. Tauran told the ambassador that the pope wished to speak to the president directly about the Cairo proposal. The Cardinal then walked Flynn through the Apostolic Palace to the pope's private chambers, where the pope gave Flynn the message himself. The personal touch indicated just how much this matter meant to the pope. Indeed, John Paul II saw the Cairo conference as a defining moment of his papacy. The inclusion of pro-abortion language in the conference's program-of-action constituted a moral catastrophe, he believed. It amounted, in the pope's word, to "a United Nations plan to destroy the family."

Flynn went back to Villa Richardson and immediately called the White House to pass along the pope's request. Then he waited—and waited—for the president to respond. After three days and numerous attempts to prod the White House, Flynn, embarrassed and frustrated, got on a plane and flew to Washington. He took a cab directly from the airport to the White House, where he planted himself in the West Wing and waited to see President Clinton personally. Then he went back the following day and waited through the morning. Finally, on the afternoon of the second day, he was called into the Situation Room to meet some of the president's staff. With considerable effort, he convinced the group that the president *had* to respond to the pope. If President Clinton did not want to talk about Cairo, fine—but he could not just ignore the pope's request for a call.

President Clinton finally placed a call to John Paul II, and Ambassador Flynn flew back to Rome. His persistence did not materially change anything, and it surely cost him a great deal politically inside the Clinton White House, but it was the right move for the diplomatic relationship between the two sovereigns.

Even as the pope worked to change Washington's mind about the Cairo platform, he pursued other tactics to defeat the abortion measure. Top Vatican officials, including Archbishop Tauran, were dispatched across the globe. As these papal emissaries pressed the pope's case, the church found allies not just in predominantly Catholic and Christian countries, but in Muslim countries as well. "It seems one of the most important aims of the conference is to facilitate sex, to undermine its passive consequences and to encourage the use of condoms to prevent the transmission of diseases caused by illegal sexual relations," said Sheik Mohammed al-Ghazali, a world-renowned Islamic scholar, expressing a concern shared by many of his fellow Muslims.

The lead-up to Cairo was, in the words of George Weigel, "another example of First World countries imposing their policies and their understanding of morality on Third World countries, using the threat of decreased foreign assistance as a weapon." But this time, instead of compliance, it found resistance and resentment. Among the harshest critics of the proposal were women delegates like Benazir Bhutto of Pakistan. These women perceived that the so-called right to abortion was anything but liberating. It could easily be turned into a coerced obligation, in which mothers were pressed by the state to abort their children for the sake of "population control," all under the aegis of UN decree.

Opposition to the abortion proposition began to gel. When the nine-day population conference opened in Cairo in early September, what had once seemed an assured victory for representatives of the developed west turned into a rout. The vote went against, and new language was inserted into the Cairo document: "In no case," read the final draft, "should abortion be promoted as a method of family planning."

Cairo was a sweet victory for the pope and the Vatican, and one of the reasons *Time* magazine named John Paul II as its 1994 Man of the Year. Few people on earth, the editors of *Time* concluded, carried as much influence as he did. Ambassador Flynn was certainly pleased. "I've always thought of politics as the art of compromise," writes Flynn. "During the Cairo controversy, though, the pope showed me that sometimes—when morality is at stake—there can be no compromise, no way to bring people together. All you can do is to try to persuade them to do what's right and pray for them if they don't."

★ ★ ★

Occasional disputes aside, the six American ambassadors who served before me facilitated and, in many instances, initiated a broad range of cooperation. The United States and the Holy See worked together on international peace solutions, as in 1999, when the Vatican brought together ambassadors from NATO countries to explore peace initiatives in Kosovo. We also worked together, through collaborations with the U.S. Agency for International Development (USAID) and Catholic Relief Services, to bring aid to places like Zambia and Haiti faced with the scourge of AIDS and other diseases like malaria. Since 25 percent of all AIDS care and treatment occurs within or by means of a Catholic-related healthcare institution, the United States, the greatest engine of charity in the world, and the Holy See, the world's preeminent humanitarian organization, are natural partners in fighting AIDS, malaria, and other pernicious diseases affecting the world's poor. Obviously this cooperation and opportunity for mutual goodwill took off under the administration of President George W. Bush, whose Emergency Plan for AIDS Relief (PEPFAR) programs brought unprecedented resources to these health problems in Africa.

Like AIDS and infectious diseases, human trafficking is a devastating international problem, though it often receives less attention than other crises. An estimated 27 million people are victims of trafficking worldwide. By far the highest rate of trafficking occurs in Asia and the Pacific region, but Africa has a growing problem. Lest Westerners dismiss this as a foreign scourge, the numbers tell a different story. At least 1.5 million trafficking victims live in virtual bondage in Europe and North America.

The United States and the Holy See share a deep commitment to ending human trafficking. This goal was championed by my immediate predecessor, Jim Nicholson, who took nascent programs and brought attention and increased resources to bear on exposing both generators and abusers of trafficked human beings. We leveraged Secretary Nicholson's work throughout 2005–2008 to expand the program, working closely with Sister Eugenia Bonetti of the Consolata Missionaries, widely recognized as one of the world's leaders in attacking this problem. With the help of Embassy Vatican and the State Department, Sister Eugenia has expanded her once-modest antitrafficking operation to include nuns working in twenty-seven countries and operating one hundred small shelters to give refuge and assistance to trafficking victims. Over the years, Sister Eugenia and her fellow nuns have rescued thousands.

When President and Mrs. Bush came to Rome in June 2007, one of the events we organized was a breakfast hosted by my wife, Kathleen, to give Mrs. Bush a chance to sit down with Sister Eugenia. The president stopped by to meet her as well. The gathering was small, personal, and successful. The State Department subsequently increased funding support for our program.

The work we did with the Holy See on trafficking was motivated by human compassion for the victims, but also by a broadly shared commitment to the concept of inalienable human rights. For the United States, the country which first explicitly encoded such rights as laws, joining the Holy See to assiduously and constantly curb violations of basic liberties around the world, wherever and in whatever form they arise, makes for a natural and potent alliance. The ultimate beneficiaries of Holy See–U.S. cooperation are those fundamental freedoms which, once lost, are not easily regained. And just as the American ideal has inspired the quest for human rights all around the world—including, in years past, within the Vatican itself—the Holy See now urges increasingly secular America to cherish these ideals and make sure we do not lose sight of them, especially when it comes to religious freedom. It reminds us, as F. A. Hayek writes in his classic, *The Road to Serfdom*, that "if the democracies themselves abandon the supreme ideal of the freedom and happiness of the individual, if they implicitly admit that their civilization is not worth preserving . . . they have indeed nothing to offer." Benjamin Franklin, with his inimitable gift for making complex ideas simple, put it another way: "those who would give up essential liberty, to purchase a little temporary safety, deserve neither liberty nor safety."

III.

The issue of religious freedom happened to come into sharp focus just a month after my arrival in Rome. In November 2005, President Bush visited China and met with President Hu Jintao. Though our Vatican embassy was only tangentially involved, the president's China visit brought into focus some of the problems that the Catholic Church, among other religions, still face in large parts of the world in the early twenty-first century.

During his trip, the third of his presidency to China, President Bush discussed a broad range of issues with the Chinese government. Among these was China's record on human rights. One basic right that President Bush addressed pointedly was the right of free worship, a matter of great personal conviction to the president. "My hope is the government of China will not fear Christians who gather to worship openly," he told reporters on Sunday, November 20, after attending a government-sanctioned Protestant service in Beijing. "A healthy society is a society that welcomes all faiths." He specifically recommended that China invite Vatican representatives to discuss Catholicism in China.

To complement and reinforce the president's message, we released a statement from the embassy on November 21:

> China has a great opportunity, following the President's visit, to become more open to the Holy See, and to work toward greater freedom for its Catholic citizens, and indeed for those of all faiths. The relationship between the Holy See and the United States is strong, and we will continue to work together to promote political and religious freedom in the world.

I noted that, in line with the president's priorities, I intended to make religious freedom in China an important focus as ambassador.

On November 22, an article in the Italian daily *La Stampa* quoted an anonymous Vatican insider disparaging American efforts to achieve religious freedom in China. "If we go to Beijing, it will certainly not be on the back of the U.S.," said the official. The comment reflected the characteristic reluctance of any sovereign to appear influenced by another. But it also raised a concern, held by some in the Vatican, that the United States, by pressing the issue of religious rights, might inadvertently upset the delicate relations between the Holy See and China, inciting Beijing to clamp down further on religious freedom. No Chinese leader would risk appearing to submit to the demands of an American president. A provoked Beijing might even make a special effort to prove its intransigence, and the Holy See would be among its targets. The Chinese government had already taken measures against the Vatican in September, when Beijing refused permission for four Chinese Catholic bishops to attend a synod in Rome. As if to demonstrate its resolve, the regime had also arrested a priest and several seminarians in the weeks before Bush's visit.

The history of the Catholic Church in China reaches back to the arrival of the Jesuit missionary Matteo Ricci in Macau in the late sixteenth century. Nearly four centuries later, in 1951, the Chinese communist government ordered Catholics to cut themselves off from Rome. Henceforth, all Catholics were to practice under the jurisdiction of a government agency, which assumed all ecclesiastic authority, including the appointment of Bishops. The government essentially claimed—as it does to this day—the right of investiture. Needless to say, this was unacceptable to the pope, just as it had been unacceptable to popes throughout the centuries. In 1958, Pius XII excommunicated all Chinese bishops not approved by Rome. Chinese Catholics then broke into two camps: those who defied the government and continued to practice in accord with the Vatican, often meeting for mass in private homes and risking severe punishment; and those who worshiped in state-approved churches under the government-sanctioned Chinese Patriotic Catholic Association. This bifurcation still exists today.

The positions of both the Chinese government and the Vatican are forcefully stated and seemingly intractable. China is determined to control the church inside its borders, while the Vatican is determined to maintain final authority on all church matters—everywhere. Particularly when questions of authority are at stake, Beijing and Rome are in conflict. A significant example of this came along shortly into my ambassadorship, in March 2006, when the Holy See elevated Joseph Zen Ze-kiun, archbishop of Hong Kong, to cardinal. China angrily retaliated by naming a Catholic bishop, Ma Yinglin, without Vatican consent.

If the relationship between these two ancient powers sometimes seems hopeless, China and the Holy See have actually found ways to accommodate each other over the years. The Vatican has explicitly disavowed government-appointed bishops but has tacitly accepted most of them. The Chinese have explicitly outlawed the underground church, but usually turn a blind eye to its members, so long as they worship discreetly, much as early American colonies like Maryland turned a blind eye to their "Romanists" and "papists" so long as the offenders kept their religion to themselves. The Chinese have made halting moves toward compromise with the Vatican— or rather they *were* making such moves until a couple of years ago, when they abruptly began to backslide.

Why this reversal occurred is not clear, but it is part of a recent push in China to restrict freedom in all of the nation's recognized religions. In addition to Catholicism, these include Protestantism, Islamism, Buddhism, and Taoism. One recent snapshot of the religious situation in China, the

U.S. State Department's 2012 Annual Report on International Religious Freedom, noted "a marked deterioration during 2011 in the government's respect for and protection of religious rights." China has ordained at least four bishops in defiance of the Vatican since 2010, all of whom were automatically excommunicated by the Vatican. None of China's bishops are permitted to freely communicate with Rome. Those who resist government control can expect to join a number of Catholic bishops already in jail or otherwise detained.

One such recent detainee is the Reverend Thaddeus Ma Daqin. In the summer of 2012, Rev. Ma celebrated his consecration as auxiliary bishop of Shanghai by immediately announcing his break from the Chinese Patriotic Catholic Association. He was immediately taken away by authorities and placed under house arrest in a seminary, where he apparently remains today.

There will doubtless be more such incidents ahead as Vatican-China relations develop. As the political scientists Ronald Inglehart and Christian Welzel have noted in their scholarship on modernization and democracy, a China that intends to join the modern world as a "knowledge society" is a nation that will have to embrace a more open society sooner or later. Knowledge societies cannot function effectively without highly educated publics that have become increasingly accustomed to thinking for themselves. Furthermore, rising levels of economic security bring a growing emphasis on a syndrome of self-expression values—one that gives high priority to free choice and motivates political action. After a certain point, accordingly, it becomes difficult to avoid democratization, because repressing mass demands for more open societies becomes increasingly costly and detrimental to economic effectiveness.

Currently an estimated 12 million Catholics live in China. Though a tiny fraction of the country's 1.3 billion population, it is a large number nonetheless, and likely to get larger. The Vatican wants to be there when the time comes for more religious freedom in China. Pope Benedict has expressed a desire to tighten ties to the Chinese Catholic community, both underground and government-sanctioned.

The Chinese government has its own reasons for eventually making peace with the Catholic Church. As the Beijing-based Italian journalist and Sino-Vatican expert Francesco Sisci has observed, a spiritual vacuum opened in China after the flaws of Mao and his version of communism were officially acknowledged. Into this vacuum flooded numerous faiths and cults, some of which, like Falun Gong, are now deemed threats by the Chinese government. Beijing may have originally miscalculated the destabilizing potential of these new religions, neglecting their spread as it sought control of older, more traditional religions, including Catholicism. The Chinese eventually came to realize, apparently, that Catholicism has the virtue of being an established and stable faith, as well as western and modern, without being driven by an explicitly political agenda. Eventually, the Chinese government is likely to appreciate the positive dynamic that Archbishop Migliore identified to me as the source of the church's soft power—Catholicism is a great social binding force—and see the value in promoting it.

The government of China also knows, however, that Catholicism can challenge state authority. In a country where late term abortions are sometimes urged upon women to keep the birth rate down, and in which thousands of men are executed every year and their organs harvested for medical use—to name just two human rights abuses—China has reason to fear, as well as embrace, the Catholic Church.

How the relationship will evolve remains unclear, but it's likely to be interesting. As noted earlier in this book, the Holy See and China diplomacy share a long-term, farsighted perspective. In his recent book, *On China*, Dr. Henry Kissinger quotes Deng Xiaopeng's twenty-four character message to the Chinese people as he neared retirement in 1997: "Observe carefully; secure our position; cope with affairs calmly; hide our capacities and bide our time; be good at maintaining a low profile; and never claim leadership." Deng's wisdom, described by Kissinger as invoking China's "ancient virtues" and instructing his people "not to evoke unnecessary fears by excessive assertiveness," has resonance in any consideration of the evolving future of the church in China and its potential diplomatic challenges.

If the Vatican opens diplomatic relations with China, it will insist that the underground church fold into the official church, a move many underground Catholics will resist. Meanwhile, Taiwan, long a Catholic stronghold in Asia, will probably see its relationship with the Vatican suffer. Indeed, the Vatican has hinted that it would be willing to end diplomatic relations with Taiwan if doing so would help it reach an agreement with China. This issue was raised during my confirmation hearing, when a senator asked whether there was any truth in the rumor that the Vatican was considering moving its nunciature from Taiwan to the mainland. I responded that any potential change in the Holy See's diplomatic representation in China could involve an expansion, or return, to the mainland but would not be an abandonment of Taiwan. Some vocal Taiwan Catholic groups were not convinced by my words and wrote me stinging letters to tell me so. Their anger was a good reminder of the delicacy of the situation.

The Holy See will have a diplomatic challenge on several fronts if or when a more formal diplomatic arrangement is undertaken with China.

For the immediate future, it appears that relations will stay more or less as they are. This was confirmed when I met Archbishop Claudio Celli not long after President Bush's visit to China. Archbishop Celli was undersecretary for relations with states (it was to him that Ambassador Melady handed President G. H. W. Bush's letter prior to the first Iraq war), and had since become the secretary of the Administration of the Patrimony of the Apostolic See, the agency that oversees Vatican properties. A leading expert on China within the Vatican, Celli had recently gone to China for backchannel negotiations with the government. The Chinese officials he met showed little willingness to concede church control to the Vatican. In fact, negotiations went so poorly that at one point Celli threatened to pack his bags and leave. He stayed, but little progress was made.

"China is like a birdcage," Archbishop Celli told me, describing the church's freedom of action in China. "The bird can fly, but not far. Sometimes the cage expands, and sometimes it narrows. But the cage is still a cage."

## IV.

The month after President Bush's visit to China—December 2005—brought not only our first Christmas in Rome, but the fortieth anniversary of *Dignitatis Humanae*, the Vatican II declaration on religious freedom that was promulgated on December 7, 1965. We recognized the anniversary by organizing a panel discussion and reception to highlight the First Amendment, the role of the American church in promoting interfaith dialogue and acceptance of other faiths, and, of course, the teachings of *Dignitatis Humanae*. Speakers included Cardinal Theodore McCarrick, who addressed the topic of religious freedom, with reflections of his personal experiences in China, Bosnia, and throughout the world; Scott Appleby of the Kroc Peace Institute at the University of Notre Dame, who summarized the evolution of the United States' view of religious freedom; and Jim Towey, the director of President Bush's White House Office of Faith-Based and Community Initiatives, who examined the First Amendment's protection of religion.

They were all great talks, and this last one particularly sticks with me. Towey pointed out that the language of the religion clause of the First Amendment—"Congress shall make no law respecting an establishment of religion, or prohibiting the free exercise thereof"—contains two equally important ideas. The first, articulated in the establishment clause, is that Congress may not back, create, or favor any religion. This is the part that everybody seems to grasp—separation of church and State. Less well understood is what comes after the comma: the free exercise clause, which tells us that Congress cannot *discourage* any religion by "prohibiting the free exercise thereof." This is the phrase that some people, particularly those of a secular bent, often gloss over. The Founders were clearly stating that government cannot prevent religious practitioners from living in accord with their faith. In stressing this second part in his talk for our panel, Towey anticipated actions that would be taken by the Obama administration, five years later, to force Catholic and other religious institutions in the United States to pay for forms of healthcare, such as birth control and pregnancy termination, that contradict fundamental Catholic beliefs—not to mention the explicit intent of the Bill of Rights.

★ ★ ★

Another important incident I recall well from that December was a meeting with Archbishop Leonardo Sandri, at the time the *Sostituto*—essentially the number three man in the Vatican—who was very knowledgeable about Latin American affairs. A native Argentinian, he had served as nuncio to Venezuela between 1997 and 2000, during the rise of Hugo Chavez. Chavez went on to distinguish himself as the most difficult leader in Latin America since Fidel Castro, spouting anti-American rhetoric, ignoring international agreements on narcotics trafficking, and using Venezuelan oil profits to fund dissension throughout the region.

Archbishop Sandri told me that he believed Chavez could be "dangerous," but he thought it unlikely that the church would speak too loudly against him. "The Holy See continues to feel that a non-confrontational approach to Chavez is the right strategy for the time being," we later explained in a cable to the State Department, "but the Vatican hierarchy is under no illusions about the danger of Chavez and kindred souls." Hugo Chavez was a problem we would come back to many times over the next months and years. Even today, following his death in March 2013, Chavez casts a long shadow over Latin America.

# 13

# MEETINGS OF MINDS

The imponderabilia often have more influence in politics than gold or military force.

—Otto von Bismarck

## I.

"So," said the pope, "we are going to see Mrs. Bush, right?"

It was my first Monday back in Rome after the holidays, the morning of the pope's annual New Year's address to the diplomatic corps and spouses, and we were gathered in the Sala Regia, the ornate marble and fresco-walled hall adjacent to the Sistine Chapel. The pope had started his address to the diplomats with a general call for peace, then devoted much of what followed to human rights, especially to freedom of religion. He was most forceful about terrorism. "No situation can justify such criminal activity," said the pope, "which covers the perpetrators with infamy, and it is all the more deplorable when it hides behind religion"

After the pope's address, we took our turns in a receiving line. This was a formal and highly ceremonial occasion, but any encounter with the pope is meaningful, and in this case the pope had news to convey—*good* news. He would grant the First Lady an audience when she came to Rome the following month.

"If you say so, Your Holiness," I replied to the pope. "We're sure looking forward to it."

I had only learned about the First Lady's visit a few days prior to the pope's address. While visiting Washington for the annual Chiefs of Mission

Conference at the State Department, I'd been contacted at my hotel by the First Lady's chief of staff, Anita McBride. She told me that Mrs. Bush very much wanted to see the pope while in Europe for the Winter Olympics in Torino in February and that it was an important priority of the White House, so please try to make this happen.

My first call to the Vatican about the First Lady's visit was not promising. I was informed that Benedict had only given formal audiences to heads of state, newly accrediting ambassadors, and recognized groups that had business with the Holy See—no First Ladies or other head-of-state spouses. Landing back in Rome on the morning of Saturday, January 7, I went to the residence, changed clothes, and headed directly to the Vatican to meet Angelo Sodano, the cardinal secretary of state, to see what arrangements could be made. Cardinal Sodano was cordial but noncommittal. The Vatican was reluctant to break precedent, he explained, even for Mrs. Bush. He suggested that one possible solution might be an unofficial "personal" visit. This sounded fine, but it wasn't until I was shaking the pope's hand on Monday that I had positive confirmation.

A meeting between a First Lady of the United States and a pope is of real consequence however it might be organized. It is the kind of personal interaction that creates goodwill, forges long-term relationships, and establishes the platform for successful diplomacy. In retrospect, Mrs. Bush's visit laid out the themes for a dramatic year ahead which would feature some of the most important incidents of the Benedict XVI's papacy.

A few days before Mrs. Bush landed in Rome that February, tensions between Christians and Muslims flared in Europe. The precipitating event was the republication, in several European newspapers, of cartoons that had originally appeared in a Danish newspaper. These were the same cartoons of Mohammed that had sparked violent protests when they were first published in September 2005. Their republication was meant to be an assertion of the right of free press against Islamic fundamentalism. To many Muslims, though, it looked like a blasphemous provocation. The result was that Mrs. Bush arrived in Europe at a time of great unrest around the world. On February 4, Muslim protestors surrounded and set fire to the Danish embassy in Damascus. The following day, protestors burned the Danish embassy in Beirut, as a sixty-one-year-old Italian missionary, Fr. Andrea Santoro, was killed in a church in Turkey. Now, on February 9—at the very moment I was accompanying Mrs. Bush through the Arch of Bells into Vatican City—hundreds of thousands of Shia Muslims were demonstrating on the streets in Lebanon.

Despite the fact that Mrs. Bush's visit had been officially designated as "personal," the First Lady was accorded all the process and ceremony of an official papal audience, from the red-carpet greeting in the Cortile San Damaso to the formal escort up the long stairs, through the Apostolic Palace to the pope's inner sanctum.

I accompanied Mrs. Bush and her daughter Barbara into the papal library. The press snapped a few pictures as we took our seats with the pope, then the doors shut. Mrs. Bush and the pope spoke warmly of shared interests in a number of humanitarian programs, including AIDS treatment and PEPFAR, and the battle to end poverty and hunger. I mentioned that Barbara had recently returned from Africa, where she worked in an AIDS clinic. This interested the pope greatly.

We then discussed the subject of the radicalizing madrasas in sub-Saharan Africa, an area that traditionally practiced a moderate form of Islam. These Saudi-backed religious schools, often located in impoverished communities in the Near East and Africa, tend to promote a version of Islam that is intolerant and extreme. The pope contrasted the madrasas' fundamentalist approach to God with American ideals of faith, in which church and state were (ideally) separated but mutually respected, and expressed his concern about what the madrasas might mean for the future.

The pope's concerns were prescient. With a continued evolution and broadening of violent expressions of Islam, incidents have occurred as recently as July 2012 in Mali, Niger, and Somalia. In Nigeria, meanwhile, the radical Islamic group Boko Haram continued to bomb churches and government buildings through the fall of 2012. The Horn of Africa is now considered by terrorism experts to be, as the *Wall Street Journal* described the area in January 2012, "the next battleground in the fight against al Qaeda and its affiliates."

Altogether, the meeting between the pope and Mrs. Bush was a productive and substantive exchange. In a half hour or so we were back in the Cortile San Damaso, stepping into the limousine to take Mrs. Bush to her next appointment. "The American people are a religious people, of course all different religions," the First Lady said in an interview with Vatican radio later that day. "But we share a lot of the same values with the Catholic Church."

## II.

As I mentioned earlier in these pages, I was fortunate to serve as ambassador at a time when the values of the U.S. government and the Holy See were particularly congruent. President Bush's views on the sanctity of life and the importance of faith in civic society, for example, found a very receptive audience inside the Vatican. The war in Iraq struck some chords of disharmony, but on the whole the Holy See sympathized with and shared our apprehensions—and our determination—regarding terrorism. Five years out from 9/11, we were all still consumed by threats rising from the Middle East, and not a day passed without these weighing heavily in all formal and informal conversations with the Holy See and other diplomatic representatives.

But if terrorism deeply concerned the Holy See, it was just one among a many subjects that demanded the pope's attention. The church is everywhere, and popes, like presidents, must handle a wide range of issues simultaneously.

One area that demanded significant attention during Benedict's early papacy and my years as ambassador was Latin America, where the Catholic Church holds a strong position and where the United States hoped to pursue common interests. The region was a special focus for us, and we had numerous interactions with the Vatican about it during my tenure.

The Catholic Church has been through several permutations in Latin America since European colonization in the fifteenth century brought waves of Catholic missionaries. By the nineteenth century, most of South America, and north through Mexico, were overwhelmingly Catholic. Many of the countries signed concordats with the Holy See, giving the church preferred legal status and endowing some of its teachings with the weight of law.

The early decades of the twentieth century often found the church in alignment with right-wing regimes, but in the mid-1960s, after Vatican II, this changed in some areas as the movement of "liberation theology" spread through local clergy. Followers of liberation theology wanted to help the poor, alleviate human suffering, push for justice, and stand up to despots, but in doing so they drew the church into domestic politics. This is what happened in Nicaragua, where Pope John Paul II reproved Fr. Ernesto Cardenal for serving as a minister in the cabinet of the Sandinista leader, Daniel Ortega. The pastoral mission of the church can become diffused and depreciated when the church becomes too closely aligned with any secular government. The fact that some regimes supported by these priests were themselves guilty of human rights abuses complicated matters greatly.

In 2006, the United States and the Holy See were in broad agreement that several regimes in power in Latin America were inhospitable to freedom and human rights. Venezuela was the most obvious instance of this, but Bolivia, Ecuador and Nicaragua, along with a few Caribbean countries, had joined Venezuela in a new organization called the Bolivarian Alliance for the Peoples of Our America, or ALBA. One leading United States think tank describes ALBA as "the fulcrum for anti-Americanism in the Americas." The organization's founding principle is to counter the Free Trade Area of the Americas, a program advanced by the United States. ALBA has been persistently hostile to U.S. interests and ideals. Meanwhile, close relations between Caracas and Tehran have given the nuclear-ambitious Iranian government access and influence as a trading partner with ALBA nations in Latin America. Hugo Chavez made it clear that he hoped to use his friendship with Iran to undermine U.S. global influence. There were even alarming press reports, not officially confirmed, that Chavez had offered arms and Venezuelan missile sites to Iran.

Whatever the truth of these reports about Iran, ALBA was apparently on the move in 2006. Daniel Ortega returned to power in Nicaragua that year, and Raphael Correa was elected in Ecuador, giving impetus to ALBA and adding to the number of countries in Latin America with no sitting U.S. ambassador. Nestor Kirchner of Argentina acted more moderately than some others, but he was dependent on Venezuela for liquidity, amply supplied by the Chavez government's purchase of Argentine debt. The wave of democratization that passed across Latin America in the 1980s, replacing a series of military dictatorships, had originally appeared as progress, but now it seemed to be moving backward. The anti-U.S., socialist-leaning movements in the region mastered the democratic process to achieve their own antidemocratic objectives.

Many Catholics in Latin America, as in Europe and the United States, had either lapsed in their practice of the faith or turned to new evangelical Protestant sects. The percentage of Latin Americans who labeled themselves Catholic fell from 80 percent in 1995 to 71 percent in 2005, while the number of self-identified Protestants rose from 3 percent to 13 percent. Nonetheless, the church remained powerful and influential. More than 300 million Latin Americans still identified themselves as Catholic. A more remarkable number, reported in a 2005 poll, was that 73 percent of Latin Americans expressed confidence in the church. The church, in other words, remained a trusted beacon in the risky world of Latin American politics, where corruption and economic collapse were common and civil institutions were fragile.

While in Washington at the Chiefs of Mission Conference in January, I had met with Latin American experts in the State Department to discuss engaging the Holy See as a more forceful partner in promoting freedom, human rights, and democracy in Latin America. Now, a month later, in early February—just a few days before Mrs. Bush's visit—Ambassador Tom Shannon, then serving as assistant secretary of state for Western Hemisphere Affairs (he is currently the U.S. ambassador to Brazil), came to Rome to discuss Latin American affairs. We went to the Vatican and met with Archbishop Sandri and Archbishop Giovanni Lajolo, the respective heads of first and second sections. Also in attendance were about half a dozen monsignors from the Secretariat of State. The presence of these monsignors reflected the serious interest the Holy See took in Shannon's visit and the issues presented by Latin America today. Here was an excellent opportunity for a high-ranking U.S. official to express our hope that the church might leverage its moral authority in Latin America to oppose Chavez's human rights violations.

We reinforced this message a few weeks after Tom Shannon's visit, on February 21, when Kathleen and I hosted a bon voyage dinner at Villa Richardson for Archbishop Pietro Sambi. Archbishop Sambi (not to be confused with Archbishop Sandri, the *Sostituto*) was about to move to Washington to become the new papal nuncio to the United States. Our guest list was composed of high-ranking members of the Curia and some other Holy See ambassadors. Dinners like these were excellent venues for relationship development. At the very least, a roomful of experienced Curial officials yields a high-level of conversation, intellectual stimulation, and valuable insights.

In part because of the guest list, the conversation veered toward Latin America and presented another chance to express our hope that the Vatican would take a firmer diplomatic stand in the region. Archbishop Sambi's previous post had been Israel, but he knew Latin America well, having launched his diplomatic career in the nunciatures in Cuba and Nicaragua. Before we sat down to dinner, I suggested to Archbishop Sambi that the church's position on Chavez would probably be the first thing President Bush asked him about when they met for his credentialing in Washington. Sure enough, a few days later, it was.

The nuncio appreciated well the danger of Chavez, but he and others at the dinner echoed the cautious tone with which Archbishop Sandri had spoken earlier of the Venezuelan leader. They doubted the church could, or would, become too involved in trying to temper him. As my now WikiLeaked cable later states, "we see no likelihood of a change in the Holy See's official (and cautious) position with regard to Venezuela." The Holy See is constitutionally averse to political confrontation when it can avoid it, on the grounds that it can backfire and make matters worse rather than better. A church that was constantly throwing itself into domestic partisan politics would lose some of the very moral authority that gives it power in the first place.

Nonetheless, my job was to push, if just a little, and that is what I tried to do.

## III.

Usually we spoke with the Vatican about our mutual interests and hopes for Latin America in general terms, but occasionally we went to them with a specific issue. In the case of Nicaragua, for example, we raised our concerns about Cardinal Miguel Obando y Bravo, the longtime archbishop of Managua. This once stalwart anti-Sandinista of the 1980s began behaving strangely after his retirement in March 2005. By the fall of 2006, he was publicly declaring his support for Daniel Ortega, the one-time Marxist guerrilla and former leader of the Sandinistas who was now campaigning again for the presidency of Nicaragua. In a blatant effort to win votes in a country where 60 percent of the population identified as Catholic, Ortega was aligning himself with the eighty-year-old cardinal, and Obando y Bravo, incredibly, was obliging, going so far as to appear in campaign advertisments with Ortega. Various rumors were circulating to supply a reason for the cardinal's conversion, but regardless of the explanation, it threatened to help Ortega achieve victory. We hoped the Vatican could convince Obando y Bravo to return to his senses.

One interesting twist in this episode: Fr. Ernesto Cardenal, the priest and former minister of culture at whom John Paul II had wagged his finger more than twenty years earlier, now spoke out against Ortega for making "a false and hypocritical use of religion" to perpetrate "one more of his charades." As Cardinal Obando y Bravo let himself get dragged in to the Sandinista mantra, Fr. Cardenal extricated himself from it.

The church's control over a retired cardinal is limited. The Holy See was reluctant to publicly reprimand Obando y Bravo, but it did ask him to step out of Ortega's campaign. Church officials also asked him to fly to Rome for a sit-down discussion about his role in Nicaraguan politics. The cardinal declined.

★ ★ ★

As we looked to the Holy See for support on certain issues, the church sometimes sought support from us. One notable example of this came in the spring of 2006, when I met with Cardinal Juan Sandoval Iniguez, the archbishop of Guadalajara. Although the meeting was not particularly noteworthy in itself, it received undue press attention in Mexico some years later due to WikiLeaks.

Cardinal Sandoval was in Rome that spring to attend a meeting of the Sacred College of Cardinals, in this case of cardinals from Latin America. These gatherings were occasions for noncurial cardinals to come to Rome and meet each other and the pope. On March 28, I met with Cardinal Sandoval in a conference room inside the Vatican. The cardinal told us that he was concerned about the "dangerous trend"—as our cable later paraphrased his comments—of leftist leaders in Latin America. Quite correctly, perhaps, the cardinal said that "the poor in Latin America do not understand the potential benefits that a free market could bring." At that time, the former mayor of Mexico City, Andreas Manuel Lopez Obrador, was running for the presidency of Mexico as the Party of the Democratic Revolution (PRD) candidate and had a good chance to win. His record as mayor of Mexico City was poor, according to the cardinal, marred by rising crime and violence. Cardinal Sandoval "asked whether President Bush could help," as our cable phrased it.

Six years later, when this cable was made public in the WikiLeaks disclosures, the press, unsurprisingly, gave it a sensational spin: "Ex-Juárez bishop worked to sway Mexican election," ran one typical headline. The leak brought a great deal of unwanted attention to the cardinal, which only distracted from his legitimate concerns regarding a victory by the PRD candidate. The cardinal had hardly been alone in expressing his concerns. Other sources in Mexico contacted the U.S. embassy in Mexico City to deliver the same message and solicit American assistance. The cardinal just had the misfortune to suffer from the WikiLeaks security breach.

IV.

Holy See–U.S. diplomacy is generally more nuanced and less tactical than the above episodes might suggest. Dialogue with the Holy See affords the United States an avenue for the moderate and careful exchange of information and opinion without, necessarily, an accompanying expectation of a specific result or time. This distinguishes diplomacy with the Holy See from what goes on at other bilateral missions.

Meetings with officials in the Curia or secretary of state's office often involved a wide variety of subjects or issues, whether broad policy or political trends or specific current events. Lost in the media's fixation on power plays inside the Vatican is the fact that leadership positions in the church are generally filled by extremely well-educated and cosmopolitan men who speak several languages and are very well informed on world events. Unlike most bilateral missions, which cover country-specific issues pertaining to U.S. interests, the Holy See mission routinely deals with core issues like religious freedom, human rights, transparency of leaders, and corruption, as these arise in all parts of the world. To grasp the breadth of the Holy See's realm of interest, consider that when President Bush met with the Vatican Secretary of State, Cardinal Tarcisio Bertone, in June 2007, they conferred about ongoing issues in more than fifteen countries around the world.

Typical of the professionalism, experience, and wide-ranging knowledge in the Vatican's Secretariat of State is Archbishop Pietro Parolin, currently papal nuncio to Venezuela, and effective October 15, 2013, the Secretary of State of the Holy See. When I served in Rome, Parolin was the undersecretary for relations between states, which made him second-in-command of the second section and our principal interlocutor. Fluent in four languages and conversant on every region of the globe, he would articulate the Holy See's positions clearly and candidly but always with consummate professionalism.

I went to see Monsignor Parolin at the Apostolic Palace one morning in mid-March to ask the Vatican to support the U.S.-backed candidates in the upcoming elections at the United Nations. As so often happened in such meetings, though, the conversation turned to other matters and regions, including China, Lebanon (which would be at war by the end of the summer), India, and Iran. A week earlier, the United States had signed a significant agreement on nuclear weapons with India, essentially recognizing India's status as a nuclear partner—despite the fact that it had never signed the Non-Proliferation Treaty (NPT) of 1968—and thus allowing the United States to sell nuclear materials to India. The Bush administration viewed the new rules and restrictions of the agreement as a means of drawing India more closely in line with the NPT. The Vatican took a less favorable view. As I later reported to the State Department, Monsignor Parolin believed the agreement sent the "wrong signal" at a time when we were trying to get Iran to halt its nuclear program, and that reacting aggressively to Iran's ambitions while nurturing India's would only alienate Iran and foreclose the possibility for further dialogue.

What the monsignor did not say in this meeting was that the Vatican was itself poised to facilitate a dialogue between the Western powers and Iran. As we had put it in an embassy cable to the State Department a few weeks earlier, the Holy See's relationship to Iran was "an East-West and Christian-Muslim link that could present an opportunity for dialogue and leverage." The Holy See and Iran enjoyed a long and mostly amicable history.

They had recently celebrated the fiftieth anniversary of diplomatic relations. People in the Vatican could still remember a more tolerant Iran. Prior to the Islamic Revolution, the country had been known for its inclusive perspective on religion, with Jews and Christians serving alongside Muslims in the Majlis. There are even today some vestiges of Zoroastrianism in the country, some fourteen hundred years after Islam superseded it in ancient Persia.

★ ★ ★

A few weeks after that meeting with Msgr. Parolin, I had the opportunity to visit with Cardinal Jean-Louis Tauran, the man who had once held Msgr. Parolin's position as undersecretary for relations between States. A native of Bordeaux, France, Cardinal Tauran had gone on to become the number one of the second section—secretary for relations between states. He is one of the most respected, admired, and important diplomatic figures in the Vatican. He was Librarian of the Holy Roman Church when I first met him. In 2007, my last full year in Rome, Pope Benedict named him as President of Pontifical Council for Interreligious Dialogue, the main body of the Catholic Church that interacts with other religions.

Even before taking on the Holy See's program for interreligious dialogue, Cardinal Tauran was a leading Vatican expert on Islam. He brought calm, intelligence, and broad experience to the subject, demonstrating a neighborly friendliness to the religion of Mohammed but firmly opposed to fundamentalists who favored violence over dialogue. Cardinal Tauran's view was not that all religions were created equal, but that all religions "which are seeking God must be respected because they have the same dignity." In other words, we don't have to agree about who or what we worship, but we have to agree to disagree civilly.

Cardinal Tauran had been one of the Vatican's harshest critics of the war in Iraq, condemning it as a "crime against peace," among other epithets. Though the fate of Iraq was the subject that still preoccupied him, he bore no ill will toward the United States. To convey the nature of pre-Saddam Iraq, and give a sense of perspective, he told me that there had once been a robust middle class whose constituents were well educated and earned a per capita income of around 3,000 euros, equal or greater to Spain at the time. In pre-Saddam Iraq, it was said that "Books are written in Egypt, printed in Lebanon, and read in Iraq," the cardinal told me in English as we sat in his office in the Vatican. Iraqis were historically a highly literate population, at least until Saddam came in and destroyed the educated middle class. Now Cardinal Tauran, like the Patriarch Delly and Ambassador Yelda, worried that the war would destroy the Christian minority. Once the Americans left, the Kurds would take care of themselves in the north, while the Shiites and Sunnis would fight for the spoils to the south. As for the Christians, they would be shut out of power completely, their rights vaporized.

The central problem of Islam, in Cardinal Tauran's view, was its failure to acknowledge the right of non-Muslims to exist. What sense was there in dialogue if the other side believed it had nothing to learn from you—that you were an infidel? I could hear in Cardinal Tauran's words a marked change in the Vatican's line on Islam. We had picked up on this in conversations with the Curia in recent months, especially following the outburst surrounding the republication of the Mohammed cartoons in February, and we suspected that it was a coordinated message. On April 20, we sent a cable to the State Department entitled "Vatican Hardening Line on Islam."

Among his other concerns about Islam, Cardinal Tauran, like others in the Holy See, lamented the lack of "reciprocity," a precondition for real dialogue and understanding. Why should it be that Western countries and cities—including Rome—welcome mosques and institutions of all faiths, while Christian churches are prohibited or severely limited in many Muslim nations? In the Vatican's own backyard, the Saudis had contributed tens of millions of dollars to build in Rome the largest mosque in Western Europe. As we informed the State Department, "the Vatican is demanding greater protection for Christians and greater freedom for religious expression." This description of the new Vatican tone turned out to be an accurate indication of where Pope Benedict XVI was headed.

★ ★ ★

One final conversation stands out from that time. In early June 2006, I was invited to a small luncheon hosted by Francis Campbell, the British ambassador to the Holy See. Also attending were British Prime Minister Tony Blair and several church leaders.

When the conversation turned to the subject of Iraq, the prime minister asked me a question that had clearly been troubling him: "Why is it that Muslims in United States are so much less confrontational than Muslims in Europe?" My response echoed the words Pope Benedict XVI had said to me the day of my credentialing: the United States has the First Amendment, which has bred religious pluralism and blessed us with a unique and extraordinary tradition of assimilating peoples and cultures.

# 14

# REGENSBURG

The clash of civilizations will dominate global politics. The fault lines between civilizations will be the battle lines of the future.

—Samuel P. Huntington (1993)

The world needs God. We need God. But what God do we need?

—Benedict XVI (2006)

## I.

Summers usually pass quietly around the Vatican. Tourists fill St. Peter's Square and the Sistine Chapel, but the papal household vacates the Apostolic Palace for the cooler climate of Castel Gandolfo, the palace in the Alban Hills south of Rome where popes have summered since the seventeenth century.

Summer 2006, however, was not without disruptions and diplomatic challenges for the Holy See. In mid-July, a war broke out in Lebanon after Hezbollah staged an ambush on Israeli troops in Northern Israel. Israel retaliated with forceful attacks on Hezbollah targets in southern Lebanon, first airstrikes and rockets, then ground troops. Hezbollah responded by sending a barrage of rockets into Israel, killing dozens of civilians. The Israel-Hezbollah conflict caused great concern in the Vatican. The church condemned Hezbollah's attack but also blamed Israel for its reprisal, which it considered disproportionate and dangerous to civilians. By the tenets of Catholic *Bellum iustum*, or just war theory, self-defense is permitted, but it must not exceed the injury against which it is meant to defend. Cardinal Sodano, the Vatican secretary of state, explained the Holy See's position on July 14:

> As in the past, the Holy See also condemns both the terrorist attacks on the one side and the military reprisals on the other. Indeed, a state's right to self-defense does not exempt it from respecting the norms of international law, especially as regards the protection of civilian populations.

Central to the church's worries was the fact that Lebanon had a large Christian community—nearly 40 percent of the population, most of whom were Maronite Catholics. Despite its long history of violence, Lebanon provided a rare example of religious freedom and cooperation in the Middle East. Muslims and Christians have lived together in relative harmony and shared power in a coalition government for years. The church worried that war would disrupt this status quo, and urged the United States, through our embassy, to push Israel to agree to a ceasefire at the earliest date.

For our part, we pressed the Vatican to encourage Patriarch Nassrallah Pierre Sfeir, head of the Maronite Catholic Church in Lebanon, to unite with his fellow Christians in defiance of Hezbollah. Lebanese Christians, including the Catholics, tended to exhibit their patriotism by supporting Hezbollah against Israel, but we had no doubt that Hezbollah was a dangerous element in Lebanon, and would become more dangerous if Christians yielded to it.

Pope Benedict addressed the Lebanon conflict at his weekly public prayer, the *Angelus* on July 30, calling for both sides to immediately lay down arms, and for the world to assist in achieving this as soon as possible. "In God's Name, I appeal to all those responsible for this spiral of violence on all sides to lay down their weapons immediately! I ask Government Leaders and International Institutions to spare no efforts to obtain this necessary cessation of hostilities and thus, through dialogue, be able to begin building the lasting and stable coexistence of all the Middle Eastern peoples."

★ ★ ★

In addition to his weekly Angelus, delivered from a balcony over the public square in front of Castel Gandolfo, the pope thought and wrote a good deal that summer. He was composing a new book—a life of Jesus—and preparing for a September journey to Germany. Benedict had been in the papacy for shortly over a year and it was still too early to tell what legacy he intended to leave. His first major work as pope, an encyclical issued at the start of the year, addressed love and charity. The encyclical's title, taken from the First Epistle of St. John, was *Deus Caritas Est*: "God Is Love."

While *Deus Caritas Est* was consistent with church dogma, the pope framed Christian truth as something positive, to be embraced and celebrated rather than imposed. As with so many of his previous speeches and comments, the encyclical was issued in the context of the conflict between the Christian (and increasingly secular) West and the Muslim (and increasingly fundamentalist) East. Though he did not mention radical Islam, Pope Benedict was writing in a world where, as he put it, "the name of God is sometimes associated with vengeance or even a duty of hatred and violence."

The key word he brought to the discussion was "reason," which appears in the encyclical twenty times. Faith without reason leads to intolerance and violence. But reason without faith is no better, for faith is "a purifying force" on reason. "From God's standpoint, faith liberates reason from its blind spots and therefore helps it to be ever more fully itself. Faith enables reason to do its work more effectively and to see its proper object more clearly."

Another way to understand this might be that reason not directed by the moral compass of faith can become a force of inhumanity and injustice. From the moment Benedict XVI took office, this view evolved consistently in his speeches and writings. It found its clearest and most dramatic articulation in September 2006, when the pope returned home to Germany.

## II.

In much the same way that Pope John Paul II defined his papacy in a journey to Poland in 1979, Benedict committed one of the defining acts of his papacy during his homecoming. His own historic journey began on the afternoon of September 9, 2006, when Benedict flew to Munich to begin a six-day visit to the Bavaria region of Germany, where he had spent most of his childhood and youth.

On Sunday, September 10, the pope gave an open air mass to 250,000 people in Munich. The subject of his homily was—no surprise—the increasing secularism of the West, a trend well documented in Germany, where regular Catholic mass attendance had fallen below 15 percent. Despite the large and exuberant crowds that met the pope, Germany and much of Western society was becoming "deaf to God," admonished the pope, and there was a great price to pay for this. "When we bring people only knowledge, ability, technical competence and tools, we bring them too little," Benedict told the crowd, picking up on the theme of *Deus Caritas Est*. As a boy in Nazi Germany—where he had been forced to join the Hitler Youth at fourteen—he had witnessed firsthand what the absence of God can mean: "All too quickly the mechanisms of violence take over: the capacity to destroy and kill becomes dominant." While the "scientific and technical prowess of the West" was admirable, a "form of rationality which totally excludes God" is equally perilous.

Pope Benedict suggested another reason that Europe needed to recall its once-fervent faith: it might relate better to those who still had such a faith. "The tolerance which we urgently need includes the fear of God—respect for what others hold sacred," said Benedict. "But this sense of respect can be reborn in the Western World only if faith in God is reborn, if God becomes once more present to us and in us." He did not mention the Danish cartoons, but it was obvious he was addressing, with some sympathy, the outrage these stirred in many Muslims.

On September 11, 2006, as Americans paused to remember the fifth anniversary of the 9/11 attacks on the United States, Pope Benedict flew by helicopter from Munich to Altotting to pray at the base of the famous fourteenth-century statue of Black Madonna, where he had often prayed as a boy. After a quick stop in the tidy little riverside village of Marktl, where he was born and baptized in 1927, he flew to the town of Regensburg. This was the site of the university where he had taught as young man in the department of theology, and where he would now make the most important speech of his still-young papacy.

By the following evening, when Benedict took the podium at Regensburg University's main hall at 5:00 p.m., a draft of his speech had already circulated, but few people seem to have read it. Indeed, according to one press account, the pope's own cardinal secretary, Angelo Soldano, was unfamiliar with its contents. Certainly nobody raised any alarms.

*Faith, Reason and the University: Memories and Reflections* was a densely packed treatise on the relationship (by now a familiar topic to pope watchers) between faith and reason. Speaking in German, Benedict began the speech with a reminiscence of his days at Regensburg, noting the "lively exchange" of ideas in the university at the time, when people of different beliefs could rationally discuss and debate faith. The pope was evidently trying to summon the spirit in which his own comments were intended—as intellectual discourse. Within the hall itself, that is exactly how the lecture was received by the audience. No one winced or objected in any way. People listened intently, then applauded enthusiastically when it was over. The trouble began later, when the speech was disseminated to the world beyond Regensburg.

The parts that were to make the speech "one of the most widely read, widely quoted and controversial lectures since the Sermon on the Mount," as one German newspaper called it, came during Benedict's brief discussion of Islam near the beginning. Addressing reason's part in religion, Benedict quoted a conversation between the fourteenth-century Byzantine emperor, Manuel II Palaeologus, and an unnamed Persian interlocutor, regarding the differences between Christianity and Islam. "Show me just what Mohammed brought that was new, and there you will find things only evil and inhuman, such as his command to spread by the sword the faith he preached."

To be clear, these were not the pope's words, but rather the emperor's words spoken more than six centuries earlier. Expressive as his language may have been, the emperor was making an important point to the Persian. A faith spread by the sword was a faith contrary to reason, and therefore, according to the Christian conception, contrary to the very nature of God. In quoting Palaeologus, Benedict was not suggesting that all of Islam embraces unreason or violence. He clearly indicated that other passages in the Quran rule out violence, quoting a surah that reads "There is no compulsion in religion."

Lost in the subsequent uproar, along with various other subtleties, was the fact that Islam was not the main topic of Benedict's lecture. Regensburg was a double-edged critique of the imbalance of reason and faith in the modern world—too little faith in secularized West, too little reason in the fundamentalist East. Indeed, the pope was far more critical of the post–Christian Europe than he was of Islamic world. As he suggests in *Deus Caritas Est*, secularism and the overreliance on reason, at the expense of faith, was as dangerous as a faith that excluded reason. Picking up where his homily in Munich left off, he returned to the point that secularism, among its other harms, fueled the clash of civilizations that scholars like Samuel P. Huntington and others had long feared. Avowed secularists could not possibly hope to reach an understanding with devout believers.

In the Western world it is widely held that only positivistic reason and the forms of philosophy based on it are universally valid. Yet the world's profoundly religious cultures see this exclusion of the divine from the universality of reason as an attack on their most profound convictions. A reason which is deaf to the divine and which relegates religion into the realm of subcultures is incapable of entering into the dialogue of cultures.

★ ★ ★

The Regensburg lecture was a reflection on the complex subject of faith in modern culture. Not surprisingly, the press quickly reduced it to a single quote and a simplistic message. One prominent news service, for example, reported incorrectly that "the Pope described Islam as evil and inhuman."

Though many Western media outlets jumped on the pope (a *New York Times* editorial suggests his speech was "tragic and dangerous"), the most outraged reaction naturally came from the Islamic world. Typical was the reaction of the leader of the Islamic Nation Party in Kuwait: "I call on all Arab and Islamic states to recall their ambassadors from the Vatican and expel those from the Vatican until the pope says he is sorry for the wrong done to the prophet and to Islam, which preaches peace, tolerance, justice and equality."

The lower house of Pakistan's parliament passed a resolution against the pope's comments at Regensburg. "This statement has hurt the sentiments of Muslims," declared the resolution. "This house demands the Pope retract his remarks in the interest of harmony among different religions of the world." A Moroccan newspaper equated the pope's remarks with the Danish cartoons, a characterization that was not only inflammatory but profoundly unjust, given the pope's own expressed disapproval of the cartoons. A top official in the Islamic party in Turkey compared Benedict to Hitler and Mussolini, while other Turks called for him to cancel a planned papal visit to their county in November. "I do not think any good will come from the visit to the Muslim world of a person who has such ideas about Islam's prophet," said Turkey's president of Religious Affair, Ali Bardakoglu. "He should first of all replace the grudge in his heart with moral values and respect for the other." Bardakoglu later admitted he had not read the text of the lecture when he made this statement.

Far worse than the verbal denunciations was the violence that occurred in the days after Regensburg. Churches were burned by Hamas in Gaza and the West Bank, and the pope was burned in effigy in Iraq, where Al-Qaeda militants promised their own special brand of vengeance on Catholics. "We shall break the cross and spill the wine," declared a statement on the Internet from Al-Qaeda in Iraq. "God will (help) Muslims conquer Rome."

The irony in all this was as rich as it was dark: to protest the pope's suggestion that certain elements in Islam were unreasonable and violent, those very elements were reacting unreasonably and violently. Pakistan's foreign minister captured the irony perfectly, if unintentionally: "Anyone who describes Islam as a religion as intolerant encourages violence."

### III.

The days after Regensburg were tense inside the Vatican. Pope Benedict XVI, a man of peace, was cast, in much of the world, as an antagonist in the central conflict of the early twenty-first century—and people were dying because of it. Those 109 acres near the Tiber, and especially those few hundred people who worked within the Secretariat of State, were suddenly under the glare of the world's spotlight and Islam's wrath. Vatican security was tighter than ever and the Curia was on edge. To assure maximum confidentiality, my meetings with some Vatican officials were held not in the usual conference rooms, but outside on walks around the piazza of St. Peter's and the Belvedere Courtyard.

Within the Curia, the reaction to Regensburg was mixed. Many applauded Benedict for his speech, but all were concerned about the effect it created. The constant demand for apologies from outside the Vatican required a united, public statement, and the spokesman of the Holy See, Fr. Federico Lombardi, soon issued a one. Lombardi insisted the pope never intended to offend Muslims and had only respect for Islam and all religions. "What is important to the pope is a clear and radical rejection of the religious motivation of violence. . . . It was certainly not the intention of the Holy Father to do an in-depth study of jihad and Muslim thinking in this field and still less so to hurt the feelings of Muslim believers."

On Sunday, September 17, back in Castel Gandolfo and appearing at his weekly public Angelus, the pope issued his own not-quite-*mea culpa*: "I am deeply sorry for the reactions in some countries to a few passages of my address at the University of Regensburg, which were considered offensive to the sensibility of Muslims. These were in fact quoted from a medieval text, and do not in any way express my personal thought." Benedict was not apologizing for what he said, in other words, but for how it might have been perceived. This papal olive branch was enough to soothe the hurt feelings of some, but others were only just warming up. An influential

Egyptian Muslim scholar Yusuf al-Qaradawi used his television show on Aljazeera to reject the pope's response as insufficient and to call for an international "day of rage" to further inveigh against Regensburg.

The pope, still not quite apologizing, took further pains on September 20 to distance himself from the sentiments of Palaeologus quote, which "lent itself to possible misunderstanding." The Vatican also adjusted the printed text of the speech to tone down Palaeologus's rhetoric, including an added phrase in which Benedict described the emperor's words as uttered with "a startling brusqueness, a brusqueness that we find unacceptable." Meanwhile, nuncios in predominantly Muslim countries approached their host governments to walk back from pope's comments.

For our own part, we advocated for calm in the Vatican diplomatic corps and cabled the State Department the pope's semi-apology as a template for any statement on the matter, "particularly the Pope's own comments confirming that his remarks have been misunderstood and disassociating himself from Manuel's words about the prophet."

My main objective was to clarify exactly what the pope meant. Many people, both inside the Curia and out, assumed the pope's comments were a mistake; that the pope did not mean to say what he said. Yet everything we knew about Pope Benedict indicated, as George Weigel has asserted, "This is a man who says precisely what he means and means exactly what he says." The Vatican officials I consulted confirmed this: the pope, while regretting the violence that came after, knew what he was saying at Regensburg and meant every word of it.

In addition to seeking clarification, I brought a message to the Vatican from the United States: we supported the pope. Indeed, with the encouragement of the State Department, our mission had recently been pushing for a stronger statement from the Vatican on Islam. Regensburg, while surprising in the harshness of the analogy used, was a variation on a theme the pope had been pursuing for years, first as Cardinal Ratzinger then as Pope Benedict XVI.

★ ★ ★

To the great majority of Muslims who chose peace over violence, the pope's message was that it is not enough to simply renounce violence. They must *denounce* it. Where were the moderate voices in Islam when Muslims acted violently? And how was it that the pope drew more furor from the Muslim community than did the terrorists who claimed to be acting on behalf of God? Pope Benedict's forceful words were not intended to provoke angry words and deeds but to invite constructive dialogue.

"We need to stop insulting Islam," Thomas L. Friedman wrote in his column in the *New York Times* a few weeks after Regensburg. "No, that doesn't mean the pope should apologize. The pope was actually treating Islam with dignity. He was treating the faith and its community as adults who could be challenged and engaged." The real insult to Islam, argued Friedman, was to treat Muslims as if they were incapable of dialogue—to tiptoe nervously around them for fear of incurring their wrath. Under the pretense of peacemaking, this tiptoeing was patronizing and only drove our distinct worldviews further apart. It meant resigning ourselves to Samuel P. Huntington's famous forecast, first made in a 1993 *Foreign Affairs* article— "The Clash of Civilizations"—that future world conflicts would fall along cultural and religious differences, rather than geographic or ideological lines. That would be a disservice to Islam and its centuries of learned scholars, libraries, and long traditions of scholarship and intellectual engagement.

★ ★ ★

As it turned out, the pope's challenge was sincerely taken up in certain quarters of the Muslim world. One early response, in an op-ed in the *International Herald Tribune*, came from Tariq Ramadan, a controversial Swiss scholar whose maternal grandfather had founded the Muslim Brotherhood. Ramadan chastised the violent demonstrators for "providing a living proof that Muslims cannot engage in reasonable debate." He then went on to engage in the kind of debate he thought was required to counter the pope. "A critical approach should not expect him to apologize but it must simply and reasonably prove to him that historically, scientifically, and ultimately, spiritually, he is mistaken." Whether you agreed with Ramadan or not, he was arguing with the pope as one rational person to another.

More significant was a letter, signed by thirty-eight Islamic intellectuals from around the world, received by the pope on October 15. One of the difficulties in engaging in interreligious dialogue with Islam was that, unlike Catholicism, it had no single individual or institution to speak for it. This committee of thirty-eight esteemed imams, muftis, and scholars came close to an authoritative body. Written "in the spirit of open exchange," the four-page letter observed that Christianity and Islam were the world's two largest religions, comprising 55 percent of the world's population between them. Such numbers made "the relationship between these two religious communities the most important factor in contributing to meaningful peace around the world." As leader of more than a billion Catholics, the pope was "arguably the single most influential voice in continuing to move this relationship forward in the direction of mutual understanding."

The letter endeavored to correct the impression that Islam was a religion of violence. Islamic law did allow for legitimate self-defense, but it forbade targeting noncombatants and called for Muslims to live peacefully with their neighbors. The signatories rejected the terrorists' interpretation of "jihad" as holy war and specifically condemned violence that had occurred following Regensburg. The Muslim God, they insisted, was merciful and loving. He was also reasonable. Islam, like Christianity, sought "a consonance between the truths of the Koranic revelation and the demands of human intelligence."

The true value of this letter came not in the clarification of Islam it provided Pope Benedict, but in its clarification of Islam for Muslims. The greatest significance of Regensburg may have been that it elicited such clarifications.

★ ★ ★

George Weigel calls the Regensburg lecture the "most important papal statement on public matters of global consequence since John Paul II's address to the United Nations General Assembly in October 1995." As Weigel adds, "no president, prime minister, king, queen, or secretary-general could have put these questions into play, at this level of sophistication, and for a world audience." That was true in 2006, and it is true now.

Weigel drew three points from Pope Benedict's speech that put Regensburg in both theological and geopolitical perspective. The first of these was that "all the great questions of life, including social and political questions, are ultimately theological. . . . How we think (or don't think) about God has much to do with how we think about what is good and what is wicked . . . and how we think about the appropriate methods for advancing the truth in a world where there are profound disagreements about the truth of things." As discussed earlier, the relationship of faith and respect for the human dignity to moral justice and good government is naturally inherent in all humans. This relationship is a core element of the doctrines of the Holy See, expressed in Vatican II documents like *Gaudium et Spes* and in the words of numerous pontiffs over the last half century. America's founding principles are variants on the same themes.

Benedict's second point, as Weigel paraphrases, was that "irrational violence" against innocents is not compatible with God and the human soul. And third, that a "western world stripped of convictions about truths that make western civilization possible cannot make a useful contribution to a genuine dialogue of civilizations and cultures, for any dialogue must be based on a shared understanding that human beings can, however imperfectly, come to know the truth of things." Here Dr. Weigel—and Benedict—echo the optimistic hope of Arnold Toynbee, as noted in this book's prologue, in recognizing that its religious basis distinguishes western civilization from failed preceding civilizations, and offers a prescription for avoiding what has historically been an inexorable pattern of decay and decline.

The pope comes to the table with no threats, no bullets, no drones; he has no sticks and no carrots. He comes simply as man of faith, armed with words and beliefs. His is the ultimate soft power. As Cardinal Donald Wuerl, archbishop of Washington, explained to me once, using words similar to Dr. Weigel's, "All basic human decisions are theological, because whether it's personal or collective, the question is: how shall I live?" Before the problem of Islamic violence can be solved on a geopolitical level, it must be solved on a theological level. Who better to engage in that theology than the pope?

# 15

# PRESIDENT AND POPE

I say that freedom is not America's gift to the world. Freedom is God's gift to everybody in the world.

—President George W. Bush

## I.

I returned to Washington at the start of 2007 to attend the annual Chiefs of Mission conference. The White House arranged for the participating European area ambassadors to see the president in the Oval Office. This was a chance for us to exchange a few quick words with George W. Bush during a busy time in the White House. On January 10, just a few days after we saw him in the Oval Office, President Bush would appear on television to announce the successful "surge" plan to add twenty thousand troops in Iraq.

When my turn came to say hello and visit briefly, the president greeted me with some news. "I'm going to come see you."

"That's great, Mr. President. We'll be looking forward to it."

A visit by the president to a foreign territory is packed with significance on many levels, practical and symbolic. It is definitely a big moment for the local American ambassador. In the case of Rome, *three* American ambassadors would be involved in a presidential visit—myself; Ron Spogli, the ambassador to the Republic of Italy; and Gaddi Vasquez, the ambassador to the United Nations Food and Agriculture Organization. President Bush already knew Rome and the Vatican well. He had visited Holy See territory four times in his presidency, once to Castel Gandolfo and twice to Vatican City, to pay his respects to John Paul II. John Paul's funeral in the spring of 2005 counted as a fourth visit. Now would be a fifth—and President Bush's first one-on-one with Benedict XVI. One more trip to the Vatican in 2008 would make it six visits—which is more than any president had ever made to the Vatican, and more than President Bush made to any other foreign state besides Mexico and Russia.

The frequency of these visits was no real surprise. The president's values aligned him closely with the Holy See and gave him a deep appreciation of the power of religion to accomplish good in the world—the soft power role that the pope plays in world affairs. President Bush was hardly alone in considering the Vatican important. A survey in 2007 found that seven out of ten Americans believed that presidents should pay at least as much attention to the popes as to other world leaders. That's a statistic that would have been unthinkable just a few decades earlier.

★ ★ ★

President Bush's comment that he intended to visit the Vatican coincided with a little known but significant step in U.S.–Holy See relations which the White House and State Department supported and worked hard to accomplish. On January 11, 2007, the president signed the Department of State Authorities Act of 2006. Approved by Congress in late December 2005 as one of the last pieces of legislation taken up by the Senate before it changed hands after the 2006 elections, this act paved the way for the president to sign an executive order granting diplomatic privileges and immunities to the Holy See's observer mission to the United Nations.

As a practical matter, the Executive Order would change little for the Holy See. Its UN mission in New York had been getting along just fine for more than four decades. Nonetheless, rights conferred by the Executive Order were important symbolic measures to preserve and protect the special position that the Holy See occupied at the United Nations.

Since joining the United Nations in 1964, the Holy See has been a "Permanent Observer State" rather than a full member. What this means is that the Holy See can participate in General Assembly and Security Council meetings and debates, can vote on procedural matters, and can even cosponsor draft resolutions. What it cannot do is vote on the passage of resolutions.

In 2002, the secretary-general of the United Nations at the time, Kofi Annan, approached the then-nuncio to the United Nations, Archbishop Celeste Migliore, and asked him to consider applying for full membership. In earlier years, the Holy See had shared the designation of Permanent Observer with more than a dozen other nations, but one by one those others had upped their status to full membership, even, at last, Switzerland. The time had come, Annan urged, for the Holy See to do the same.

Undoubtedly the Holy See could have achieved full membership had Migliore and his colleagues pursued it, as it had been offered and encouraged not just by Annan, but by previous secretary-generals as well. Furthermore, as we have seen, the Holy See has a long history of diplomatic relations, global engagements, and recognized sovereignty that confer on it the status required for full membership in the United Nations. The Holy See could easily have accumulated the necessary votes to be accepted as a full member.

Archbishop Migliore took Annan's suggestion to some of his UN counterparts to feel them out on the matter, as a matter of due diligence. But these conversations only confirmed what Migliore already believed, which was that membership, rather than enhancing the role of Holy See, would detract from it. Unlike other nations, the Holy See represents a constituency from around the world, scattered among countries that are often in fierce disagreement with each other. Membership would inevitably compromise the Holy See's impartiality, forcing it into political alliances and voting blocs. It would also force it to tacitly accept, for the sake of those alliances and blocs, positions it did not hold. Neither of these were acceptable options for the Holy See. By maintaining its status as Permanent Observer, the Holy See could continue to advocate for its own universal agenda, exerting influence but staying above the fray—the deal making, the dog fighting—and preserving its universality and moral authority.

The challenge was making sure the status really remained *permanent*. To prove its legitimate place at the United Nations the Holy See possessed just a single piece of paper, a 1964 letter from then Secretary-General U Thant inviting the Holy See to join as a Permanent Observer State. The Holy See's status had been occasionally contested over the years, not by states but by outside organizations (notably a pro-abortion group called Catholics for Free Choice) that hoped to see its influence reduced or abolished at the United Nations. Now that the Vatican was the lone sovereign without Member designation, it seemed wise to bolster its Permanent Observer status and make it official. On July 1, 2004, the fortieth anniversary of the Holy See's participation in the United Nations, the General Assembly took less than ten minutes to adopt by consensus a resolution confirming the "rights and privileges" of the Holy See as Permanent Observer.

By extending to the Holy See all of the privileges and immunities enjoyed by full UN members, the president was offering an additional guarantee of the Holy See's permanence at the United Nations and confirming its unique status. When President Bush signed Executive Order 13427 on March 7, 2007, the United States publicly acknowledged Holy See diplomacy to be important—both to the interests of the United States and to the world at large.

★ ★ ★

The soft power of Holy See diplomacy came to bear just a few weeks after President Bush signed the Executive Order, during a tense drama involving Iran. Characteristically, the Vatican's actions to resolve the conflict went, and remain, virtually unnoticed.

The incident began on March 23, 2007, when a small patrol of fifteen British navy personnel conducted a search on a vessel in the Shatt al-Arab, in what the British sailors believed to be Iraqi waters. As far as the Brits were concerned, they were conducting a routine operation to deter smugglers, as permitted by UN mandate. But as the British sailors were completing the search, they noticed two speed boats racing toward them. These boats, soon joined by half a dozen others, belonged to the Iranian National Guard. Aboard were men heavily armed with machine guns and RPGs. The Iranians accused the British of trespassing on their national waters and placed them under arrest. To avoid bloodshed, the outmanned and outgunned British sailors submitted. They were blindfolded and transported to Tehran, where they were imprisoned and interrogated for more than two weeks.

Given their strained relations with Iran, the British government had few diplomatic options to get its sailors released. The solution came from Rome. A man named Denis MacShane, a British member of Parliament and a former Minister for Europe in the British Foreign Office, happened to be in the city on government business at the time and staying with the British Ambassador to the Holy See, Francis Campbell. Seeking a neutral party to deescalate the crisis, MacShane and Campbell turned to the Holy See. As Mr. MacShane described it to me, "when the news broke about our sailors, as soon as I could, I caught up with the prime minister and asked, 'Why don't we get Francis to make an informal approach, under the radar, to the Vatican to see if the pope can help get them released?'"

Prime Minister Blair was supportive and gave approval to the ambassador to approach the Vatican. The pope agreed to help. He immediately wrote a letter to the religious leader of Iran, Ayatollah Khamenei, asking that the sailors be freed as an "Easter gesture of good will." This letter was delivered to the Iranian ambassador to the Holy See, who received it "with great happiness," as he remembers, due to the "spiritual importance the Vatican has throughout the world." Hours later, as the British captives were freed by President Mahmoud Ahmadinejad, the Iranian president seemed to quote directly from the papal communiqué, calling the release a "gift" to Britain. He echoed the very words the pope had used in his letter to Ayatollah Khamenei.

As in most of its diplomatic ventures, the Vatican received little credit for its assistance in freeing the British sailors. But the truth is that not many figures in the world could have accomplished what the pope did, for he is one of very few world leaders—perhaps the only one—who combines global stature with a neutrality acknowledged both in the West and in the East; he was the only Western leader who could have gotten the respectful attention of the government of Iran. And because the Holy See functions below the radar and without seeking credit or acknowledgment, its particular exercise of soft power was uniquely effective.

## II.

The Holy See's bias is always for neutrality, morality, and truth. This is precisely the source of its soft power, but these virtues can cut both ways, as was the case in its vocal opposition to the Iraq War. As noted previously, by the time I arrived at the Holy See the Iraq situation had evolved and the pope indicated that he hoped to focus on the future and to work with us. As the war slogged on and casualties mounted, though, we picked up a strong sense from the Vatican that Pope Benedict would probably feel compelled to speak out critically in the near future. We cabled the State Department to warn of such a rebuke.

It finally came on Easter Sunday, April 8. In his traditional *Urbi et Orbi* address, Pope Benedict XVI commented on the challenges facing the international community. He spoke of the "grievous crisis" in Zimbabwe, of strife in Lebanon, and of the unfolding "catastrophic" humanitarian crisis in Darfur. And then he turned to the war. "Nothing positive" was coming out of an Iraq, he told the audience packed into St. Peter's Square, as Iraq was a country "torn apart by continual slaughter."

The following Sunday, April 15, I was attending a papal mass in St. Peter's on the occasion of the pope's eightieth birthday when our political officer, Peter Martin, informed me that the State Department wanted us to register a *demarche* to the Holy See objecting to the pope's characterization of the situation in Iraq. A few days later, meeting with the recently appointed new foreign secretary, Archbishop Dominique Mamberti, I delivered our note. We did not see the pope's comment as "constructive under the circumstances," I told him. Mamberti responded sympathetically. The pope did not seek to criticize America, he told me, but was speaking generally of the tragedy of the war.

★ ★ ★

Popes have been objecting to war for centuries, and have been adamantly antiwar since Vatican II. The exchanges concerning both of the Iraq interventions are well known, so the pope's comments weren't surprising, especially following many months of silence on this issue. The Vatican's response to the planning for President Bush's visit was more unexpected.

A date was chosen for the visit—June 9, 2007, following the G8 summit in Germany. We suggested that the president visit the Community of Sant'Egidio, a Catholic lay organization active in humanitarian aid and peace building. Embassy Vatican had been working closely with Sant'Egidio for several years, beginning in the late 1980s, when the embassy, along with the Departments of State and Defense, participated with the group in peace talks to end war in Mozambique. Continuing to expand the relationship, we had recently connected Sant'Egidio with Georgetown University to collaborate on some projects of mutual interest.

Founded in Rome in 1968 by a small group of Catholic high school students, and now based on the grounds of a former sixteenth-century Carmelite nunnery in the Trastevere section of the city, Sant'Egidio has grown into a highly influential NGO of more than sixty thousand volunteers in seventy-three countries. In addition to spreading the message of the gospel, Sant'Egidio was, and is, devoted to putting into practice the Christian message of charity and peace. Helping the homeless, advocating for the poor, tending to the sick—this is the work of Sant'Egidio. Their "Dream Project," partly funded by American PEPFAR money, is an important, highly successful program in the fight against HIV/AIDS in Africa, providing antiretroviral drugs and compassionate care in at least ten countries. Sant'Egidio is sufficiently volunteer-driven that it spends just 4 percent of its budget on administration, an unusually low amount in the universe of charities.

While their focus is treating the poor, the community has made a reputation for itself as a peace negotiator, consistent with the Holy See's position that peace is a fundamental the precondition for human rights. The community has been successful in many peace missions in the last three decades, from its role in brokering the end of civil war in Mozambique in 1992 to subsequent efforts in the Balkans, Latin America, and Uganda. Sometimes called the "United Nations of Trastevere," Sant'Egidio, with the tacit encouragement of Pope John Paul II, went to Albania and Bosnia in the 1990s to act as a diplomatic back channel in solving civil strife in those countries. As an NGO and not a state, Sant'Egidio acts from a bargaining position that entails no hegemonic or threatening agenda, making it in some sense analogous to the Holy See itself. As we have seen, sometimes the greatest form of power is powerlessness.

Sant'Egidio is perceived as utopian, but its members deny it. "We're not dreamers," Andrea Riccardi, the founder, says. "We need to convince people that peace is the best situation for them and that war is madness."

Given the nature of their work and our mission's history of support, a presidential visit to Sant'Egidio was a good fit. It was an ideal venue to highlight the serious and sometimes overlooked commitment to charity by the first-ever American president to create an office in the White House devoted to advancing the works of faith-based initiatives. President Bush had spoken consistently and passionately in support of compassion and human rights around the world.

About two weeks before the president was due to arrive in Rome, I received a call from a prominent cleric in Rome, insisting that we reconsider the president's visit to Sant'Egidio and stating that the Vatican opposed it. The core of the objection, I was told, was that the president's meeting at Sant'Egidio's offices in Trastevere would create a false perception of parity between Sant'Egidio and the Vatican, raising Sant'Egidio to the stature of a "state institution" like the Vatican or the government of Italy. At the very least, the Holy See preferred that the visit should occur at a more neutral setting than Sant'Egidio's property.

In the end, the Vatican got more or less what it desired, not because anyone gave in but because outside events dictated the outcome. The Italian government could not guarantee the security of the president in the narrow alleys and cobblestone courtyards of the Trastevere neighborhood around Sant'Egidio. The possibility of being trapped among the demonstrators and tourists expected to descend on Rome during the president's visit was a legitimate concern. Rumors suggested that the Vatican's nuncio to Italy urged the Italian government to find a way to make the visit impossible, but regardless of how it came about, the meeting site was moved at the last minute to Embassy Rome. It was probably for the best.

### III.

President Bush touched down in Rome on the evening of June 8, at the end of six-country tour that included the G8 summit in Germany, along with stops in Czechoslovakia, Bulgaria, Albania, Poland, and now Italy. Kathleen and I went out to Fiumicino Airport to greet President Bush and the First Lady. We stood on the tarmac with the American ambassador to Italy, Ronald Spogli, and his wife, Georgia. Also with us was the American ambassador to the United Nations Food and Agriculture Organization, Gaddy Vasquez, and his wife, Elaine. Two high-level representatives from the Vatican, Monsignor Peter Wells, an American from my home state of Oklahoma, and an archbishop named Peter Paul Prabhu, an Indian who had served as nuncio to Zimbabwe, were also present. We had not expected Archbishop Prabhu at the airport, but we welcomed his presence as an extra signal of the Vatican's respect and appreciation for the Bush administration. Shortly, an Italian protocol officer came over and announced the Vatican had too many representatives on the tarmac and one would have to go. I sought out the lead White House advance officer, Therese Burch, who was very experienced in these matters. She set the protocol officer straight. "The reason we're here is to see the pope," she told him. "If the Vatican had an airport, we'd go there." The protocol officer went away, and the archbishop stayed.

Air Force One landed and taxied up to the red carpet. After descending the airplane stairs, the president visited along the receiving line. He told Monsignor Peter Wells how much he looked forward to seeing the pope. The following morning, after the antitrafficking breakfast mentioned earlier, Kathleen and I went to meet President and Mrs. Bush at the Quirinale, once the palace of popes—more than thirty of them had lived there between the sixteenth century and the nineteenth century—and now the residence of the Italian president. President Bush finished his meeting with the president of Italy, then we rode in the motorcade with the president and Mrs. Bush to the Vatican. Normally, this would be a quick drive, even in the usual bustling Italian traffic. Now the roads were closed to other traffic and we sped, but our route was long and circuitous, no doubt for security reasons. The ride was a unique opportunity for us to visit with the Bushes. One topic we discussed was reasonable comprehensive immigration reform in the United States, which the president had worked hard to accomplish and which remains (in my opinion) both a practical necessity and a significant human rights issue. I also took the opportunity to brief him on the Vatican. Among other things, I mentioned that the first man to greet him would be Archbishop James Harvey, a native of Wisconsin and the prefect of the papal household. I knew the president always appreciated personal details about the people he met.

After crossing the Tiber, we rode down the Via della Conciliazione, crossed St. Peter's Square and passed under the Arch of Bells. Archbishop

Harvey was at the red carpet to greet the president in the Cortile San Damaso. "How about those Brewers?" asked the president with a grin.

Inside the papal library, the president and the pope discussed AIDS and famine in Africa and our mutual commitment to end these. They also addressed immigration and, of course, Iraq, the pope expressing his concerns about the treatment of Christians inside the country. As *Time* magazine put it at the time, both men were "straight talkers who act according to what they see as simple truths."

After about almost forty-five minutes, a longer than customary papal visit, we went in the library and the president introduced the American delegation to Benedict XVI. He and the pope then exchanged gifts. Pope Benedict gave the president a seventeenth-century etching of St. Peter's Square. President Bush gave the pope a walking stick engraved with the Ten Commandments, carved and hand-painted by a former homeless man in Dallas named Roosevelt Wilkerson. He also gave Benedict a book of writings by Archbishop John Carroll, the man with whom we began this book in chapter 1—and the man first responsible, in many ways, for the extraordinary relationship between the Holy See and the United States.

"Sometimes I'm not poetic enough to describe what it's like to be in the presence of the Holy Father," President Bush later told reporters. "It is a moving experience."

★ ★ ★

As if arranging the president's meeting with Sant'Egidio had not already been challenging enough, there remained one last obstacle: on the way there, the president's limo, a heavy, armored Cadillac called The Beast, came to a stop in the middle of the crowded street. The motor had died. People with phones and cameras came packing in toward the limo, amazed to find the president of the United States suddenly in their midst, just a few yards away. The limo driver tried to start the engine, but it would not turn over. It was a nervous moment for the U.S. Secret Service and a long five or so minutes for the rest of us. To calm the surrounding crowd, the president opened the door and waved, which seemed to work wonders. Fortunately, the driver soon managed to get the limo powered up again and we were on our way.

The round table with Sant'Egidio was a success. Representatives of Sant'Egidio spoke of various programs the community ran to alleviate poverty and bring dignity to the lives of the poor, particularly in Darfur and Kosovo. One very important contribution of Sant'Egidio addressed at the meeting was the BRAVO program. Through BRAVO, Sant'Egidio works with governments to build civil birth registration systems where they are lacking and to create awareness among parents and children of the need for birth documentation. The program, now operating in several African countries, offers the promise of access to government services, including health and education, and better protection of essential human rights to the more than 50 million children that UNICEF counted as unregistered in 2007. A young woman named Beatrice, who had been born without documentation in Liberia but was now living in the Ivory Coast, spoke movingly about the program and the opportunities it afforded her and others in Africa. The president listened carefully to Beatrice and all the participants, asking questions and offering encouragement. "You are part of the international army of compassion," he told the group before the meeting ended. Later, the president of Sant'Egidio, Marco Impagliazzo, told reporters that getting the opportunity to sit down with the president was "like a fairy tale."

Looking back at the president's visit, putting the distractive territorial issues behind, both the Holy See and Sant'Egidio have much to offer for the good of the world and can accomplish feats that would be unachievable for territorial sovereigns and others with more hegemonic or less selfless agendas. The last section of this book, accordingly, leaves us to consider what role the Holy See can and may play in international relations and the global diplomacy of the future.

# V

# CONCLUSIONS

# 16

## FAITH AND FREEDOM

Religion in America takes no direct part in the government
of society, but nevertheless it must be regarded as the foremost of the political institutions of that country; for if it
does not impart a taste for freedom, it facilitates the use
of free institutions.

—Alexis de Tocqueville

I.

The morning after President Bush met Pope Benedict XVI at the Vatican, Kathleen and I went to see him and Mrs. Bush off at Fiumicino
Airport. I thanked the president for his visit and for the opportunity to be
part of his team. Then we stood on the tarmac and watched Air Force One
lift off and turn for home. For all the bumps in the road, the visit had been
a success. Looking back over my time in Rome more broadly, I felt good
about the work we'd done in fulfilling my promise to President Bush to
represent him and the country to the best of our abilities. But after several
years away from my business and our children, the time had come, as I'd
discussed earlier with the White House, for Kathleen and me to start thinking about returning home.

That summer the pope decamped as usual to Castel Gandolfo in the
hills outside Rome. Vatican business slowed to a crawl, and the "canicular
heat"—to borrow the phrase used by the American consul Jacob Martin
160 years earlier—settled over the city. The pace picked back up in September. On November 5, the White House announced the nomination

217

of my successor: Mary Ann Glendon, a highly regarded Harvard Law professor specializing in human rights who previously served on President Bush's Commission on Bioethics. It was gratifying to know that someone of such high caliber would follow me in representing the United States to the Holy See, and that the relationship would be in such capable hands. In the meantime, I still had several months to serve.

A standout moment that autumn occurred the day after Dr. Glendon's nomination, November 6, 2007, when King Abdullah of Saudi Arabia visited the pope at the Vatican. This first-ever visit by a Saudi monarch to a pope was evidence that the pope's strong words at Regensburg had promoted, rather than discouraged, dialogue with Islam. Already, the previous May, the United Arab Emirates had established diplomatic relations with the Holy See, an important step in Catholic-Muslim relations. Now this visit by the Saudi king, who came not simply as a civic leader but as the guardian of the Islamic holy sites of Mecca and Medina, bore even more symbolic importance. As we later phrased it in our cable to the State Department, "The most important aspect of the King's visit was the fact that a visit took place."

The pope and the king discussed a number of topics of mutual concern, including the treatment of some 1.6 million Christians in Saudi Arabia, 80 percent of whom were Catholic. These Christians were forbidden to practice their faith publicly, a particular hardship for Catholics, who are supposed to regularly receive sacraments from clergy. The Vatican did not expect an instant reversal in the religious policies of Saudi Arabia, but it did hope for greater tolerance for Christians. In the meantime, the pope and king found common ground in exalting the important role of morality in public affairs and in agreeing on the need for dialogue among Christian, Muslims, and Jews.

The pope conceptualized a new approach toward Islam that fall, as Cardinal Tauran told me when I saw him in September. Intent on forging closer relations, Benedict decided to focus on areas in which both religions shared views, such as the sanctity of life, culture, and human needs. The pope's new approach would start with the Ten Commandments, a foundational text for all three Abrahamic faiths—Judaism, Christianity, and Islam. From this common ground, Benedict would seek greater rapport. "It just might work," Cardinal Tauran said with the air of someone who has seen too much to expect miracles but never stopped praying and hoping for them.

★ ★ ★

Those last months in Rome, as we waited for Dr. Glendon to pass through the nomination and confirmation process, were punctuated with farewell receptions and holiday parties. Our time in Rome had brought us many new friends, and I enjoyed warm relations with many Vatican officials and a number of my fellow diplomats. One diplomat, Nicolay Sadchikov, the ambassador from Russia, told me I would be missed because I was "not on a leash." I took this as high praise. While I had duly and completely executed all directives from the State Department, I had also tried to generate new ideas and measures to advance and leverage our relationship with the Holy See.

I joined my fellow members of the diplomatic corps in the Sala Reggia one last time in early January 2008 to hear the pope's annual address. Though *pro forma* in some respects, the pope's speech was packed, as always, with meaningful insights. "The factors of concern are varied, yet they all bear witness to the fact that human freedom is not absolute, but is a good that is shared, one for which all must assume responsibility," the pope said after giving a brief overview of the world's hotspots. "It follows that law and order are guarantees of freedom. Yet law can be an effective force for peace only if its foundations remain solidly anchored in natural law, given by the creator."

The American Founding Fathers could not have stated it any better. Given that the Vatican had recently announced the pope's intention to visit the United States the following spring, these words seemed to set the stage for Benedict's appearance before an American audience.

As per Vatican protocol, I was invited in those last weeks for exit visits by the leadership of Secretariat of State, including Cardinal Bertone, Archbishop Sandri, and Monsignor Parolin. On our way to my final meeting with the pope, the "congedo" visit (from the Italian verb *congedare*: to leave), Kathleen and I, along with our children, retraced the route we had taken on credentialing day in 2005—the same route through the loggias and halls of the Apostolic Palace that I took with Mrs. Bush and President Bush when accompanying them on their visits to the pope.

Pope Benedict XVI took my hand and smiled warmly as we entered the papal library. So much had passed since he had settled into the papacy in the spring of 2005. He had started his reign under a cloud of scandal and suspicion and had met many hard challenges since. He turned out to be nothing like the fierce "Rottweiler" his pre-papal critics had warned he would be. Now, instead, his critics portrayed him as too passive. He was a poor administrator, they said, a misplaced academic who preferred quiet contemplation to governance and politics, a weakness exacerbated by a few unfortunate appointments he had made in the personnel who worked under him. It was a fair critique up to a point. This is not the place to belabor the Vatican scandals and squabbles of the last several years, except to acknowledge that they distract the Holy See it from its mission and likely diminish its moral authority. To borrow Harry Truman's phrase about the presidency, the buck stops at the pope's desk; he is ultimately responsible for what happens under his watch, even if not personally to blame.

But if we are to acknowledge some of the flaws of his papacy, we must also grant that Benedict XVI, far from being the passive placeholder of his critics' imagination, was a pope who displayed tremendous resolve and integrity in charting the church's course, even if this sometimes meant courting controversy and bad press. He turned out to be a very complicated pontiff, which made him frustrating to journalists who wanted to pigeonhole him with some sort of "personality," but also fascinating to watch. Trained as a classical pianist as a child, Benedict had the traits of mental discipline, precision, and respect for tradition that such a pursuit requires; but he was also willing to sometimes put aside the musical score and follow his own less expected tune. Regensburg was one instance of this, and there were plenty of others. His surprise resignation was really no surprise at all if you reflect on his long a record of doing what he believed to be right, always putting the church ahead of his own popularity. Sometimes the press interpreted his refusal to court public affection as a lack of warmth. Actually, his humility came before public affection, and that same humility led him to resign when he knew his health required it for the good of the church. He served slightly less than eight years—just five months longer than his World War I–era namesake, Benedict XV. Perhaps, like the last Benedict, he will be a "forgotten" pope. Or perhaps history will remember him as a pope who held firm in the face of immense challenges and served the church well.

But back to 2008, when Benedict XVI's resignation was still very much in the future. As I met with him for the final time, the pope looked strong and healthy. He was bit more stooped than when we first met—he was now eighty, after all—but he was totally in command. He told me he was looking forward to visiting the United States in April. Then he greeted my family, speaking to my wife and children individually. We left him as we had come, walking out through the Apostolic Palace to the Cortile San Damaso, then drove out of the Vatican.

II.

I was back in the United States when Benedict XVI touched down at Andrews Air Force Base on April 15, 2008, to begin his first visit as pope to the United States. The visit held personal significance for me, reaffirming themes of Benedict's papacy that had emerged during my tenure in Rome. Indeed, every major speech and homily the pope gave in the United States was a variation of the theme he had pursued since becoming pope: the relationship between faith and reason in the twenty-first century, and the need to treat these not as a polarity but as a symbiosis.

Benedict's motorcade pulled into 1600 Pennsylvania Avenue on April 16, only the second time a pope had ever visited the White House (the first being John Paul II's visit during the Carter administration). The day happened to be Benedict's eighty-first birthday. The visit coincided with a number of other significant dates, including the two hundredth anniversary of John Carroll's installment as the first archbishop in the United States and Baltimore's elevation as the first archdiocese in America. Also in that momentous year of 1808, four other American cities—Boston, New York, Philadelphia, and Louisville—became dioceses. Benedict's visit in many ways marked the bicentennial of the American Catholic Church, which made it an ideal time to reflect on the long and remarkable history of the relationship between the United States and the Holy See.

The country in which Benedict XVI arrived in 2008 was far more welcoming to popes than the United States of 1808, when anti-Catholicism was rampant and increasing, and "popery" was roundly condemned as un-American. Today, in the early twenty-first century, Catholicism is woven into every aspect of American culture, and overt anti-Catholicism is all but erased. Although John F. Kennedy was the last Catholic president, Catholics now serve in the highest levels of government, including the six Catholics who sit on the Supreme Court and nearly a third of the members of Congress. Catholic institutions form a large part of the nongovernmental public institutions in this country as well. Today, 630 hospitals, including a quarter of the top-ranked hospitals in the country, are Catholic, as are 244 colleges and universities. The Catholic Church is the single largest charitable organization in the United States.

Catholicism has given much to America, and America, in turn, has given much back to the Catholic Church. Materially, Americans still donate the lion's share of Peter's Pence—money donated by Catholics to the Vatican—and as much as 60 percent of the wealth of the church is reported to come from the United States.

The church has gained more than money from the United States: As America became more Catholic during the twentieth century, the Catholic Church became more American. Not in the majority of its leadership, which even today remains heavily Italian, nor in deference to American power, but in its goals and views. Without the influence of American thought, the church would not have evolved as it did between the nineteenth and twentieth centuries. That influence was especially apparent, as we have seen, during Vatican II, when key documents, most notably the declaration on religious liberty, *Dignitatis Humanae*, were drafted by Americans like John Courtney Murray and were informed by American perspectives of civil rights and democracy. Of course, as we have also seen (in this book's first chapter), those seminal American ideals were themselves originally drawn from the Catholic concepts of natural law. Before America influenced the church, the church influenced America.

Over the previous century, the relationship between America and the church has prospered, but as Pope Benedict XVI visited in 2008 the prospects for the future of the American Catholic Church were mixed—and so they remain today. The number of Catholics in the United States has held steady and even climbed in recent years, from about 46 million in 1965 to 65 million by 2005, and now to more than 66 million. As a percentage of Americans, Catholics comprise about 25 percent of the adult U.S. population. Those numbers tell a positive story, but other numbers are less encouraging. Regular mass attendance among Catholics in the United States has declined from roughly 60 percent in that late 1950s to less than 30 percent today. At the same time, the number of American priests fell from almost 60,000 in 1965 to 43,000 in 2005, and was down to 39,000 by 2012—a steep drop indeed given that the population of the United States has grown by more than a 100 million since 1965. The American Church is reverting, as the American Catholic historian James O'Toole notes, to the priestless church of colonial America.

The pedophilia scandals have caused grave damage. Legally and practically, the Vatican cannot be blamed for the actions of bad priests, but the church could have more aggressively managed the crisis from a more centralized and consistent approach as it was unfolding in parishes around the world in the 1990s. As noted earlier, the Holy See understands this and has made significant efforts to repair the damage and improve response with candor and action. Benedict XVI wisely addressed the scandal head on during his trip to the United States. In fact, he started addressing it while still on the plane from Rome, telling the travelling press corps that he was "deeply ashamed" of the acts of abusive priests.

★ ★ ★

Recent troubles aside, Catholicism, like most major Western religions, is facing a long-range crisis in the secularization of the developed world. This damage is likely to be felt long after the current scandals have faded. The pope addressed the trend toward secularization frequently and urgently over the course of his five days in the United States.

Benedict gave a number of lectures and homilies in Washington, then in New York, where he spoke before the United Nations, visited Ground Zero, and presided over an outdoor mass at Yankee Stadium. He was met with adulation and delight—and huge crowds—wherever he went. In turn, he expressed his great appreciation for the American people, not just Catholics but Americans of every faith. In the ecumenical spirit of *Dignitatis Humanae*, he met with groups of Jewish leaders, along with Hindus, Buddhists, and Muslims. He stressed, again and again, the role that religion played in the founding of America, a nation whose history is wedded to faith and is drawn (see chapter 1) from the traditions of Catholic natural law.

Kathleen and I were present at the White House on the morning of April 16 when this alignment of natural law theology and American ideals was dramatically highlighted in an exchange between Pope Benedict XVI and President Bush. Following a twenty-one-gun salute and a performance by opera singer Kathleen Battle, the president spoke. "Here in America you'll find a nation that welcomes the role of faith in the public square," President Bush told the pope. "When our founders declared our nation's independence, they rested their case on an appeal to the laws of nature and of nature's God."

The pope expanded on the president's words in his own remarks. "Democracy can only flourish, as your founding fathers realized, when political leaders and those whom they represent are guided by truth and bring the wisdom born of firm moral principle to decisions affecting the life and future of the nation." The pope then addressed, like President Bush, the lessons of American history:

> From the dawn of the Republic, America's quest for freedom has been guided by the conviction that the principles governing political and social life are intimately linked to a moral order based on the dominion of God the Creator. The framers of this nation's founding documents drew upon this conviction when they proclaimed the "self-evident truth" that all men are created equal and endowed with inalienable rights grounded in the laws of nature and of nature's God. The course of American history demonstrates the difficulties, the struggles, and the great intellectual and moral resolve which were demanded to shape a society which faithfully embodied these noble principles.

Here was the president of the United States quoting the Holy Father, and the Holy Father referring back to the work of American's Founding

Fathers. These complementary speeches were neither previewed nor coordinated in advance. They were, rather, a natural recognition, many years after the founding of the United States, of the deep intellectual roots shared by the American republic and the Catholic Church.

In his mass at Yankee Stadium on April 20, the pope urged sixty thousand worshipers to reject "a false dichotomy between faith and political life." Benedict XVI quoted from the Second Vatican Council: "there is no human activity—even in secular affairs—which can be withdrawn from God's dominion."

It will come as news to many Americans that the men who founded this country shared Benedict's view. We are generally misled about the Founders' opinions on religion, despite the fact that the First Amendment of the Constitution is quite clear in its meaning. The Founders gave primacy of place to freedom of religion not because they thought religion mattered little to civil society, but because they understood that it was absolutely *vital*—that, in fact, civil society could hardly function without it.

In his book *God and the Founders*, the scholar Vincent Phillip Muñoz shows that the three Founders with the most to say about the relationship between religion and the state—Madison, Jefferson, and Washington—each had his own distinct thoughts on the matter but agreed that recognition of a deity was critical in a democratic country, where, as Washington stated, "virtue or morality is a necessary spring of popular government." Even Jefferson, the man most commonly associated with the term "wall of separation between church and state," recognized that civil government benefited from popular belief in a Supreme Being. "Religion, as well as reason," he wrote in a letter in 1815, "confirms the soundness of those principles on which our government has been founded and its rights asserted."

The religious beliefs of American citizens were never dismissed as irrelevant by the Founders; nor did they expect church and state to exist in isolation from each other. They would almost certainly have agreed with Pope Benedict XVI's remarks to U.S. bishops in 2012: "The legitimate separation of Church and State cannot be taken to mean that the Church must be silent on certain issues, nor that the State may choose not to engage, or be engaged by, the voices of committed believers in determining the values which will shape the future of the nation."

What were the Founders telling us about church and state in the First Amendment? As Jim Towey explained at our conference on religious freedom in 2007, the religion clause of the First Amendment is fundamental to the whole idea of the United States. If we focus exclusively on the establishment clause, though, we fail to appreciate the second part—the free exercise clause. Which means we fail to grasp the full meaning of the amendment. The primary intent of the religion clause of the First Amendment was not to limit religion's influence on government; it was to limit government's interference in religion.

The freedom to worship according to one's conscience—to believe what you believe—is the very essence of freedom. A government may have enormous power over its citizens, but as long as it cannot tell its citizens what to think, as many totalitarian countries have tried to do, its power will be limited. Religious liberty is called the "first freedom" because civil liberties begin with freedom of conscience and freedom of worship. No wonder so many Catholic Americans were dismayed by the Obama administration's effort to force Catholic institutions to obey government healthcare laws contrary to Catholic teaching. The reason for dismay was not that the mandate ran counter to the tenets of the Catholic faith but that it contradicted the core principle of American civil liberties. Water down the freedom to worship by forcing Catholic institutions to support practices they deem immoral, and you debase the First Amendment. A proponent of ObamaCare might argue that abridging the rights of Catholic institutions is justified by the national health benefits the new plan is promised to offer, but even people who sincerely believe that should worry about such a bargain. Consider, again, the words of Ben Franklin: "Those who would give up essential liberty to purchase a little temporary safety deserve neither liberty nor safety."

No one understood better the roles of faith and freedom in America than Alexis de Tocqueville, the French writer who visited in 1831. "Upon my arrival in the United States, the religious aspect of the country was the first thing that struck my attention," wrote Tocqueville in *Democracy in America*, "and the longer I stayed there the more did I perceive the great political consequences resulting from this new state of things." Tocqueville was struck by the way Americans' religion was directly related to their remarkable civic life. "In France I had almost always seen the spirit of religion and the spirit of freedom pursuing courses diametrically opposed to each other; but in America I found that they were intimately united, and that they reigned in common over the same country."

That unique collaboration of faith and freedom has defined America. As freedom has allowed individual Americans to achieve prosperity, the moral vision imparted by faith has endowed the nation with a collective calling greater than any material wealth. This has made America a powerful adversary against dictators and zealots, and a nation that continually rights itself when it veers off the track.

## III.

What does any of this have to do with international relations in the twenty-first century? A great deal, actually, because the future of international relations will be determined in large part by the values that drive nations, including the United States, toward their individual and collective destinies. As I have tried to show in these pages—and as recent history has demonstrated—religion is not incidental to the practicalities of geopolitics. On the contrary, it is often decisive. So we, like the pope, must take note of current trends of religious faith in the world; and, like the pope, we should be concerned.

Right now the developed Western world, especially that part of the globe that used to be known as *Christendom*, is witnessing a dramatic uncoupling of faith and society. Young Europeans are tossing aside the religion of their parents and grandparents and embracing the orthodoxy of secularization, not realizing that a freedom cut loose from faith will not be stronger but will be, rather, profoundly attenuated, condemning people, as Tocqueville writes, "in some way to confusion and impotence."

Perhaps it would not surprise Tocqueville—though it would surely dishearten him—to know that his homeland of France, where he saw freedom and faith marching in opposite directions, is now among the most secular nations on earth. Compared to 73 percent of Americans, just 27 percent of French people now believe in God or Supreme Being. Much of Europe is following in France's footsteps. Just 35 percent of British citizens believe in God or a Supreme Being, with over half calling themselves agnostics or atheists.

In the early fall of 2010, Pope Benedict XVI went to the UK and delivered at Westminster Hall his most important speech since Regensburg. As in Germany in 2006, he spoke before an audience comprised mostly of lay people, including British leaders. As then, his subject was the proper role of faith in society—"the perennial question of the relationship between what is owed to Caesar and what is owed to God." Democracies could not pretend to solve the dilemma by appealing to the will of the people, as if suffrage obviated faith. "If the moral principles underpinning the democratic process are themselves determined by nothing more solid than social consensus, then the fragility of the process becomes all too evident—herein lies the real challenge for democracy." Reason-based government profits from religion, which can "help purify and shed light upon the application of reason to the discovery of objective moral principles." Conversely,

Without the corrective supplied by religion, reason too can fall prey to distortions, as when it is manipulated by ideology, or applied in a partial way that fails to take full account of the dignity of the human person. This is why I would suggest that the world of reason and the world of faith—the world of secular rationality and the world of religious belief—need one another and should not be afraid to enter into a profound and ongoing dialogue, for the good of our civilization.

If the pope is right, and if the trend toward secularization continues, then the West is heading into a morass. Religion is already leaving the public sphere, taking its "corrective" influences with it. Increasingly, secular states are nurturing cultures of relative morality—the "dictatorship of relativism" that Pope Benedict described in 2005. Moral equivocation is a theological problem, but it is also a political problem. "Individuals, communities and states, without guidance from objectively moral truths," said Benedict in June 2010 during a visit to Cyprus, "would become selfish and unscrupulous and the world a more dangerous place to live." Sacrificing moral truth to political expediency or popular whim creates a vacuum into which, sooner or later, extremism will likely enter. Here is Tocqueville stating this in different terms, almost two centuries ago:

> When a nation's religion is destroyed, doubt takes a grip upon the highest areas of intelligence, partially paralyzing all others. Each man gets used to having only confused and vacillating ideas on matters which have the greatest interest for himself and his fellows. . . . As everything in the domain of their intelligence is shifting, they crave at least for a firm and stable state in their material world. Being unable to recover their ancient beliefs, they find a ruler.

Secularists may eschew the orthodoxies of Christianity, but before they cast the old beliefs aside they might consider the history of alternative dogmas and the governments that propagate these, usually with little concern for reason or rights or separation of church and state. The Christian tradition that gave rise to Europe recognizes, as no civilization had before, the distinct spheres of government and faith—what is owed to Caesar and what is owed to God—while reconciling reason with religion. It is a tradition, Pope Benedict XVI has said, that "does not speak from blind faith, but from a rational perspective which links our commitment to building an authentically just, humane and prosperous society to our ultimate assurance that the cosmos is possessed of an inner logic accessible to human reasoning."

Already, as noted by the historian and foreign policy expert Robert Kagan, the world provides numerous examples of "toxic nationalism," the violence and tribalism that cultures fall back on in the absence of moral truths. "We are in a battle between two epic forces," writes Kagan: "Those of integration based on civil society and human rights, and those of exclusion based on race, blood and radicalized faith. It is the mistake of Western elites to grant primacy to the first force, for it is the second that causes the crises with which policy makers must deal."

Beyond the implications of secularization for individual nations are its global ramifications, especially at a time when radical Islam is growing and spreading. Islamic fundamentalists are taking root not only in the Middle East and Africa, but in Europe. The developed world makes a mistake if it believes its modernity and high standard of living secure it against extremist sects of Islam. The British writer and devout Catholic, Hilaire Belloc, made exactly this point in 1937. Although his perspective was born of a now outdated colonialist mindset, his words are still worth considering:

> The story must not be neglected by any modern, who may think in error that the East has finally fallen before the West. . . . Islam survives. Its religion is intact; therefore its material strength may return. *Our* religion is in peril, and who can be confident in the continued skill, let alone the continued obedience, of those who make and work our machines? . . .
>
> We worship ourselves, we worship the nation; or we worship (some few of us) a particular economic arrangement believed to be the satisfaction of social justice. . . . Islam has not suffered this spiritual decline; and in the contrast . . . lies our peril.

Islam is an illustrious religion with over 1 billion adherents, most of whom who cherish peace and respect human dignity. However, Islamic fundamentalism is a different story. Radical groups in the Middle East and Africa impose Sharia law and commit atrocities in the name of God. Madrasas sponsored by the fundamentalist Wahhabis indoctrinate young people in a hate-filled version of Islamic faith that feeds terrorism. The West faces the challenge of simultaneously respecting moderate Islam while refusing to appease violent radicals. This will be one of the great geopolitical challenges of the twenty-first century.

Which brings us back to the Holy See, and to the final conclusions of this book.

# 17

# THE ART OF HOPE

Diplomacy is, in a certain sense, the art of hope. It lives from hope and seeks to discern even its most tenuous signs. Diplomacy must give hope.

—Benedict XVI (2008)

## I.

Five years have passed since I ended my tenure as the American ambassador to the Holy See. These years have seen cordial but cooling relations between the United States and the Holy See. President Obama has visited the Vatican just once since becoming president, while his administration seems to exhibit little more than a perfunctory interest in the Holy See's diplomatic role in the world.

This is regrettable. As I have argued throughout this book, U.S. foreign policy has much to gain from our relationship with the Holy See, and vice versa. No institution on earth has both the international stature and the global reach of the Holy See—the soft power, the people power—to promote religious freedom, human liberties, and related values that Americans and our friends around the world believe in and rely on. "There is no other universally regarded voice of moral authority on the planet," in the words of Cardinal Wuerl, the archbishop of Washington. "Even the people who disagree with the pope recognize this."

As I complete the manuscript of this book, a newly elected pope, Francis, is commencing his papacy. Despite ongoing scandals and challenges facing the church, a spirit of fresh hope and renewal is discernible in the Vatican. Francis is by no means a young pope at seventy-six, but already he has demonstrated that he intends to bring a new perspective to church leadership. Indeed, given his background, it is almost inevitable that he will. Unlike Benedict XVI, he is not a veteran of the Curia, having spent most of his life not in Rome but in his native Argentina. Yet he is experienced in church administration and Vatican politics. He has visited Rome often over the years to participate as a member of several important congregations, as well as the Synod of Bishops. He is an outsider, but he knows the ropes.

An important and possibility pivotal moment leading up to Francis's election was a brief speech he gave in the Vatican's Paul VI grand hall one week before the conclave. Cardinal Bergoglio, as he was known before becoming pope, told his fellow cardinals that the church had to stop being "self-referential" and must turn its attention from itself to the poor and others in need. His message seems to have piqued the interest especially of the American cardinals, one of the decisive voting blocs in the conclave.

Francis promises to be a firm adherent to church dogma, but he is likely to bring a more conciliatory style to the papacy. Claudio Betti of the Community of Sant'Egidio, which worked often with Cardinal Bergoglio in programs to assist the poor in Buenos Aires, describes him as a pope "who, thanks to his great spiritual liberty, could smooth the corners and allow space for debate," an opinion shared widely by those who know him personally. This blend of firm leadership and thoughtful compassion was a hallmark of many great popes, such as Leo XIII, in centuries past, and it is likely to have diplomatic implications in coming years. Francis's stated desire to shift the church toward a more outward-looking approach, along with his Southern Hemisphere background, will place the Holy See in a more robust engagement with the world beyond the Vatican, including, perhaps, with the United States.

In fact, Pope Francis has already undertaken several important initiatives to address issues that have surfaced recently. These include an advisory board of eight cardinals to focus on reform of the Roman Curia; a five-member commission to analyze weaknesses in internal control and to propose reforms for the operation of the Vatican Bank; and a Financial Security Committee headed by the Assessor, Monsignor Peter Wells, to ensure compliance with international norms for detection and prevention of money laundering and tax evasion. Now, with the appointment of Pietro Parolin to succeed Cardinal Tarcisio Bertone as the secretary of state, the pope has made his most decisive move to date. An individual who shares the pope's simplicity of life and philosophy of externality, looking outward to service in the world rather than looking inward at the centrality of the church in Rome, Archbishop Parolin is sure to guide an active and valuable engagement by the Holy See in world affairs. He is truly the diplomat's diplomat.

In the short term, the strategic value of America's relationship with the Holy See may not always be apparent, but in the long term it is of great potential value. Most saliently, in both short and long terms, the pope is in a unique position to mediate between the secular west and the Islamic east: to put pressure on secular democracies to cherish fundamental values, and to persuade fundamentalist regimes to better appreciate freedom's virtues. As Benedict XVI suggested in speeches during his 2006 trip to Germany, the gap between the Western secularized nations and those nations that remain theocratic is wider than ever. The pope, a neutral sovereign of the Christian West, has a unique capacity (as demonstrated by his success in securing the release of the British sailors from Iran) to speak to Islamic nations. Muslims may vehemently disagree with him at times, but many respect him as a man of God. Pope Francis, with his disarming candor and informality, may be able to take the message of reason and religion, of secularism and fanaticism, to a broader audience and deeper understanding than ever.

The word pontiff is derived from the Latin word for bridge—*pons*—and aptly so. Few men alive are better suited to bridge the great divide than the pope.

★ ★ ★

An immediate goal of the church in the Middle East, where Christianity was born centuries before Islam became the region's predominant religion, is to promote the rights of Catholics whose safety, security, and religious freedom is threatened. In standing up for religious and cultural minorities, the church carries the torch of liberty into places darkened by repression and violence. The Holy See is also a strong proponent, like the United States, of a two-state solution in Israel. Not only would such an arrangement between Israelis and Palestinians do much for peace in the region, it would also help protect and preserve the holy sites of Bethlehem and Nazareth, which mean at least as much to Christians as they do to Jews or Muslims. The Holy See has played a little known but significant role in attempting to broker peace in the Middle East.

Looking beyond the Middle East, there are many areas of the world in these early years of the twenty-first century where the Catholic Church, especially if backed by American goodwill, can make a positive impact. One of the most important of these is Africa, where the pope, whether Francis or his successor, will likely be an important moderating influence in the twenty-first century.

Islam remains the dominant organized religion in much of Africa, but Christianity is a close second, and Catholicism is deeply rooted. In the twentieth century, the Catholic population in Africa grew from less than 2 million to 130 million. Today, according to some estimates, as many as 185 million Catholics live on the continent, and countries like Uganda and Nigeria are overflowing with seminarians and priests. This is a bright spot for the church. It's also good news for Africa, where the church has given great material and spiritual aid to end poverty, illiteracy, disease, and war. *Caritas Internationalis*, the Catholic charity organization, is a leading and necessary presence in humanitarian emergencies in Darfur, the Democratic Republic of Congo, and Zimbabwe, among many other countries. As noted earlier, Catholic organizations provide roughly 25 percent of all AIDS treatment and care throughout the world; in some parts of Africa, the proportion is closer to 100 percent.

Neither the good works nor the faith of Catholics is a panacea to the tribalism and despotism that too often plague Africa. Sadly, Catholics, even Catholic priests, participated on both sides of the Rwandan massacres in the 1990s. But the church has made great strides in establishing a unified collective vision that offers a spiritual alternative to extreme Islam and other forms of radicalism: a message of peace, unity, and charity that shows Africa a path into the future.

Latin America, where Catholicism has been entrenched for centuries, presents a very different set of challenges and opportunities, but the Vatican can have an important impact here as well, especially after the installation of Pope Francis. An Argentinian of Italian Ancestry, Francis is perfect bridge from Rome to Latin America. For the moment, the future status of the church in the region remains an open question. Will Latin Americans continue to leave the church for Protestant evangelical sects, as they have over the last several decades, or will they return to the fold? Shortly before Benedict XVI's resignation, Cardinal Theodore McCarrick, the retired archbishop of Washington and an expert on Latin America, told me that the region must be the focus of the church's pastoral mission in years to come, to "reignite" the faith. The election of Francis suggests that many other cardinals agree with him.

In decades past, the Latin American Church has often been associated with domestic politics, first on the right and then on the left. Occasionally, local churches have supported governments that are democratic in name but repressive in practice. But now a new chapter is opening in the history of the Latin American Church. Foregoing politics and leading through moral principles and theology, the church can reevangelize and enrich the lives of those Latin Americans who have been alienated from the church and who feel forgotten by the power structures and economic progress of their countries. Latin Americans will benefit in turn, as will the interests of the United States.

We can see a recent, poignant example of the good the church can do in the successful  mediation and negotiation of a truce among rival gangs in El Salvador in March 2012. Working together with a former FMLN deputy, Raul Mijango, Salvadorian Biship Colindres, and the papal nuncio to Salvador, Luigi Pezzuto, accomplished what had theretofore been impossible despite many efforts of civil authorities and NGOs. Archbishop Pezzuto credited the successful building of trust and openness to the church's authority "based on two pillars," the pastoral and the humanitarian.

As noted earlier, several Latin American countries have evolved away from freedom and respect for individual rights and liberties despite the existence of an ostensibly democratic process. The ability of the United States to affect change in some of these countries is very limited. We no longer have embassies in Venezuela, Bolivia, or Ecuador, each having expelled our ambassadors as *persona non grata*, and we have not had an ambassador in Cuba since President Eisenhower broke off diplomatic relations with Fidel Castro in January 1961. The church can be a moderating influence in these countries and, as it was in Nicaragua at the time of Pope John Paul II's visit in 1983, a force for change and voice for freedom of religion. This has certainly been the case in Venezuela the last few years.

As for Cuba, change will come sooner or later. The Cuban people may well seek freedom and a more democratic regime. Here, too, the Holy See will have important opportunities to promote and shape the future. The Cuban revolution, beginning in 1959, was hard on the local Catholic Church. The Castro government confiscated church property, closed Catholic schools, and jailed clergy. Catholics fought back, but in the end most dissidents were imprisoned or fled the country, or learned to practice their faith privately, away from the prying eyes of Cuba's government. A policy of state-enforced atheism was finally revoked in 1992, and in 1998 the Cuban Catholic Church was revitalized by a visit from Pope John Paul II, a watershed moment that brought Catholics back into the mainstream. Pope Benedict XVI made his own trip to Cuba in the spring of 2012, speaking before crowds of tens of thousands in Revolution square. Cuba today is largely Catholic; the church estimates that 60–70 percent of Cubans are believers, including some members of the ruling Communist party.

The Catholic Church maintains a nuanced relationship with the Cuban government, staying true to its mission and values on the one hand, not rashly provoking the government on the other. There are Cuban dissidents and Cuban Americans who believe that Cardinal Jaime Ortega, archbishop of Havana, has been too compliant with the Castro government, in contrast to those heroic Cold War Eastern European prelates—like Karol Wojtyla, the future John Paul II—who stood up to their nation's despots. Likewise, many people regret that while he was in Cuba, Pope Benedict XVI did not meet with *Las Damas en Blanca* (the Ladies in White), a group of wives, mothers, and other women who formed in 2003 to protest the imprisonment of political dissidents.

But if the Cuban Church has acquiesced in some circumstances, it has hardly been silent or inactive. Cardinal Ortega helped negotiate the release of dozens of political prisoners in 2009 and 2010, and the church has used its publications to air social problems in Cuba, including articles that are frankly critical of the government. On a very practical level, the archdiocese of Havana, in collaboration with a Spanish university, has begun offering graduate courses in business to help Cubans transition to a free market economy, while Caritas-Cuba works to provide much needed pharmaceuticals and medical equipment. Perhaps its most important role will come in the future: the Cuban Catholic Church, as the de facto alternative to the Communist party—as the only organized social institution with the infrastructure and moral authority to act independently of the state—will be a critical institution to lead and guide the transition to a free Cuba.

Looking deeper into the future, perhaps the most dynamic evolution of the church will occur in another communist country, China. Catholics remain a small fraction of the Chinese population but are likely to grow in numbers and influence in the coming century. In some ways, the situation in China is an anomalous throwback, requiring the church to fight battles settled long ago in most of the world regarding, for example, the right of investiture. On the whole, the challenge is much as it is in other parts of the world. The church is pressing for religious freedom where civil rights are in short supply. The Chinese government is keeping a tight handle on the church, but the Holy See represents a patient yet persistent voice for freedom of religion. As the American founders understood—and as the Chinese rulers evidently fear—oppression ends where freedom of religion begins.

Dealing with China will require all of the Vatican's diplomatic ingenuity. Not only must it find accommodation with the government, but it will also have to reconcile the state sanctioned "official" church with the underground church and, finally, appease Taiwanese Catholics. In the end, though, I suspect that both China and the church will make each other stronger.

★  ★  ★

There are limits to the church's ability to influence the behavior of societies. It cannot force its will, having no economic or military leverage. Nor is it likely to motivate great spontaneous uprisings, in the manner of revolutionary movements, since its message is essentially conservative, grounded in thousands of years of tradition. It cannot even dependably deliver political blocs to election booths, since Catholics are found all along the political spectrum. But it is precisely in these failings that its greatness lies. The church appeals above and beyond might, money, or political power to a deeper recognition in human beings of what is good and right. The influence of the church springs from the same well that gives it endurance. It stands for something—the same thing every day, every year, every place. Its message is universal through time and through space.

The Catholic Church is at a crossroads. Challenges bear down from all directions in the forms of secularization and scandals. The message of the Catholic Church is one of hope—for peace, charity, love, and the good news of Christianity—but not a lot of good news reaches the Vatican these days. Certainly not from the Western media, which lavishes coverage on papal transitions but otherwise seldom carries a positive story about the church. This is understandably frustrating for the vast majority of Catholic prelates, who give their lives to serving God as best they can, for the church seems at times to be under siege. Both friends and enemies of the church might recall the lesson that Napoleon and Stalin each learned in his own way. As the author and historian Hilaire Belloc put it, "The Church is a perpetually defeated thing that always outlives her conquerors." There is much good still to come from the church, especially in areas where the Holy See and the United States find themselves in alignment.

As discussed in earlier pages, the United States was born of many of the same convictions that define the Catholic Church: a belief in laws that transcend human power and caprice—those God-given "unalienable rights" on which Thomas Jefferson based his argument in the Declaration of Independence. The relationship between the Holy See and the United States is a story of two powers failing for years to recognize what was best in the other and how much they shared in common. Only recently has the church shaken off its monarchial fears of democracy and come to embrace the very values it inspired in United States; likewise, only recently has the American public rejected the prejudices, so contrary to American ideals, that poisoned its view of the church. Having each gained from the other, we are now in a position to recognize what is best in ourselves, and to appreciate our mutual interests and objectives. Where the Holy See possesses leverage and tools unavailable to the United States—the unique "soft power" of a sovereign lacking territorial or hegemonic agendas—the United States should encourage and assist the Holy See in putting forth its message. Likewise, as the only nation founded upon the unalienable rights of humans, including the right to unfettered religious freedom, the United States merits the support and cooperation of the Holy See in advancing these shared values throughout the world.

# AFTERWORD: POPE FRANCIS
# AND THE GLOBAL VATICAN

"You all know that the duty of the Conclave was to give a bishop to Rome. It seems that my brother Cardinals have come almost to the ends of the Earth to get him . . . but here we are."

By these few words in his initial speech from St. Peter's Basilica, Pope Francis began a new era at the Holy See: the world's first pope from the New World, and from the Southern Hemisphere as well. For an organization steeped in continuity and stability, the election of Pope Francis has awakened many new voices around the world. It has generated much enthusiasm and optimism globally, and has brought a new perspective to the Holy See itself.

From the very beginning, Pope Francis took a different tack, referring to St. Ignatius of Antioch's view of Rome as a source of charity rather than control, and of himself solely as Bishop of Rome, not pope.

In these first two years of his pontificate, Pope Francis has pursued Holy See diplomacy in continuity with his predecessors and the longstanding principles of protecting human dignity and religious freedom, albeit with some occasional misunderstanding. His initial forays into social justice and capitalism were often misquoted, or taken out of context. And a recent reference to forms of justifiable retaliation for harsh versions of free expression quickly called for Vatican nuancing and spin control. As noted earlier, the appointment of Cardinal Pietro Parolin as Secretary of State was an enlightened one. He has been exceptionally effective in shaping the diplomatic message in circumstances like this, in making sure, for example, that the visit of President Obama left the intended message from the Holy See, and in leading the behind the scenes intermediation between Cuba and the United States.

The pope waded into the issue of how the world should deal with radicalized Islamic terrorists on his return from a papal visit to South Korea in August of 2014, saying that, with backing of the international community, "it is right to stop an unjust aggressor." His words were amplified by the papal nuncio to the United Nations, Archbishop Silvano Tomasi, to the effect that "all the force that is necessary to stop this evil and this tragedy" is justified under the UN charter. In this respect the pope went further than anyone had to date, implicitly suggesting that a military response to Islamic terrorism would be a "just war" under Vatican doctrine. He has reaffirmed the position of Pope Benedict in offering clear and unequivocal support to the position that this terror is a war that the modern world must confront by denouncing clearly its perpetrators, on one hand, and working with Muslim scholars and leaders on the other to find "developing" constructions of Koranic teachings which align with modern values and respect for humanity.

Pope Francis used three papal visits in 2014 to reinforce these messages: May to Jordan and Israel, September to Albania and November to Turkey.

First, the trip to Jordan and Israel: The pope broke new ground by beginning his trip in Jordan, affirming King Abdullah's critical role in the search for peaceful solutions in the Middle East and underscoring Jordan's history of religious tolerance and pluralism. He then went to Bethlehem, which has become a walled off enclave surrounded on three sides by Israeli controlled lands, comparing this situation to the Jewish Ghettos in Warsaw during Nazi occupation. Later, in addition to calling on the grand mufti of the Al Aqsa Mosque, he invited Israeli president Shimon Peres and Palestinian Authority President Mahmoud Abbas to join him in Rome to pray together. What better way to promote interreligious dialogue than this?

His next trip was to Albania, formerly the most repressed and poorest of all the Warsaw Pact nations, under the government of Enver Hoxha, and now a model of a successful coalition government among Catholics, Orthodox Christians and Muslims—embracing free enterprise and the opportunities which capitalism affords society. Illustrative of this new identity, the government of Albania has named a street after President George W. Bush. The pope reflected that "the climate of respect and mutual trust between Catholics, Orthodox and Muslims is a precious gift to the country."

While in this eastern outpost of Europe, dismissing threats which had been made against his personal safety, Pope Francis also took another opportunity to condemn the "distortion and manipulation" of religion by extremists like ISIL.

Lastly, the pope followed Pope Benedict's footsteps in visiting Turkey and praying with the Grand Mufti of Istanbul in the Blue Mosque, again embracing the promise of interreligious cooperation. He also called for Muslim leaders to speak up against the violence which has threatened to pervert the message of Islam, building carefully upon the case articulated by his predecessor, Pope Benedict, in his address at Regensburg in September 2006. Just as many Muslim leaders came together after Regensburg and spoke up about the need for Islam to come to terms with life and the cultural mores of the 21st century, so have numerous clerics and political leaders from the Muslim world been recently closing ranks and speaking up clearly in opposition to religiously-linked terrorism and violence perpetrated by ISIL, Al-Qaeda cells, and the like around the word.

Grand Mufti Abdul-Aziz, the leading Muslim cleric in Saudi Arabia, spoke out clearly against radicalism in response to King Abdullah's public call for all clerics to raise their voices on this issue. While it is true that King Abdullah visited Pope Benedict in the aftermath of Regensburg, this is the clearest expression of Saudi opposition to radicalism to date.

In late-2014, some two dozen American Muslim leaders met in Washington with officials from the Department of Homeland Security and spoke out against Islamic terrorism and the recruitment of young Muslim Americans to extremism. More recently, in a direct reference for the need to develop "soft power" solutions to the conflict, the Minister of Religious Affairs for Jordan, Hayil Abdelhafeez Dawoud, told the *Wall Street Journal* that "to fight terrorism, we need to fight its ideology. It can't be solved militarily."

The Holy See's leadership has found resonance in many parts of the world. In early 2015, Egyptian President Abdel-Fattah el-Sisi challenged Muslim leaders to confront radicalism in the faith. "We are in need of a religious revolution. . . . You, imams, are responsible before Allah. The entire world, I say it again, the entire world is waiting for your next move . . . because this umma [Islamic world] is being torn, it is being destroyed, it is being lost—and it is being lost by our own hands."

Perhaps there exists an analogy between the growing number of calls for religious institutions to weigh in on the Islamic terror threat and the effort that President Truman undertook at the beginning of the Cold War to catalyze a concerted opposition to Communism among the major religions of the world. At that time, among the major Christian Churches only the Catholic Church was united, unambiguous and forceful in opposing everything for which Communism stood. There was an unfortunate reluctance and cognitive dissonance among many protestant leaders to oppose communism. In fact, some embraced it. Ironically, the staunchly Baptist President Truman was consigned to rely on the Catholic Church to be the tip of the spear in this "soft power" diplomatic effort.[1]

In his papal trips and pronouncements, therefore, Pope Francis continues to reinforce the message Pope Benedict laid out in Regensburg in 2006: that religiously-inspired violence has no place in the twenty-first century; that Islam needs to come to terms with this reality; and that the teachings of the Koran must be developed, or interpreted, in a manner which is aligned with modern culture and values of human life.

Once again building upon the legacy of Pope Benedict, this pope has continued the Holy See diplomacy of opposing secularism, or as Pope Francis has called it, "materialism," in the Western world. Speaking to the European Parliament in November 2014 the pope described Europe as "elderly and haggard . . . a grandmother, no longer fertile and vibrant."

In all of this the pope has continued to advance the fundamental themes characteristic of Holy See diplomacy in recent years—oppose any and all abrogations of human rights—whether by Communists in Poland or the purveyors of radicalized Islamic terrorism, seek to insure that all people enjoy religious freedom and related freedoms, and work to create conditions wherein all people share in the basic human dignity which stems from having gainful employment, providing for their family and contributing to the betterment of their communities. It is noteworthy that when his comments on social justice were mistaken to assume he opposed capitalism, the pope made clear that he was not calling for a "welfare mentality."

The influence of Holy See diplomacy continues to be felt in other areas of the world as well—as in the role played by Pope Francis and Holy See diplomats in successfully convening the United States and Cuba, resulting in a historic shift in U.S.–Cuba relations. Though it remains to be seen whether this incipient dialogue will result is a good bargain for the United States, creating a platform for the rule of law, protection of a free press and religion freedom, assuring internet access to the world, and that Cuban workers' wages are paid directly to them by their employers, rather than being intermediated by the state, there can be no doubt that the Holy See has played an indispensable role in stimulating dialogue and creating conditions for a possible diplomatic solution in Cuba.

Apart from his diplomatic and theological work, Pope Francis has pursued internal reforms aimed at improving the efficiency and effectiveness of decision-making of the Roman Curia and at reorganizing the Vatican Bank to respond to procedural deficiencies which in part led to the "Vatileaks" disclosures in 2013. The fact that the pope comes from the new world, and looks at the historic governance architectures with a clean perspective, has been invaluable in moving these initiatives forward. Consistent with his desire, as expressed during the Albania trip, to reach out to the "peripheries" of the world he has broadened the College of Cardinals and has named twenty-five new Cardinals from small regions of the developing world.

In 2015, Pope Francis will make important visits to Latin America, including Bolivia and Ecuador, countries with large indigenous populations, and in September to the United States, where he will address the United Nations as his predecessors have, and make an unprecedented address to a Joint Session of the U.S. Congress. While the principal objective of the trip is to attend the World Council on the Family in Philadelphia, building upon the recent Extraordinary Synod on the Family in Rome, these two addresses offer major diplomatic opportunities to advance the Holy See's vision for a more just and peaceful world, and thereby once again demonstrate the effectiveness of its "soft power" approach.

The Holy See's influence and reach is perhaps more visible in Latin America than in any other region. With highly Catholic populations, Latin leaders have routinely sought the approval of the Holy See for their actions, and have often turned to the Holy See to mediate regional disputes. From the Treaty of Tordesillas which was sanctioned by the Church in 1506 through the Beagle Channel dispute of the 1970s and beyond, the Holy See has an established track record of mediation in Latin America. As conditions continue to deteriorate in Venezuela, for example, both the Union of South American Nations (UNASUR), a coalition of South American states, and Corina Machado, a Venezuelan dissident, have called upon Pope Francis to mediate between the sharply contending factions that threaten to tear the country apart. With wisdom derived from centuries of experience and its characteristic long term diplomatic perspective, the Holy See has thus far determined, discretely and without fanfare, that the conditions to negotiate in good faith are not present, and remains on the sidelines.

In just two short years, Pope Francis has accomplished many things both diplomatically and regarding internal Church organization. His new-world openness and ease of communication bring promise that he will continue to broaden and deepen the fundamental Holy See diplomatic message and positively influence world events.

# ACKNOWLEDGMENTS

Writing this book has been a fascinating journey, and I owe a debt of gratitude to the many people who have served as my teachers and guides along the way. I am appreciative beyond words for the valuable time and wisdom that a number of American Church leaders shared with me, including Cardinal Timothy Dolan, archbishop of New York; Cardinal Donald Wuerl, archbishop of Washington; and Cardinal Theodore McCarrick, former archbishop of Washington. I also greatly appreciate the encouragement and support of Bishop William Murphy of Rockville Center, New York, and Bishop Frank Dewane of Venice, Florida.

In Rome and Vatican City, many leaders of the Curia and the Holy See diplomatic corps kindly met with me and offered information, perspective, and advice. My thanks to Cardinal Leonardo Sandri, formerly nuncio to Venezuela and *Sostituto* in the Secretariat of State, and currently prefect of the Congregation for the Oriental Churches; to Cardinal Jean-Louis Tauran, former secretary for Relations with States and current president of the Pontifical Council for Interreligious Dialogue; to Cardinal Bernard Law, archbishop emeritus of Boston; to Cardinal Renato Martino, president emeritus of the Pontifical Council for Justice and Peace; to Cardinal William Levada, former prefect of the Congregation for the Doctrine of the Faith; and to Cardinal James Harvey, former prefect of the Papal Household. In Warsaw, Archbishop Celestino Migliore, now serving as the papal nuncio to Poland and formerly posted at the United Nations in New York, spent an afternoon answering many questions about Holy See diplomacy. Thank you, all.

This project began in January 2011 at the Vatican's nunciature in Washington, D.C., where I interviewed Archbishop Pietro Sambi, then serving as the nuncio to the United States. (Sadly, Archbishop Sambi passed away the following summer.) Monsignor Peter Wells, the most senior American in the Vatican's Secretariat of State, was terrifically helpful in explaining the Holy See to his fellow Oklahoman. Long before I began this book, while still serving as ambassador, I gained insight and knowledge in conversations with Archbishop Claudio Maria Celli, former undersecretary for the Relations with States and current president of the Pontifical Council for Social Communication, and with Archbishop Tommaso Caputo, the man in charge of the diplomatic corps accredited to the Holy See during my tenure, now serving the Holy See as nuncio to Malta and Libya.

On recent trips to Rome I had the good fortune to interview knowledgeable friends like Prince Hugo Windisch-Graetz, an ambassador of the Knights of Malts diplomatic service and a Gentleman of His Holiness; Fr. James Grummer, SJ, of the Jesuit Curia; and Monsignor Charlie Burns, former historian of the Vatican Secret Archives and currently a Canon of St. Peter's Basilica. Claudio Betti and Cardinal Vincenzo Paglia, both leaders in the Community of Sant'Egidio, gave me their thoughtful perspective over a pleasant lunch at their headquarters in Trastevere. Memorable and candid discussions with two veteran Holy See ambassadors, George Poulides of Cyprus and Nikolay Sadchikov of Russia, added to my understanding of the diplomatic corps from a global perspective. Jorge Dezcallar de Mazarredo, who served as Spain's ambassador to the Holy See and subsequently to the United States, lent his significant experience and insight to our effort. Our good friend Francis Campbell, former UK ambassador to the Holy See and now serving as head of the Policy Unit, Foreign and Commonwealth Office in London, helped make our time in Rome pleasurable and memorable and assisted me on several occasions in preparing this book. Also, my close friend from El Salvador, Francisco R. R. de Sola, was a great help concerning events in Central America.

I am likewise indebted to a number of scholars who guided me in these explorations, including Fr. Thomas Reese, SJ, who was also one of the very first people I went to see when embarking on this project; Fr. Gerald Fogarty, SJ, of the University of Virginia; Fr. Drew Christiansen, SJ, former editor-in-chief of *America Magazine*; and America's preeminent papal scholar, George Weigel, who spoke with me early on and then reviewed the book in draft form, offering advice and corrections. The book was also read in draft by Fr. Tim Scully, CSC, founder of the Alliance for Catholic Education at the University of Notre Dame, and Monsignor Dan Mueggenborg, formerly the vice rector of the Pontifical North American College in Rome and now at Christ the King parish in Tulsa, Oklahoma. Their efforts saved me from committing numerous errors. Any that remain are mine.

Of course, scholars would be nothing without archives, as I learned in writing this book. The staffs at the three Vatican archives where I spent a number of happy hours buried in old papers were all helpful and patient. I especially thank Archbishop Dominique Mamberti, the secretary for the Holy See's Relations with States, and Monsignor Ettore Balestrero, current nuncio to Colombia and former undersecretary for Relations with States, for organizing such open and complete access. My thanks also go to Georgetown University's Fr. John P. Langan, SJ, for leading us to the Woodstock Theological Center Library, and to Fr. Leon Hooper, SJ, senior fellow and library director at Woodstock, for guiding us to Vatican records uniquely possessed by America's oldest Jesuit university.

Peter Martin, our political officer at the embassy during my ambassadorship, and Michael Napolitano, my special assistant at the embassy, helped me recall many events and facts and lent significant detail to the project. I was fortunate to consult with Michael Sulick, former director of the U.S. National Clandestine Service, on intelligence activities during the Cold War. The veteran American diplomat, John Negroponte, who served as U.S. ambassador to the United Nations under President George W. Bush—and then later as the first director of National Intelligence—not only read the manuscript and offered valuable advice, but also honored this book by writing its foreword. I am deeply thankful to this brilliant American diplomat who has been an inspiration to me and many other American ambassadors over the years.

I also want to thank Dina Powell, head of presidential personnel for George W. Bush, and Michael Meece, chief of staff at President Bush's office in Dallas. Therese Burch, who advanced President Bush's 2007 visit to the pope, kindly gave her time helping recollect the details of that episode. The author Jim Rasenberger assisted me in shaping the book, and Andrew Steele provided research and editing. Both were introduced to me by friends at the Center for the Study of the Presidency and Congress, the think tank led by Dr. David Abshire, a former ambassador to NATO, Special Counselor to President Reagan (during Iran-Contra), and cofounder of the Center for Strategic and International Studies. Dr. Abshire first encouraged me to start this project, gave me much support and advice, and discussed it with me on many occasions.

The book had the good fortune to land in the hands of Jed Lyons, CEO and president of Rowman and Littlefield Publishers, and his excellent staff, including Jon Sisk, senior executive editor; Benjamin Verdi, assistant editor; and Elaine McGarraugh, senior production editor. I also want to thank Sharon Cherry in our Tulsa office and Mary Stein in our Naples office for their efforts in helping keep this project, and many others, on track.

Of course, none of this would have happened were it not for President George W. Bush, who has given so much to our country and much to me and our family, including the unique opportunity to serve as his ambassador to the Holy See.

Our sons, Larry and Michael, and our daughter, Kathleen, made Rome feel like home during our time there, and made our experience truly a happy one. My wife and partner, Kathleen, supported completely my work as ambassador in Rome and has given her invaluable support and advice to this project. She encouraged me to write this book, offered her keen insights all along the way, and represented herself, our family, and President Bush capably while we were serving our country.

# NOTES

Published books are identified here by author and page numbers; see the bibliography for more information. In the case of periodicals, archival materials, and all unpublished sources, full citations are provided here.

## ABBREVIATIONS

APP American Presidency Project: papers of presidents available at www.presidency.ucsb.edu

AUTH. INT. interviews conducted by Francis Rooney. (For a full list of interviewees, see the bibliography.)

CNS *Catholic New Service* at www.catholicnews.com

FOIA/CIA Generated by the Central Intelligence Agency, released under Freedom of Information Act, and accessed at www.foia.cia.gov.

FRUS *Foreign Relations of the United States*

NYT *The New York Times*

VATICAN.VA Website of the Holy See, with collected papal papers and utterances, at www.vatican.va

## PROLOGUE

xiv. "He is at heart a teacher": AUTH. INT. with Father Reese, January 2011.

xiv. Of approximately 65 million American Catholics: Center for the Applied Research in the Apostolate (CARA), "Frequently Requested Church Statistics: Catholic Population (The Official Catholic Directory)," via cara.georgetown.edu. See also "Sunday Morning: Deconstructing Catholic Mass Attendance in the 1950s and Now," *1964* (research blog for CARA), posted March 21, 2011. And see "Church Struggles with Change," *USA Today*, November 7, 2004.

xiv. A similar wave of secularism: "Catholic Church Withers in Europe," *Boston Globe*, May 2, 2005.

xv. "Congress will probably never send": Quoted in Pfeffer, 302.

xvi. The historian Arnold Toynbee: see Toynbee, 401–404.

xvii. to borrow a phrase coined by the political scientist Joseph Nye: see Nye's *Soft Power*.

xvii. "congruence on values": Kissinger, *On China*, 266.

xviii. "the meticulous preparation": Kissinger, *On China*, 273.

xviii. The church's ban on artificial birth control: *Reuters*, April 13, 2011.

xix. The pope even has his own Twitter account: NYT, December 3, 2012.


## PART I: FAITH AND REVOLUTION

## CHAPTER 1: THE GREATEST EVILS TO BE FEARED

3. "By reputation, the United States": Novak, 85.

5. "Jesuit or Ecclesiastical person": O'Toole, 39.

5. "popish recusants": Ellis, 110–111.

5. "mutual love and Amity": Dolan, *The American Catholic Experience*, 69, 73.

5. The persecution of Catholics varied: Ellis, 115; Pfeffer, 91; Dolan, *The American Catholic Experience*, 84–85.

6. "You must not imagine": Shea, 62–63.

6. John Carroll was born: see biographies of John Carroll by Shea and Guilday for detailed descriptions of Carroll's youth. See also Birzer, 3–4.

6. The school offered an extraordinary education: Birzer, 3–6; Guilday, 22.

6. "Most of our Merylanders": Birzer, 4.

7. Given events on the political horizon: Birzer, 11–15.

7. By the early 1770s, Charles was caught up: Ellis, 128–129; Dolan, *The American Catholic Experience*, 96–97.

7. John Carroll took a very different route: see Shea, 32–38.

7. "the papacy's most shameful hour": Duffy, 246.

7. "I am not, and perhaps never shall be": Shea, 39; see also Guilday, 37, 43, 57.

8. We have to imagine: Shea, 46; Dolan, *The American Catholic Experience*, 103; see also *Catholic Encyclopedia* entry on John Carroll.

8. One auspicious sign: Birzer, 96.

9. "impiety, bigotry, persecution": quoted in Michael Sean-Winters, "Anti-Catholicism and the Founders," *National Catholic Reporter*, September 1, 2010.

9. "poor wretches fingering their beads": Ellis, 132–133.

9. "the greatest of evils": McSorley, 729.

9. "that ridiculous and childish custom": Ellis, 136; see also Beneke, 279–280.

10. In a letter to Abigail: Birzer, 107.

10. "distinguished and unexpected honour": Guilday, 96–97.

10. "I find I grow daily more feeble": Guilday, 103.

11. Now, one by one, the former colonies: Beneke, 277–279; Ellis, 137.

11. "Thoughtful persons could not fail": Pfeffer, 97.

12. "History, I believe, furnishes no example": Muñoz, 100.

12. The renowned Medievalist: see Brian Tierney, *The Idea of Natural Rights: Studies on Natural Rights, Natural Law and Church Law 1150–1625* (Atlanta: Scholars Press, 1997). See also Cornell Law Review, accessed at www.lawschool.cornell.edu/research/cornell-law-review/upload/Reid.pdf. See also Novak, 83–85.

12. Jefferson's words *are* strikingly similar: Rev. John C. Rager, "Catholic Sources and the Declaration of Independence." *Catholic Mind* Vol. 28, no. 13 (July 8, 1930).

13. "the deepest bias": Jenkins, 23.

## CHAPTER 2: THE LAST POPE

15. "When we reflect": Hales, *The Catholic Church*, 17.

15. There is an intriguing story: Illing, 36.

17. "when non-Catholic states": Graham, 37.

17. "a venerable anachronism": Bokenkotter, 277.

19. "a subject which increases in time and develops": Pope Benedict XVI's *Address to the Roman Curia* (December 22, 2005), VATICAN.VA.

19. "the basic principles stay the same": AUTH. INT. with Cardinal Harvey.

19. "The Holy See, which enjoys international juridical status": Cardinal Jean-Louis Tauran lecture: "The Presence of the Holy See in International Organizations" (April 22, 2002), VATICAN.VA.

19. "the science and art": Graham, 10.

20: "if you don't know truth you cannot build peace": AUTH. INT. with Archbishop Sambi.

20. "the art of creating and maintaining the international order": speech by Archbishop Giovanni Battista Montini (future Paul VI) at the 250th anniversary of the founding of the Pontifical Ecclesiastical Academy (April 25, 1951), VATICAN.VA.

20. "It is true that the aims of Church and State": Pope Paul VI's *Sollicitudo Ominum Ecclesiarum* (June 24, 1969), VATICAN.VA.

21. "lever of opinion": Duffy, 262.

21. "Deal with the Pope": Graham, 24.

21. "How many divisions has the Pope?": Graham, 24.

21. "feverishly engaged in a race": Manhattan, 9–10.

22. "When they are free to render": Van Doren, 91.

23. "Western Christendom . . . was now composed": McSorley, 137.

24. "Descend and relinquish": Bokenkotter, 117. Re: Gregory VII, see also Duffy, *Saints and Sinners*, 121–128.

25. "nothing less than a complete revolution": MacCaffrey, 293. See also Hales, *The Catholic Church in the Modern World*, 19.

27. "You are not ignorant": Guilday, 172.

27. "Resolved, that Doctor Franklin be desired to notify": Propoganda Fide Archives, Sc America Centrale, Vol. I, pos. 47, folio 407; see also Pfeffer, 121.

27. Franklin was not above giving private advice: Dolan, *The American Catholic Experience*, 105.

27. In the summer of 1784: Dolan, *The American Catholic Experience*, 105.

28. The French Revolution did not appear: see Hales, *The Catholic Church*, 33–50, for an excellent account of the Catholic Church in France during the Revolution.

29. "As the supreme head of a religion": Graham, 39.

30. "A man can die anywhere": Duffy, 259.

30. Some prognosticators saw: Duffy, 259; Kelly, 302.

## CHAPTER 3: RETURN TO ROME

31. "Does he imagine": Hales, *The Catholic Church*, 70.

32. One of Napoleon's first official acts: Duffy, 262.

32. "I wished to see you all gathered": Neilsen, 219.

32. "France has had her eyes opened": quoted in Norwich, 383.

32. "Of all the dispositions": George Washington's *Farewell Address*, September 19, 1796, APP.

33. "My political method": Hales, *The Catholic Church*, 56.

33. "Go to Rome": Bokenkotter, 290–291.

33. "There has seldom": Hales, *The Catholic Church*, 57.

33. "If Henry VIII, who had not a twentieth part": Neilsen, 238–239.

34. Napoleon and his retinue poured: Englund, 184–185.

34. Accompanied by six cardinals: Hales, *The Catholic Church*, 62–63.

35. "Nobody thought of the Pope": Duffy, 267. See also Hales, *The Catholic Church*, 64.

35. "Your Holiness is the sovereign of Rome": Norwich, 385.

35. The pope bore his captivity stoically: Duffy, 269–271; Hales, *The Catholic Church*, 67; Kelly, 303.

36. "imbecile old man": Hales, 67.

37. All of Rome: Duffy, 272; Neilsen, 340.

37. As Europe's rulers met: see Bokenkotter, 292, for discussion of Congress of Vienna.

37. Carroll himself witnessed: Guilday, 808.

37. Carroll also had one odd but not insignificant brush: Shea, 511. See also the "History" of the Patterson-Bonaparte Collection at the Maryland Historical Society: www.mdhs.org/findingaid/patterson-bonaparte-collection-pp70.

38. The shift in Carroll's attitude: Dolan, *The American Catholic Experience*, 112–117; Glazier and Shelley, entry for John Carroll, 226.

38. "anarchy and insurrection": Dolan, *The American Catholic Experience*, 117.

38. It was still a small church: O'Toole, 43.

39. Charles Carroll was still robust: Birzer, 189–194.

39. "fervent and zealous in the belief": Tocqueville quoted in Massa and Osborne, 42–43.

39. Such sentiments were fanned: DePalma, 66; O'Toole, 90.

39. More damaging than the pamphlets: regarding Lyman Beecher's campaign against the Catholic Church, see DePalma, 54, 76, 82–83. See also Rugoff, 152–153.

39. "moral destiny" of the nation: DePalma, 76.

39. "arouse themselves and shake off the drowsy stupor": DePalma, 76, 83.


# PART II: THE MODERN WORLD

## CHAPTER 4: PIO NONO AND THE TURNING POINT

43. "If, with Shakespeare, we were to choose": Hales, *Pio Nono*, ix.

43. Gregory XVI . . . despised newness: Kelly, 307.

43. For his papal appellation: Hales, *Pio Nono*, 19.

44. Pius was a natural *bon vivant*: Hales, *Pio Nono*, 18; Schofield, 112. See also *St. Louis Medical Review*, edited by Clarence Loeb and Albert Miller. Vol. 49 (April 23, 1904), 262.

44. Pius IX seemed determined to change this: see Hales, *Pio Nono*, 57–68; Kelly, 309.

45. The United States was not immune: Stock, *United States Ministers*, xxi–xxii; D'Agostino, 19. For quotes by Lester and Fuller, see D'Agostino, 26.

45. "You may recollect": Stock, *United States Ministers*, xxii; Moore, *Works of James Buchanan*, 4.

46. "interesting political events": Polk's third annual message, December 7, 1847, APP.

46. Inevitably, perhaps, the debate in Congress: for the transcript, see *The Congressional Globe*, March 8, 1848, 439–445. See also the footnote on page 104 of Leo Francis Stock's "The United States at the Court of Pius IX" in *The Catholic Historical Review* Vol. 9, No. 1 (April, 1923).

47. Secretary Buchanan nominated Jacob L. Martin: see Stock, "The United States at the Court of Pius IX," 103–107.

47. "Tomb of the mighty dead": *Choice Specimens of American Literature and Literary Reader*, Benjamin Nicholas Martin (ed.), 429.

47. "There is one consideration": Buchanan to Martin, April 5, 1848, in Moore, 42.

47. "I am fully aware": Martin to Buchanan, May 1, 1848, in Stock's *United States Ministers*, 5.

48. The truth was that the pope: Riccards, 12–17. Re: change in Pius IX's views, see Hales, *Pio Nono*, 63–69, 74–75.

49. Realizing he had been misunderstood: Hales, *Pio Nono*, 76–77.

49. The unfortunate Jacob Martin: Martin to Buchanan, August 20, 1848, in Stock's *United States Ministers*, 8–15.

49. "Young liberty should not exhaust herself": Martin to Buchanan, Stock's *United States Ministers*, 14.

49. The heat and chaos of Rome: for description of Martin's death, see Hooker to Buchanan, August 26, 1848, in Stock's *United States Ministers*, 15–16.

50. The city had become too dangerous: Hales, *Pio Nono*, 90–94; Bokenkotter, 306; Kelly, 309.

50. In the ecclesiastical realm: Kelly, 309.

50. The number of American Catholics was rising rapidly: Hales, *The Catholic Church*, 157; Crocker, 376.

51. "The Catholic Church . . . opposes everything which favors democracy": McGreevy, 39.

51. "the foe of all progress": McGreevy, 34.

52. A more significant crimp: for a narrative of the Bedini visit, see O'Toole, 86–87; DePalma, 105–107; Franco, 6–9; Feiertag, 74–85.

52. "a blunder from every point of view": quoted in Timothy M. Dolan, "Hence We Cheerfully Sent One Who Should Represent Our Person," *U.S. Catholic Historian* Vol. 12, No. 2, The Apostolic Delegation/Nunciature 1893–1993.

53. Perhaps the strangest episode of anti-Catholic mischief: for an overview of the story of the pope's stone, based on historical newspaper descriptions, see "The Readex Blog" by August Imholtz Jr., posted May 18, 2010, at http://blog.readex.com/the-pope%e2%80%99s-stone-part-one. Also see the National Park Service's history, "Catalogue of Lost, Stolen, Never Sent, or Otherwise Missing Commemorative Stones" at www.nps.gov/wamo/photosmultimedia/upload/WAMO%20Stones%20Section%206.pdf

53. In the fall of 1862, he wrote letters: Feiertag, 111–115.

53. "the papal government never wavered": Stock, "The United States at the Court of Pius IX," *The Catholic Historical Review* Vol. 9, No. 1 (April, 1923), 116.

53. The only evidence: Stock, "The United States at the Court of Pius IX," 116–118. See also Feiertag, 115–125.

53. Davis wrote to Rome in September: Feiertag, 116. The original of J. Davis's letter is in the Vatican Secret Archives.85. "Illustrious and Honorable Sir": Feiertag, 117.

54. Judah P. Benjamin . . . dismissed the letter: Stock, "The United States at the Court of Pius IX" in *The Catholic Historical Review* Vol. 9, No. 1 (April 1923), 117.

54. Jefferson Davis believed he received: *The Papers of Jefferson Davis: June 1865–December 1870*, edited by Lynda Lasswell Crist, et al., Louisiana State University Press, 2008, 162. See also Felicity Allen, 441–442.

54. The perception that the pope favored the Confederacy: McGreevy, 50; Feiertag, 135–137.

54. "The only government in the world": NYT, January 25, 1867. See also Feiertag, 144–165.

54. By the end of the month Congress had voted: *The Congressional Globe*, 39th Congress, 2nd session, 850–851, 882–885.

54. He was "at a loss": the Rufus King correspondence with Sec. of State Seward is in Stock, *United States Ministers*, 426–440.

55. "Rome is about to pass off the stage": quoted in Feiertag, 139.


# CHAPTER 5: THE NEW CONCEPT OF SOVEREIGNTY

57. "What the Pope has already destroyed": Hales, *Pio Nono*, 137.

57. "It was necessary that the whole world": Graham, 176.

57. They filed into St. Peter's: for description of First Vatican Council, see NYT, December 9, 1869; Hales, *Pio Nono*, 296–297; Kertzer, 27; and for names and faces of participants, see "First Vatican Council Photographic Album" from the WRLC Libraries Digital and Special Collections, available online at www.aladin0. wrlc.org/gsdl/collect/vatican/vatican.

58. His first salvo was an extraordinary document: McGreevy, 96–97; Riccards, 23–30.

58. E. E. Y. Hales, while acknowledging the syllabus to be "irritating": Hales, *Pio Nono*, 256. See also Duffy, 296.

59. As the council proceeded: Duffy, 297; for a detailed narrative regarding the issue of infallibility, see Kertzer, 22–32.

59. "monstrous assault on the reason of mankind": Kertzer, 29.

59. "universal monarchy": Graham, 159.

59. "We will not go to Canossa": Duffy, 303.

59. A number of Catholic prelates expressed their own concerns: Kertzer, 25.

59. "This question has already set Europe": Hales, *Pio Nono*, 301.

59. "I am the tradition": Duffy, 299. See also Kertzer, 30–31.

60. "the beauty of inflexibility": Duffy, 305.

60. Sheets of rain ripped: Kertzer, 31; Hales, *Pio Nono*, 309–310.

60. Immediately after the vote, Fitzgerald fell: Hales, *Pio Nono*, 309–310; Duffy, 300.

60. "If the Lord wants me to lose the Papal States": Bokenkotter, 274.

61. The attack began: a detailed description is in Kertzer, 51–58; see also Hales, *Pio Nono*, 315.

61. "The great scandal of the ages is wiped out": O'Toole, 139–140.

61. "monster demonstration": NYT, December 5, 1870.

61. "Pope Pius IX, as simple head": NYT, September 15, 1870; NYT, September 22, 1870.

62. "For one thing": Graham, 179.

62. "it would take a particular kind of obtuseness": George Weigel, "Italy at 50," posted March 17, 2011 on *National Review Online* (www.nationalreview.com).

62. "The supreme head of the Church": Graham, 176.

63. "Never will I accept it": quoted in Hales, *Pio Nono*, 318.

63. When his body was moved: Hales, *Pio Nono*, 330–331; Kelly, 310.

64. "He had the grittiness and determination": AUTH. INT. with Cardinal Dolan.

64. The new pope, born Gioacchino Vincenzo Pecci: Kelly, 311.

65. He was the first pope to allow electricity: Riccards, 36. See also Duffy, 306–307, and Bokenkotter, 331.

65. Otto von Bismarck, who had been waging war: Duffy, 308; Norwich, 418–419.

65. From the United States, meanwhile, came an emissary: NYT, March 31, 1878.

65. "It cannot be called in question": *Immortale Dei: Encyclical of Pope Leo XIII on the Christian Constitution of States* (November 1, 1885), VATICAN.VA.

66. It is a recognized sovereign: see "Vienna Convention on Diplomatic Relations Done at Vienna on 18 April 1961," article 16(3), accessible online at United Nations Treaty Collection at www.treaties.un.org.

66. Even Vatican detractors: Robertson, 94.

66. One legal treatise cited: Duursma, 386.

66. "The distinct legal personality": Duursma, 388.

67. Otto von Bismarck was among those who now saw: McSorley, 811.

67. Leo's name was later raised: NYT, October 23, 1889.

67. "As the Pope has no troops": quoted in Graham, 89.

67. Leo's *Libertas* was another step: *Libertas: Encyclical of Pope Leo XIII on the Nature of Human Liberty* (June 20, 1888), VATICAN.VA.

68. His 1895 encyclical *Longinqua* chided: *Longinqua:Encyclical of Pope Leo XIII on Catholicism in the United States* (January 6, 1895), VATICAN.VA. See also Riccards, 48.

68. Leo genuinely seemed to admire: see NYT, April 7, 1891. See also "The Papal Policy Toward America," *The Catholic World*, July 1895.

68. Perhaps this is what President Grover Cleveland: NYT, December 30, 1887.

68. "ask the King of Italy for a stay": Henry Brann, "The American College in Rome," *The Catholic Encyclopedia*, Vol. 1. New York: Robert Appleton Company, 1907.

69. In 1891, Leo issued what is commonly believed: *Rerum Novarum* (May 15, 1891), VATICAN.VA.

69. "Magna Carta of social Catholicism": Bokenkotter, 329.


## CHAPTER 6: THE WORLD AT WAR: PART ONE

71. "Is this civilized world to be turned": full text of Benedict's Peace Note is in FRUS, 1917, "Supplement 2, The World War (1917) Part I: The continuation of the war—participation of the United States," 162–164.

71. painted a white line at the edge: J. P. Gallagher, 32.

72. "War alone keeps up": Riccards, 113.

72. "the role of the intermediary": NYT, January 31, 1915.

73. "neither spiritual or temporal majesty": Pollard, 71. See also Riccards, 73.

73. "Who's he?": Pollard, xii.

73. "prophet of peace": Benedict XVI's General Audience ("Reflection on the name chosen: Benedict XVI"), April 27, 2005.

73. Benedict XV's humanitarian efforts alone: Pollard, 112–113.

73. "the profound moral, ethical and religious influence": Letter from American Jewish Committee to Pope Benedict XV, 12/30/1915. Archives of Vatican Secretariat of State, *Sacra Congregazione degli Affari Ecclesistici Staordinari (AAEESS) 1915–1916*, Pos. 195, Fasc. 108.

74. "The Pope must actually place himself": NYT, September 6, 1914.

74. "The combatants are the greatest": the full text of *Ad Beatissimi Apostolorum* (November 1, 1914), VATICAN.VA. See also Riccards, 77.

74. "Remember, Nations do not die": Pollard, 117.

74. To the French, he was *pape boche*: McBrien, 356–357.

75. "Anyone suggesting peace now": Zivojinovic, 38.

75. The Allies had made a deal with Italy: Pollard, 101–102.

75. "I think that the chances of a just and lasting peace": Cooper, 276.

75. "peace without victory" speech: Zivojinovic, 63.

76. "he reserved for himself": Zivojinovic, 181.

76. "not only in European but also in American politics": McGreevy, 109.

76. "Is the Roman Catholic element in the United States": Cooper, 35.

76. "multitudes of men of the lowest class": quoted in Zivojinovic, 19.

76. Whatever the reasons: see Zivojinovic, 65–66.

77: Copies were prepared for the heads: Archives of Vatican Secretariat of State, *Stati Ecclesiastici 216*, "*Guerra Europa 1914-1916, Vol. XII.*

77. "Unfortunately our appeal was not heeded": full text of Benedict's Peace Note is in FRUS, 1917, "Supplement 2, The World War (1917) Part I: The continuation of the war—participation of the United States," 162–164.

77. "He goes into details": *The Nation*, August 16, 1917.

78. "so that a similar attitude be observed": FRUS, 1917, "Supplement 2, The World War (1917) Part I: The continuation of the war—participation of the United States," 165.

78. With millions of their young now dead: see Riccards, 82.

78. Wilson consulted his advisors: Zivojinovic, 84.

78. Benedict later told friends: Pollard, 128.

78. "Every heart that has not been blinded": for Wilson's full published reply, August 27, 1917, see Wilson's papers, APP.

78. President Wilson's response, soon made public: Zivojinovic, 92.

79. "mutual guarantees of political independence": see Wilson's Address to a Joint Session of Congress on the Conditions of Peace, January 8, 1918, APP.

79. "rearranged them and proposed them more explicitly": Peters, 163.

79. "I can assure you": Balfour to Gibbons, April 3, 1918. This letter is in the archives of the Vatican Secretary of State, *Sacra Congregazione degli Affari Ecclesistici Staordinari (AAEESS), pos. 1317, fasc. 470.*

79. They demanded onerous reparations: Kissinger, *Diplomacy*, 239, 245, 257.

80. An interesting and ironic coda: Cooper, 465.

80. The papacy would continue to be more actively engaged: Pollard, 155, 157.

## CHAPTER 7: THE WORLD AT WAR: PART TWO

81. "Gone are the proud illusions": *Summi Pontificatus: Encyclical of Pope Pius XII on the Unity of Human Society* (October 20, 1939), VATICAN.VA.

81. By the following morning: NYT, February 13, 1922; Kelly, 116.

81. He was a robust, barrel-chested athlete: Cuddihy, 201; NYT, February 7, 1922.

82. "For the first time in my life": Riccards, 103.

82. "Look at this multitude": Riccards, 103.

82. "always and in every case": Article 24 quoted in Graham, 318.119. There were other benefits to the Church: Cuddihy, 199; Norwich, 431; see also Vatican Radio, "Our History," http://en.radiovaticana.va/chisiamo.asp.

83. Hitler intended to use the Church: Riccards, 122.

83. "between an agreement on [Nazi] lines and the virtual elimination": Robert A. Krieg, "The Vatican Concordat with Hitler's Reich," *America Magazine*, September 1, 2003.

83. A number of unsavory conditions: Hales, *The Catholic Church*, 271–272; Norwich, 433–434.

84. It was not communism: see Hales, *The Catholic Church*, 268.

84. "Religion is the opium for the people": Marx and Engels, 10.

84. In Russia, by one Vatican official's calculation: Riccards, 119.

84. None of this suggests: Hales, 271; Norwich 433–434; Riccards, 122.

85. "especially significant in the urgent struggle": Cornwall, 152.

85. "nobody quite believed": Hales, *The Catholic Church*, 272.

85. Pius XI gradually wakened: Hales, *The Catholic Church*, 273; *Mit Brennender Sorge: Encyclical of Pope Pius XI on the Church and the German Reich* (March 14, 1937), VATICAN.VA.

85. "the only bright spot in Italy": "Goldhagen v. Pius XII" by Ronald J. Rychlak, *First Things*, June–July, 2002.

85. "push them back": quoted in Crocker, 393.

86. In the fall of 1936: for details of Pacelli's visit to the United States, see NYT, October 24, 1936; NYT, October 26, 1936; NYT, November 6, 1936. See also Riccards, 132; Nasaw, 252; and Gerald P. Fogarty's "The United States and the Vatican, 1939–1984" in Kent and Pollard.

87. While the precise topics: Gerald P. Fogarty's essay "The United States and the Vatican, 1939–1984" in Kent and Pollard. See also "The Future Pope Comes to America: Cardinal Eugenio Pacelli's visit to the United States" by Leon Hutton, *U.S. Catholic Historian*, Vol. 24, No. 2 (Spring 2006). Nasaw, 252, writes of Pacelli: "While he insisted otherwise, the reason for the visit was to discuss with the president the possibility of the United States renewing diplomatic relations with the Vatican."

87. "Ever in my personal judgment": FRUS, 1938, "*General*, Volume 1," 474–476.

87. "I think it is unquestionable": FRUS, 1939, "General, the British Commonwealth and Europe (1939)," Vol. 2, 869. See also Charles R. Gallagher, 71.

88. The conduit for these speeches was Father Joseph P. Hurley: Charles R. Gallagher, 78–81.

88. Franklin Roosevelt wrote a memo: FRUS, 1939, "*General, the British Commonwealth and Europe* (1939)," Vol. 2, 869–870.

88. Sending an American envoy: see Graham, 343.

89. Taylor was one of the most highly regarded: see *Time*, June 8, 40; see also "President Franklin D. Roosevelt's 'Ambassador Extraordinary'" by W. Davis Curtiss and C. Evan Stewart, *Cornell Law Forum*, Winter 2007 (www.lawschool.cornell.edu) and "The Man Nobody Knew" by C. Evan Stewart in New York Archives, Summer 2009 (www.nysarchivestrust.org).

89. Most immediately, per Roosevelt's wishes: Tittmann, 7.

89. A second key task for Taylor: "President Franklin D. Roosevelt's 'Ambassador Extraordinary'" by W. Davis Curtiss and C. Evan Stewart, *Cornell Law Forum*, Winter 2007 (www.lawschool.cornell.edu).

89. In 1937, Pius XI had declared: *Divini Redemptoris: Encyclical of Pope Pius XI on Aesthetic Communism* (March 19, 1937), VATICAN.VA.

90. grew frustrated: Charles R. Gallagher, 99.

90. "We would like to utter words of fire": quoted in Riccards, 135.

90. "not only an untrustworthy scoundrel": Hurley, 88; see Riccards, 133–135.

90. Any doubt that Pius XII meant these words: Cornwall, 234–240.

90. Even so tough a critic: Cornwall, 240.

90. "Pope-Speak": AUTH. INT. with Father Fogarty.

90. "Vatican observers, including the press": Reese, 167.

90. *Summi Pontificatus* is a good place to start: *Summi Pontificatus: Encyclical of Pope Pius XII on the Unity of Human Society* (October 20, 1939), VATICAN.VA.

91. "It should always be remembered": Tittmann, 95. See also Tittmann, 41.

92. After Dutch priests had denounced: Duffy, 348.

92. "sugar the pill": quoted in Charles R. Gallagher, 90.

92. Pius XII believed: Charles R. Gallagher, 90.

92. "He was operating Benedict XV's policy": Duffy, 347.

92. "[I]f I denounce the Nazis by name": Tittmann, 125; see also Tittmann, 118–119.

92. Making the moral distinction even blurrier: see Blet, 159–160, 165.

93. "to develop into an organization": Tittmann, 119.

94. "without comment": Tittmann, 76; see also Tittmann, 75–76, 80.

94. "it is of very great importance": Tittmann, 77.

94. "It is, in my opinion, much more useful": Tittmann, 43.

94. The issue that dominated: Tittmann, 137–158; and for U.S. State Department cable traffic regarding the bombing of Rome, see FRUS, 1942, "Europe," Vol. 3, 791–800.

94. The response from President Roosevelt: Tittmann, 148, 151–152.

95. the relationship between the Holy See and Japan: Tittmann, 102–109; and for U.S. State Department cable traffic regarding Holy See–Japan relations, see FRUS, 1942, "Europe," Vol. 3, 778–791.

95. "ostrich-like policy": Tittmann, 116–118; FRUS, 1942, "Europe," Vol. 3, 772–773.

95. "would have laid himself open": Tittmann, 118.

95. His two most urgent goals: FRUS, 1942, "Europe," Vol. 3, 775–776.

96. "The Holy See is still apparently convinced": Tittmann in FRUS, 1942, "Europe," Vol. 3, 777.

96. "I regret that the Holy See": Tittmann in FRUS, 1942, "Europe," Vol. 3, 777.

96. "hundreds of thousands, who, through no fault of their own": Cornwall, 268.

96. "Germany does not lack physical means": Riccards, 143.

96. "Flying in perfect formations": Tittmann, 165–166.

97. The pope prayed tearfully: Riccards, 139.

97. Events moved very fast: Tittmann, 172, 175, 177–178.

97. "The German military authorities occupying Rome": NYT, September 26, 1943; details of St. Peter's Square drawn also from NYT, September 11, 1943; NYT, September 13, 1943; September 17, 1943; October 9, 1943.

97. The Germans had every reason: Riccards, 140; Tittmann, 189.

98. "nest of spies": Kurzman, 12.

98. "The Governor of Vatican City, on the orders of the Secretary of State": NYT, October 14, 1943. See also Graham, 318.

99. Others who have studied the matter: Michael Tagliacozzo's biography and views are described in Dalin, 83–85.

99. "If he had spoken out": Tittmann, 122.

99. "Not one plan or proposal": Rubinstein, 84.

100. Donovan had realized: Waller, 256–258.


# PART III: THE COLD WAR

## CHAPTER 8: COMMON GROUND

103. "Both religion and democracy are founded": Truman's Address in Columbus, March 6, 1946, APP.

104. "In our relations abroad and in our economy at home": Truman's Address in Columbus, March 6, 1946, APP.

105. "This is the supreme opportunity": Truman's Address in Columbus, March 6, 1946, APP.

105. "Truman was beginning to lay": Inboden, 109–110.

105. As Truman writes in a letter: Inboden, 121.

106. Spellman turned down the pope: Kent, 93–95.

106. "Looks as if he and I may get": Truman, 554; see also Inboden, 124.

106. "had his friend Hugh Gibson": from the diary of Herbert Hoover, in the Truman Library (www.trumanlibrary.org/hoover/world.htm), item 48, June 1946. See also Duffy and Gibbs, *The Presidents Club*, 36–37.

107. Ties between state and church remain tight: NYT, October 31, 2012.

107. The most infamous: Waller, 297–302; National Archives Record Group 226, Entry 210, Box 23, Vessel Reports.

108. the recently organized CIA: Kent, 196–198. See also Weiner, 30, and footnote on page 622.

108. "Socialist-Communist bloc could very easily win a plurality": CIA memo: "Italy: Pope concerned over coming elections," January 29, 1948, FOIA/CIA.

108. "There would follow a discreet, but rapid": Central Intelligence Agency, "Consequence of Communist Accession to Power in Italy by Legal Means," March 5, 1948, FOIA/CIA.

108. "the most ancient seat of Western Culture": Weiner, 29–30.

108. "We had bags of money": NYT, July 6, 2006 (Mark Wyatt obit). See also Colby, 109; Weiner, 30–31; and Trevor Barnes, "The Secret Cold War: The CIA and American Foreign Policy in Europe, 1946–1956," *The Historical Journal* Vol. 24, No. 2 (June, 1981), 412–413.

108. Circumstances in Eastern Europe: see Chadwick, *The Christian Church in the Cold War*, for a detailed portrait of Christianity in the Soviet Bloc.

109. "bitter disgrace": NYT, June 7, 1948. See also Chadwick, *The Christian Church in the Cold War*, for a detailed portrait of Christianity in the Soviet Bloc in 1940s.

109. "liquidation of clerical reaction": NYT, November 22, 1948.

109. "wanton persecution": NYT, February 10, 1949.

110. The State Department favored: FRUS, 1950, "Western Europe, Volume III," 1790–1792.

110. "The President feels": FRUS, 1950, "Western Europe, Volume III," 1794.

110. Dean Acheson tried to talk him out of it: Acheson, 574–575.

110. On October 20, the White House announced: Truman News Conference, October 25, 1951, via APP; see Truman's comments and footnote.

110. Telegrams to the White House: F. William O'Brien, "General Clark's Nomination as Ambassador to the Vatican: American Reaction." *The Catholic Historical Review* Vol. 44, No. 4 (January 1959), 437. See also Pfeffer, 309.

111. "The fuss over the appointment": Arthur M. Schlesinger Jr., "Relations with the Vatican: Why Not?" *Atlantic Monthly* 189 (January 1952), 55–56.

111. "When any president begins to flinch": Schlesinger, "Relations with the Vatican," 55–56.

111. President Truman wrote a long regretful letter to Pius XII: Truman's letter, dated May 14, 1952, is in FRUS, 1952–1954, "Western Europe and Canada, Volume VI, Part 2," 2003–2006.

111. "If opposition of such a nature": Pius XII's response to Truman, dated July 10, 1952, is in FRUS, 1952–1954, "Western Europe and Canada, Volume VI, Part 2," 2010–2012.

112. "The Vatican is fated to be a continual object": Graham, 348.

113. "There is a moral or natural law": Inboden, 232.160. The alliance became personal in 1956: Avery Dulles would go on to become an important voice of American Catholicism, and would be made a cardinal by Pope John Paul II in 2001.

113. As James O'Toole points out: see O'Toole, 194–196.

114. "prima facie evidence of loyalty": quoted in O'Toole, 196.

114. Spellman played an important behind-the-scenes role: Kent, 65–66; Cooney, 244–246.

114. The agency asked him to arrange: Cooney, 297.

115. "to demonstrate that secret aid could help": Colby, 109. See also Nasaw, 699–701, regarding involvement of Joseph P. Kennedy in this program.

115. One glimmer of good news: "Personal Reminiscences about 1956 and Cardinal Mindszenty." Accessed at http://hungary.usembassy.gov/reminiscence.html.

## CHAPTER 9: WAR AND *PACEM*

117. "Peace on Earth": John XXIII's encyclical *Pacem In Terris* (April 11, 1963), VATICAN.VA.

117. Born in a rural village: see Chadwick, *The Christian Church in the Cold War*, 115–117.

118. "Catholic-baiting": Dallek, 232.

118. According to a 1959 Gallup poll: Dallek, 232.

118. "open negotiations for that Trans-Atlantic Tunnel": Dallek, 231.

118. "I'm getting tired of these people": Dallek, 283–284.

119. Richard Nixon, himself a fervent anticommunist: Richard M. Nixon, "Cuba, Castro, and John F. Kennedy: Some Recollections on United States Foreign Policy," *Reader's Digest*, November 1964.

119. "Above all": Schlesinger, 108.

119. St. Peter's Basilica was specially decorated: NYT, October 9, 1962.

119. "From Nicaea to the Space Age": NYT, October 10, 1962.

120. More than three times that number came: for numbers and backgrounds of council participants, see NYT, October 8, 1962; NYT, October 10, 1962; NYT, October 11, 1962; October 12, 1962. Most major American news outlets covered the opening of Vatican II in detail.

120. Pope John's appeal to "separated brethren": see Chadwick, *The Christian Church in the Cold War*, 119–120.

121. "render an account to God": NYT, October 13, 1962.

121. "unmistakable evidence": President Kennedy's "Radio and Television Report to the American People on the Soviet Arms Buildup in Cuba," October 22, 1962, APP.

122. "horrors of a war": NYT, October 26, 1962.

122. The following day, the Soviet premier wrote: Ronald J. Rychlak, "A War Prevented: Pope John XXIII and the Cuban Missile Crisis," *Crisis Magazine*, November 11, 2011.

122. "But stranger things have happened": quoted by Dean Rusk in memorandum to President Kennedy, February 19, 1963, in FRUS, 1961–1963, "Volume V, Soviet Union," Document 295, 631.

122. Pope John stunned the world: NYT, May 20, 1963; Riccards, 181–182; and re: Soviet–Holy See relations, see Pierre Salinger's memorandum to President Kennedy, November 16, 1962, at the John F. Kennedy Memorial Library.

123. Pope John XXIII soon surprised the world again: John XXIII's encyclical *Pacem In Terris* (April 11, 1963), VATICAN.VA.

123. "It is *the* document": AUTH. INT. with Father Christiansen.

123. "As a Catholic I am proud of it": NYT, April 21, 1963.

124. Murray's argument that Catholic faith: *Time*, December 12, 1960.

124. "The Catholic Church rejects nothing": *Nostra Aetate* (Declaration on the Relation of the Church to Non-Christian Religions), proclaimed by Pope Paul VI (October 28, 1965), VATICAN.VA.

124. "This Vatican Council declares": *Dignitatis Humanae* (Declaration on Religious Freedom), promulgated by Pope Paul VI (December 7, 1965), VATICAN.VA.

125. "The question is sometimes raised": Murray, *We Hold These Truths*, xiii.

125. "The human person's right to religious freedom cannot be proven": Murray, *Religious Liberty*, 241–242.

125. "that you can only truly claim": Chadwick, *The Christian Church in the Cold War*, 119–121.

126. *Gaudium et Spes* is perhaps the defining document: *Gaudium et Spes* (Pastoral Constitution on the Church in the Modern World), promulgated by Pope Paul VI (December 7, 1965), VATICAN.VA.

126. "No pope since the times of Gregory the Great": Duffy, 363.

127. New York virtually bowed: NYT, October 5, 1965.

127. "No more war!" NYT, October 5, 1965.

127. "It was not that he said anything new": NYT, October 7, 1965.

127. The pope responded by stepping up: Wynn, 196.

128. A meeting with Pope Paul had been hastily arranged: for an inside view of Johnson's visit to the Vatican, see Jack Albright Oral History (December 11, 1980), 103–106, Lyndon Baines Johnson Oral History Collection, accessed online at www.lbjlib.utexas.edu.

128. It was well into the evening: President Johnson's Daily Diary for December 23, 1967, accessed online at www.lbjlib.utexas.edu. See also NYT, December 24, 1967.

128. the president's helicopter began to sink: Jack Albright Oral History.

128. "disastrous": Kent and Pollard, 213; *Time*, December, 29, 1967.

128. the transcript drafted by the president's aid: Jack Valenti's *Aide-Memoire* is in FRUS, 1964–1968, "Volume XII, Western Europe," Document 309. Quotes also come from "Memorandum of Conversation," Document 310, also drafted by Valenti.

129. Before they parted: Kent and Pollard, 213–214.

129. In late April 1968, President Johnson: see Joseph A. Califano Jr., "The President and the Pope: L.B.J., Paul VI and the Vietnam War," *America*, October 12, 1991.

129. "This is a beautiful message": Califano Jr., "The President and the Pope"; see also FRUS, 1964–1968, "Volume XII, Western Europe," Document 215 and Document 216.

130. Among other accomplishments: Illing, 132; see also "Memorandum from Helmut Sonnenfeldt," FRUS, 1969–1976, "Volume XXIX, Eastern Europe; Eastern Mediterranean, 1969–1972," Document 122.

131. "The Soviet collapse in 1991": Gates, 170.

131. "At one moment": Kissinger, *Diplomacy*, 763.

## CHAPTER 10: PARALLEL INTERESTS

133. "Overwhelmingly Catholic Poland": Graham, 382.

134. Analysts at the Central Intelligence Agency issued a report: Memorandum: "The Impact of a Polish Pope on the USSR." Generated by the Central Intelligence Agency, National Foreign Assessment Center, October 19, 1978, FOIA/CIA.

134. Should this destabilization succeed: Weigel, *Witness to Hope*, 279–280.

134. "our enemy": Weigel, *Witness to Hope*, 304. See also O'Sullivan, 92–96.

134. "How can I not receive a Polish pope": Koehler, 65.

135. Over the course of his 9,665 days as pope: Weigel, *The End and the Beginning*, 434.

135. "nine days": Weigel, *The End and the Beginning*, 111.

135. "dictated by strictly religious motives": full text of John Paul II's "Welcoming Ceremony" in Warsaw" (June 2, 1979), VATICAN.VA.

135. "Christ cannot be kept out": Kohler, 73.

135. Wherever John Paul went in Poland: for a detailed and stirring description of John Paul II's visit to Poland, see Weigel, *Witness to Hope*, 291–324.

136. "The Holy Father told us": quoted in Kohler, 74. See also Weigel, *Witness to Hope*, 323.

136. "My theory of the Cold War": O'Sullivan, 91.

136. "The United States would no longer be content": Richard Allen, "The Man Who Changed the Game Plan," *The National Interest*, Summer 1996.

136. "Reagan, nearly alone, truly believed": Gates, 197.

137. "in fact, fundamentally a disarmer": Richard Allen, "The Man Who Changed the Game Plan," *The National Interest*, Summer 1996.

137. "Reagan believed that relations": Kissinger, *Diplomacy*, 778.

137. "I have decided": O'Sullivan, 87.

138. The leading theory: for detailed exploration of assassination theories, see works by Henze, Kohler, and West.

138. Gordon Thomas, in his book: Thomas, 236–237.

138. "without the church": O'Sullivan, 130.

138. "All of us are deeply alarmed": Kohler, 95.

139. the CIA's investigation revealed little: Gates, 354–356.

139. A final CIA report: Memorandum: "The Papal Assassination Conspiracy Trial: Inconclusive Results," April 1, 1987, FOIA/CIA.

139. According to at least one source: Kohler, 132.

139. It began late on the evening: for brief descriptions of the Polish crackdown leading to martial law, see Gates, 234–236; Schweizer, 67–68.

139. The CIA had a highly placed mole: for detailed analysis of Kuklinski's role, see Mark Kramer, "Jaruzelski, the Soviet Union, and the Imposition of Martial Law in Poland: New Light on the Mystery of December 1981," *Cold War International History Project Bulletin 11*. See also Gates, 227–239; Kohler, 109; West, 90, 95–110.

140. Walters shared some intelligence with the pope: O'Sullivan, 178.

140. The possibility exists: Weiser, 267.

140. In interviews with Polish media: "Pulkownik Ryszard Kuklinsi mowi" [Colonel Richard Kuklinski Speaks], *Tygodnik Solidarnosci*, No. 49, December 9, 1994, 1, 12–14; similar comments in "Wojna z narodem widziana od Srodka [The War with the Nation as seen from inside], *Kultura* Vol. 4, No. 475 (April 1987), 48–49.

140. As John Kohler details: Kohler, 31–32, 41, 173–173.

140. By 1980, the KGB was making a concerted effort: Kohler, 165–173.

141. John Kohler identifies three priests: Kohler, 153–169.

141. The unfortunate result: Gates, 238.

141. One of the first calls: Schweizer, 70.

141. The term Holy Alliance: Carl Bernstein, "The Holy Alliance," *Time*, February 24, 1992.

141. "In that meeting": Bernstein, "The Holy Alliance."

142. "I went to great pains": Richard Allen interview for the Ronald Reagan Oral History Project at the Miller Center, May 28, 2002, 58–59. Available at www.millercenter.org.

142. He approached his job: Schweizer, xvi–xvii, 35.

142. The CIA then channeled funds: for detailed descriptions of the CIA's work with the Catholic Church and Solidarity, see Gates, 237–238, 358–359, 450–451; Schweizer, 70–89.

143. "there was considerable sharing of information": Gates, 237.

143. "He always received me alone": West, 211.

143. A 1984 KGB report: West, 214.

143. In the early spring of 1983, John Paul II took a historic trip: details of this trip are in Weigel, *Witness to Hope*, 452–457.

144. "Regularize your position with the Church": Weigel, *Witness to Hope*, 454.

144. "Silencio!": Weigel, *Witness to Hope*, 456.

144. "one great concentration camp": Weigel, *The End and the Beginning*, 161.

144. "If I can't see him, then I'm going back to Rome": Weigel, *The End and the Beginning*, 161.

144. In the Able Archer affair: Gates, 270–273.

144. On January 10, 1984, the Reagan administration announced: NYT, January 11, 1984.

145. "a sensible and long overdue move": *Washington Post*, January 13, 1984.

145. Congress approved Wilson's appointment: Kent and Pollard, "The United States and the Vatican, *1939–1984*, by Gerald P. Fogarty, SJ, 240.

145. "We respect the great moral": NYT, January 11, 1984.

## PART IV: ACROSS THE TIBER

## CHAPTER 11: TO THE VATICAN

149. "If diplomacy is the art of persuading others": Albright, 75.

149. The first hint: personal reminiscences and conversations regarding the author's appointment and assignment as ambassador to the Holy See are largely drawn from his daily journal in which events and dialogue were recorded. When necessary, the author has confirmed and supplemented his recollections with interviews with other participants, observers, and, in some cases, State Department cables made public by WikiLeaks.

150. "The star most of us navigated by": Albright, 7.

150. "Since the terror attacks": Albright, 9.

152. "You must always remember": AUTH. INT. with Monsignor Peter Wells.

153. "Our commitment to freedom": Instruction letter from George W. Bush to Francis Rooney, October 12, 2005, in possession of author.

155. The Crusaders were successful: Madden, 32.

155. "Where the Church itself": Ratzinger, 162.

156. "Politics must be a striving for justice": Address of His Holiness Benedict XVI, Reichstag Building, Berlin (September 22, 2011), VATICAN.VA.

156. "dictatorship of relativism": *Washington Post*, April 19, 2005.

158. Now, with Saddam gone, the Patriarch feared: cable from Embassy Vatican to U.S. State Department: "Iraq; Patriarch Concerned about Constitution, Christian Community," November 25, 2005 (accessed via WikiLeaks).

158. by August 2006, half of all Christians: CNS, August 3, 2006. When General Maude of the British army captured Baghdad from the Ottomans in 1817, the

city was 40 percent Jewish and highly diverse; as late as 2003, 1 million Christians lived there.

159. Conditions for Christians did indeed deteriorate: U.S. State Department's "2006 Report on International Religious Freedom," accessed via state.gov.

160. "the Vatican is a ball of wool": "Exhausted in the Vatican," *Spiegel Online*, June 15, 2012.

162. "to take 100 pages and turn it into three": AUTH. INT. with Monsignor Peter Wells. This is similar to an admonishment General Eisenhower reportedly gave his D-Day commanders concerning the presentation of their invasion plans.

## CHAPTER 12: NEW FRIENDS

165. "Everything that happened in Eastern Europe": Rev. John J. Coughlin, OFM, "The Practical Impact of the Common Good in Catholic Social Though," *St. John's Law Review* Vol. 75, No. 2 (Spring 2001).

166. "People came to church to find out": Weigel, *Witness to Hope*, 529.

166. "We have a theological concept": AUTH. INT. with Archbishop Migliore, March 2012, Warsaw.

167. By the end, things had turned: O'Sullivan, 295–297.

167. "I recall with deep gratitude": O'Sullivan, 328.

168. "It is a question": NYT, December 30, 1989.

168. "My instructions were clear": Melady, 20.

168. Ambassador Melady spelled out: Melady, 20.

169. Ambassador Melady warned: Melady, 21.

169. "appalled by the attacks": NYT, December 30, 1989.

169. At least one prominent official: Bose and Perotti, 181.

169. He composed a letter: this letter was briefly seen by, and later described to, the author.

169. "psychological environment": NYT, January 6, 1990.

169. "He closed all the doors": NYT, January 5, 1990.

170. He personally delivered a letter: Melady, 95.

170. "The United States (the world's only real superpower)": Melady, 123; see also Weigel, *Witness to Hope*, 619–624.

171. Prior to the Cairo conference: for a detailed overview of the Cairo conference, see Weigel, *Witness to Hope*, 715–727.

171. "pregnancy termination": Weigel, *Witness to Hope*, 724.

171. "I found myself between": Flynn, 102.

171. Tauran told the ambassador: Flynn, 107–108.

171. "a United Nations plan to destroy the family": Flynn, 103.

171. Flynn went back to Villa Richardson: Flynn, 109–112.

172. President Clinton finally placed a call: Flynn, 112.

172. "It seems one of the most important aims": *Los Angeles Times*, July 23, 1994.

172. "another example of First World countries": Weigel, *Witness to Hope*, 717.

172. Among the harshest critics: Weigel, *Witness to Hope*, 725; see also Flynn, 116.

172. "In no case": Weigel, *Witness to Hope*, 725.

173. *Time* magazine named John Paul II: *Time*, December 26, 1994.

173. "I've always thought of politics": Flynn, 118.

173. Since 25 percent of all AIDS care: "Vatican Hosts AIDS Meeting in Wake of Condom Controversy," *The Rundown—PBS Newshour* (www.pbs.org/newshour/rundown), May 27, 2011.

173. An estimated 27 million people: U.S. States Department, "Trafficking in Persons Report 2012," June 2012, 6.

174. Sister Eugenia has expanded: *Rome Reports* (romereports.com), April 8, 2012.

174. "if the democracies themselves abandon": Hayak, 221.

174. "those who would give up essential liberty": Franklin, 254.

175. "My hope is the government of China": NYT, November 21, 2005.

175. "A healthy society": *Washington Post*, November 20, 2005.

175. "China has a great opportunity": U.S. Embassy to the Holy See, "Statement by Francis Rooney, Ambassador of the United States to the Holy See," November 21, 2005.

175. "If we go to Beijing": the *La Stampa* article is quoted by John L. Allen Jr., *National Catholic Reporter*, November 25, 2005.

176. The history of the Catholic Church in China: see John A. Worthley, "A Bridge to Beijing: Can a 16th-Century Jesuit Help Rebuild Chinese-Vatican Relations?" *America*, April 2, 2012,

176. In 1958, Pius XII excommunicated: Christopher Beam, "Is Catholicism in China Different from Elsewhere?" *Slate*, November 19, 2010. See *Ad Apostolorum Principis: Encyclical of Pope Pius XII on Communism and the Church in China* (June 29, 1958), VATICAN.VA, for the "automatically incurred" excommunication: "From what We have said, it follows that no authority whatsoever, save that which is proper to the Supreme Pastor, can render void the canonical appointment granted to any bishop; that no person or group, whether of priests or of laymen, can claim the right of nominating bishops; that no one can lawfully confer episcopal consecration unless he has received the mandate of the Apostolic See. Consequently, if consecration of this kind is being done contrary to all right and law, and by this crime the unity of the Church is being seriously attacked, an excommunication reserved *specialissimo modo* to the Apostolic See has been established which is automatically incurred by the consecrator and by anyone who has received consecration irresponsibly conferred."

177. "a marked deterioration": U.S. State Department, Bureau of Democracy, Human Rights and Labor, "International Religious Freedom Report for 2011," accessed via state.gov.

177. One such recent detainee: *Wall Street Journal*, July 26, 2012.

177. "Knowledge societies cannot function": Ronald Inglehart and Christian Welzel, "How Development Leads to Democracy," *Foreign Affairs*, March–April, 2009.

177. Currently an estimated 12 million: U.S. State Department, Bureau of Democracy, Human Rights and Labor, "International Religious Freedom Report for 2011," accessed via state.gov.

177. The Chinese government has its own reasons: Francesco Sisci, "China's Catholic Moment," *First Things*, June–July 2009.

178. "Observe carefully": Kissinger, *On China*, 438, footnote 40.

179. In fact, negotiations went so poorly: cable from Embassy Vatican to U.S. State Department: "Holy See: Foreign Minister Says 'No Progress' in Relations with China," July 31, 2006 (accessed via WikiLeaks).

180. "The Holy See continues to feel": cable from Embassy Vatican to U.S. State Department: "Vatican Wary of Leftist Latinos," December 23, 2005 (accessed via WikiLeaks).

## CHAPTER 13: MEETINGS OF MINDS

181. "The imponderabilia often have more influence": Graham, 25.

181. "No situation can justify": "Address of His Holiness Benedict XVI to the Diplomatic Corps Accredited to the Holy See for the Traditional Exchange of the New Year Greetings" (January 9, 2006), VATICAN.VA.

182. great unrest around the world: see NYT, February 4, 2006; NYT, February 5, 2006.

182. at the very moment: *BBC News* (news.bbc.co.uk), February 9, 2006.

183. The Horn of Africa is now considered: *Wall Street Journal*, January 23, 2012.

183. "The American people are a religious people": *USA Today*, February 9, 2006.

184. The Catholic Church has been through several permutations: for a review of the church's evolution in Latin America over the last fifty years or so, see Scott Mainwaring, "The New Catholic Church in Latin America: A Conference Report," (December 1983), The Helen Kellogg Institute for International Studies. See also "Catholicism in Latin America: 5 Key Facts," *Christian Science Monitor*, posted March 23, 2012, on CSMonitor.com.

185. "the fulcrum for anti-Americanism": Ray Walser, "Time Is Ripe for U.S. Policy to Address Anti-Americanism in Latin America," Issue Brief #3740, The Heritage Foundation.

185. Meanwhile, close relations between Caracas and Tehran: see Stephen Johnson, "Iran's Influence in the Americas," Center for Strategic and International Studies, March 12, 2012.

185. The percentage of Latin Americans: CNS, June 23, 2005.

186. "we see no likelihood of a change": cable from Embassy Vatican to U.S. State Department: "Vatican on Sumate, Venezuela," February 22, 2006 (accessed via WikiLeaks).

187. "a false and hypocritical use": *Fox News Latino*, August 19, 2011.

188. "dangerous trend": cable from Embassy Vatican to U.S. State Department: "Holy See: Prominent Latin American Cardinals Seek USG Help in Promoting Free Trade," April 3, 2006 (accessed via WikiLeaks).

188. "Ex-Juarez bishop worked to sway": *El Paso Times*, July 23, 2011.

189. "wrong signal": cable from Embassy Vatican to U.S. State Department: "Holy See Concerned by US–India Nuclear Cooperation, Iran," March 27, 2006 (accessed via WikiLeaks). See also "The U.S.–India Nuclear Deal," Council on Foreign Relations backgrounder, November 5, 2010 (accessed via cfr.org).

189. "an East-West and Christian-Muslim link": cable from Embassy Vatican to U.S. State Department: "Vatican-Iran: Possible Engagement on Nuclear Issue," February 22, 2006 (accessed via WikiLeaks).

190. "which are seeking God": CNS, August 7, 2007.

190. "crime against peace": *Time*, March 2, 2003.

191. "Vatican Hardening Line": cable from Embassy Vatican to U.S. State Department: "Vatican Hardening Line on Islam," April 20, 2006 (accessed via WikiLeaks).

191. One final conversation: see cable from Embassy Vatican to U.S. State Department: "Conversation with Prime Minister Blair," June 7, 2006 (accessed via WikiLeaks).

## CHAPTER 14: REGENSBURG

193. "The clash of civilizations": Samuel P. Huntington, "The Clash of Civilizations?" *Foreign Affairs*, Summer 1993.

193. "The world needs God": Benedict XVI, "Homily of the Holy Father," Munich (September 10, 2006), VATICAN.VA.

194. "As in the past": *Zenit* (zenit.org), July 14, 2006.

194. nearly 40 percent of the population: Central Intelligence Agency, *The World Factbook*, "People and Society: Lebanon" (accessed via cia.gov; last updated February 5, 2013).

194. "In God's Name": Benedict XVI, "Angelus," Castel Gandolfo (July 30, 2006), VATICAN.VA.

195. His first major work as pope: Benedict XVI, *Deus Caritas Est*, delivered in St. Peter's in Rome (December 25, 2005), VATICAN.VA.

196. "When we bring people only knowledge": Benedict, XVI, "Homily of the Holy Father," Munich (September 10, 2006), VATICAN.VA. See also NYT, September 10, 2006.

196. On September 11: NYT, September 12, 2006.

196. Indeed, according to one press account: "Reconstruction of a Global Crisis: How the Pope Angered the Muslim World," *Spiegel Online International*, November 24, 2006.

196. "lively exchange": Benedict XVI, "Lecture of the Holy Father: Faith, Reason and the University—Memories and Reflections," Regensburg (September 9, 2006), VATICAN.VA.

197. "one of the most widely read": "Reconstruction of a Global Crisis: How the Pope Angered the Muslim World," *Spiegel Online International*, November 24, 2006.

197. "In the Western World it is widely held": Benedict XVI, "Lecture of the Holy Father: Faith, Reason and the University—Memories and Reflections," Regensburg (September 12, 2006), VATICAN.VA.

198. "the Pope described Islam": BBC World Service, quoted in "The Pope, Faith, and Reason," *National Review Online*, September 22, 2006.

198. "tragic and dangerous": NYT, September 16, 2006.

198. "I call on all Arab and Islamic states": NYT, September 14, 2006.

198. "This statement has hurt": *Spiegel Online International*, September 15, 2006.

198. A top official in the Islamic party: NYT, September 15, 2006.

198. "I do not think any good": NYT, September 14, 2006.

198. Bardakoglu later admitted: "Reconstruction of a Global Crisis: How the Pope Angered the Muslim World," *Spiegel Online International*, November 24, 2006.

198. "We shall break the cross": *Spiegel Online International*, September 18, 2006.

199. "Anyone who describes Islam": "The Benedictine Rule," *Brussels Journal*, September 17, 2006, via brusselsjournal.com.

199. "What is important to the pope": *Spiegel Online International*, September 15, 2006.

199. "I am deeply sorry": Benedict XVI, "Angelus," Castel Gandolfo (September 17, 2006), VATICAN.VA.

200. "day of rage": ABC News, September 18, 2006, via abcnews.go.com.

200. "lent itself to possible misunderstanding": *Catholic News Agency*, September 20, 2006.

200. "particularly the Pope's own comments": cable from Embassy Vatican to U.S. State Department: "Vatican: Controversy Continues, Tone Shifting," September 22, 2006 (accessed via WikiLeaks).

200. "This is a man who says": George Weigel, "Reading Regensburg Right," speech for the Ethics and Public Policy Center, November 30, 2007.

201. "We need to stop insulting Islam": Thomas L. Friedman, NYT, September 29, 2006.

201. "providing a living proof": Tariq Ramadan, editorial, *International Herald Tribune*, September 20, 2006.

201. More significant was a letter: "Open Letter to His Holiness Pope Benedict XVI," accessed via *Thinking Faith: The Online Journal of the British Jesuits* (thinking-faith.org).

202. "most important papal statement on public matters": George Weigel, "Reading Regensburg Right," speech for the Ethics and Public Policy Center, November 30, 2007.

203. "All basic human decisions": AUTH. INT. with Cardinal Wuerl, March 2011.

## CHAPTER 15: PRESIDENT AND POPE

205. "I say that freedom is not America's gift to the world": Woodward, 88–89.

206. A survey in 2007: *USA Today*, June 7, 2007.

206. Department of State Authorities Act of 2006: this act reads, in part: "Under such terms and conditions as the President shall determine, the President is authorized to extend, or to enter into an agreement to extend, to the Permanent Observer Mission of the Holy See to the United Nations in New York, and to its members, the privileges and immunities enjoyed by the diplomatic missions of member states to the United Nations, and their members, subject to corresponding conditions and obligations." 109th Congress Public Law 472, U.S. Government Printing Office.

206. In 2002, the secretary-general: AUTH. INT. with Archbishop Migliore. See also Msgr. Leo Cushley, "A Light to the Nations: Vatican Diplomacy and Global Politics," Lecture for the Joseph and Edith Habiger Endowment for Catholic Studies, delivered February 26, 2007, University of St. Thomas in St. Paul, Minnesota.

207. To prove its legitimate place: CNS, July 2, 2004.

207. "rights and privileges": UN General Assembly Resolution A/58/314 ("Participation of the Holy See in the work of the United Nations"), Fifty-eighth session, July 16, 2004. Full text of the resolution is available at holyseemission. org.

208. The incident began: "Royal Navy captives: Key quotes," *BBC News*, last updated April 6, 2007, via news.bbc.co.uk.

208. "when the news broke about our sailors": AUTH. INT. with Denis MacShane.

208. "Easter gesture of good will": Edward Pentin, "Vatican Diplomacy," *Diplomat Magazine*, March 2010. See also *Catholic Herald*, May 4, 2007 (archive. catholicherald.co.uk).

209. "Nothing positive": Pope Benedict XVI, "Urbi et Orbi," Easter 2007, VATICAN.VA.

210. "constructive under the circumstances": cable from Embassy Vatican to U.S. State Department: "Holy See: Ambassador Presses Vatican on Iraq," September 25, 2007 (accessed via WikiLeaks).

210. "United Nations of Trastevere": see "Andrea Riccardi," *Time*, April 3, 2008. See also Weigel, *Witness to Hope*, 670.

211. "We're not dreamers": *Time*, April 3, 2008.

213. Inside the papal library: "Bush and Benedict: First Meeting," *Inside the Vatican*, June 10, 2007.

213. "straight talkers who act": "Bush and Benedict: First Meeting," June 7, 2007.

213. "Sometimes I'm not poetic enough": *USA Today*, June 11, 2007.

214. "like a fairy tale": CNS, June 11, 2007.

## PART V: CONCLUSION

## CHAPTER 16: FAITH AND FREEDOM

217. "Religion in America takes no direct part": de Tocqueville (Reeve, 1904), 329.

218. "The most important aspect": cable from Embassy Vatican to U.S. State Department: "Holy See Pleased about Saudi King Meeting with Pope, Interested in Inter-Religious Dialogue," November 30, 2007 (accessed via WikiLeaks).

218. These Christians were forbidden: see "Pope discusses Christians, Middle East peace with Saudi Arabia's king," CNS, November 6, 2007. See also Elliot Abrams, "'Destroy All the Churches': Saudi Arabia's Poor Treatment of Christians," *The Atlantic* (theatlantic.com), posted March 18, 2012.

219. "The factors of concern are varied": "Address of His Holiness Pope Benedict XVI to the Diplomatic Corps Accredited to the Holy See for the Traditional Exchange of New Year Greetings" (January 7, 2008), VATICAN.VA.

221. nearly a third of the members of Congress: "The Pew Forum: Faith on the Hill: The Religious Composition of the 113th Congress," Council on Foreign Relations (cfr.org), updated January 2, 2013.

221. Today, 630 hospitals: *The Economist*, August 18, 2012.

221. as much as 60 percent of the wealth: *The Economist*, August 18, 2012.

222. The number of Catholics in the United States: Center for the Applied Research in the Apostolate (CARA), "Frequently Requested Church Statistic: Catholic Population (The Official Catholic Directory)," via cara.georgetown. edu.

222. Regular mass attendance: "Sunday Morning: Deconstructing Catholic Mass attendance in the 1950s and now," *1964* (research blog for CARA), posted March 21, 2011.

222. the number of American priests: CARA, "Frequently Requested Church Statistics: Total Priests," via cara.georgetown.edu.

222. The American Church is reverting: O'Toole, 305.

222. Legally and practically, the Vatican cannot be blamed for actions of bad priests: A federal court in Oregon determined exactly this in 2012, ruling that the Holy See is not liable for the actions of individual priests.

222. "deeply ashamed": NYT, April 16, 2008.

223. "Here in America": "Transcript: President Bush Welcomes Pope Benedict XVI to U.S.," Foxnews.com, posted April 16, 2008.

223. "Democracy can only flourish": "Transcript: President Bush Welcomes," April 16, 2008.

224. "a false dichotomy": Benedict XVI, "Celebration of the Eucharist," Yankee Stadium (April 20, 2008), VATICAN.VA.

224. "virtue or morality is a necessary spring": Muñoz, 55.

224. "Religion, as well as reason": Jefferson, 283. See also Novak, 31.

224. "The legitimate separation": Pope Benedict XVI, "Address to U.S. Bishops," January 19/2012, quoted in *Inside the Vatican*, February 2012.

225. "Those who would give up essential liberty": Franklin, 254.

225. "Upon my arrival in the United States": Tocqueville (Reeve, 1904), 331.

226. "in some way to confusion and impotence": Tocqueville (Bevan, 2003), 510.

226. Compared to 73 percent of Americans: "Religious Views and Beliefs Vary Greatly by Country," *Financial Times/Harris Poll*, December 20, 2006, via harrisinteractive.com.

226. "the perennial question": "Address of His Holiness Benedict XVI," Westminster Hall, City of Westminster (September 17, 2010), VATICAN.VA.

227. "Individuals, communities and states, without guidance": "Address of His Holiness Benedict XVI," Presidential Palace Gardens in Nicosia (June 5, 2010), VATICAN.VA.

227. "When a nation's religion is destroyed": Tocqueville (Bevan, 2003), 511–512.

227. "does not speak from blind faith": Pope Benedict XVI, "Address to U.S. Bishops," January 19, 2012, quoted in *Inside the Vatican*, February 2012.

228. "toxic nationalism": Robert Kagan, "The Return of Toxic Nationalism," *Wall Street Journal*, December 23, 2012.

228. "The story must not be neglected": Belloc, 320–321.

## CHAPTER 17: THE ART OF HOPE

229. "Diplomacy is, in a certain sense": "Address of His Holiness Pope Benedict XVI to the Diplomatic Corps Accredited to the Holy See for the Traditional Exchange of New Year Greetings" (January 7, 2008), VATICAN.VA.

229. "There is no other universally regarded voice": AUTH. INT. with Cardinal Wuerl.

230. "self-referential": *Wall Street Journal*, March 16, 2013.

231. In the twentieth century, the Catholic population in Africa: Philip Jenkins, "The World's Fastest Growing Religion," *Real Clear Religion* (realclearreligion. org), November 13, 2012.

232. As noted earlier, Catholic organizations provide roughly 25 percent: Francis Phillips, "The Lesson That Jesuits Could Give Aid Organizations in Africa," *Catholic Herald* (catholicherald.co.uk), August 23, 2012.

232. "reignite" their faith: AUTH. INT. with Cardinal McCarrick, December 2012.

232. Mediation in El Salvador: *El Diario de Hoy*, March 21, 2012, 1–3; March 27, 2012, 6–7. See also *Nacional*, March 23, 2012, 7; December 12, 2012, 1.

233. A policy of state-enforced atheism was finally revoked: CNS, February 29, 2012; CNS, March 9, 2012. See also Margaret E. Crahan, "Back from the Margins," *America*, September 24, 2012.

233. The Catholic Church maintains a nuanced relationship: "Cuba's Cardinal Jaime Ortega under Fire for Comments," June 12, 2012, APP.

## CHAPTER 17: THE ART OF HOPE

240. See William Inboden, *Religion and American Foreign Policy, 1945–1960: The Soul of Containment* (New York: Cambridge University Press, 2008).

# SELECT BIBLIOGRAPHY

*For other materials consulted, please see notes.*

Acheson, Dean. *Present at the Creation: My Years in the State Department.* New York: W.W. Norton, 1969.

Albright, Madeleine. *The Mighty and the Almighty: Reflections on America, God, and World Affairs.* New York: Harper Perennial, 2007.

Allen, Felicity. *Jefferson Davis: Unconquerable Heart.* Columbia: University of Missouri Press, 1999.

Allen, John L., Jr. *All the Pope's Men: The Inside Story of How the Vatican Really Works.* New York: Doubleday, 2004.

Belloc, Hilaire. *The Crusades: The World's Debate.* Milwaukee: Bruce, 1937.

Beneke, Chris, and Christopher S. Grenda. *The First Prejudice: Religious Tolerance and Intolerance in Early America.* Philadelphia: University of Pennsylvania Press, 2011.

Birzer, Bradley J. *American Cicero: The Life of Charles Carroll.* Wilmington, Del.: ISI Books, 2010.

Blet, Pierre. *Pius XII and the Second World War.* New York: Paulist Press, 1999.

Bokenkotter, Thomas. *A Concise History of the Catholic Church.* New York: Doubleday, 2004 (1977).

Bose, Meena, and Rosanna Perotti, eds. *From Cold War to New World Order: The Foreign Policy of George Bush.* Westport, Conn.: Praeger, 2002.

Brown, Anthony Cave. *The Last Hero: Wild Bill Donovan.* New York: Times Books, 1982.

Bush, George W. *Decision Points.* New York: Broadway Paperbacks, 2010.

Carroll, John. *Eulogy on George Washington (Delivered in St. Peter's Church, Baltimore, February 22, 1800).* New York: P. J. Kenedy & Sons, 1931.

Chadwick, Owen. *A History of Christianity.* New York: St. Martin's Press, 1995.

———. *The Christian Church in the Cold War.* London: Penguin, 1993.

Colby, William, and Peter Forbath. *Honorable Men: My Life in the CIA.* New York: Simon & Schuster, 1978.

Cooney, John. *The American Pope: The Life and Times of Francis Cardinal Spellman.* New York: Dell, 1986.

Cooper, John Milton, Jr. *Woodrow Wilson: A Biography.* New York: Vintage Books, 2009.

Cornwell, John. *Hitler's Pope: The Secret History of Pius XII.* New York: Penguin Books, 2008.

Crocker, H. W., III. *Triumph: The Power and the Glory of the Catholic Church: A 2,000-Year History.* New York: Three Rivers Press, 2001.

Cuddihy, Robert J., and George N. Shuster. *Pope Pius and American Public Opinion.* New York: Funk & Wagnalls Company, 1939.

D'Agostino, Peter R. *Rome in America: Transnational Catholic Ideology from the Risorgimento to Fascism.* Chapel Hill: University of North Carolina Press, 2003.

Dalin, David G. *The Myth of Hitler's Pope: How Pope Pius XII Rescued Jews from the Nazis.* Washington, D.C.: Regnery Publishing, 2005.

Dallek, Robert. *An Unfinished Life: John F. Kennedy 1917–1963.* New York: Little, Brown and Company, 2003.

DePalma, Margaret C. *Dialogue on the Frontier: Catholic and Protestant Relations, 1793–1883.* Kent, Ohio: Kent State University Press, 2004.

Dolan, Jay P. *The American Catholic Experience: A History from Colonial Times to the Present.* Garden City, N.Y.: Doubleday, 1985.

Duffy, Eamon. *Saints and Sinners: A History of the Popes.* New Haven, Conn.: Yale University Press, 2006.

Duffy, Michael, and Nancy Gibbs. *The Presidents Club: Inside the World's Most Exclusive Fraternity.* New York: Simon & Schuster, 2012.

Duursma, Jorri C. *Fragmentation and the International Relations of Micro-States: Self-determination and Statehood.* Cambridge: Cambridge University Press, 1996.

Ellis, John Tracy. *Documents of American Catholic History: 1493–1865.* Vol. 1. Wilmington, Del.: Michael Glazier, 1987.

Englund, Steven. *Napoleon: A Political Life.* New York: Scribner, 2004.

Feiertag, Loretta Clare. *American Public Opinion on the Diplomatic Relations between the United States and the Papal States (1847–1967).* Washington, D.C.: Catholic University, 1933.

Flamini, Roland. *Pope, Premier, President: The Cold War Summit That Never Was.* New York: Macmillan, 1980.

Flynn, Ray. *John Paul II: A Personal Portrait of the Pope and the Man.* New York: St. Martin's Griffin, 2001.

Fogarty, Gerald P. *The Vatican and the American Hierarchy: 1870–1965.* Stuttgart: Anton Hiersemann, 1982.

Franco, Massimo. *Parallel Empires: The Vatican and the United States: Two Centuries of Alliance and Conflict.* New York: Doubleday, 2008.

Franklin, Benjamin. *The Works of Dr. Benjamin Franklin: In Philosophy, Politics, and Morals.* Vol. 2. Philadelphia: William Duane, 1809.

Gallagher, Charles R. *Vatican Secret Diplomacy: Joseph P. Hurley and Pope Pius XII.* New Haven, Conn.: Yale University Press, 2008.

Gallagher, J. P. *The Scarlet and the Black: The True Story of Monsignor Hugh O Flaherty, Hero of the Vatican Underground.* San Francisco: Ignatius Press, 2009.

Gates, Robert M. *From the Shadows: The Ultimate Insider's Story of Five Presidents and How They Won the Cold War.* New York: Simon & Schuster, 2006.

Glazier, Michael, and Thomas J. Shelley, eds. *The Encyclopedia of American Catholic History.* Collegeville, Minn.: Liturgical Press, 1997.

Graham, Robert A. *Vatican Diplomacy: A Study of Church and State on the International Plane.* Princeton, N.J.: Princeton University Press, 1959.

Guilday, Peter. *The Life and Times of John Carroll: Archbishop of Baltimore, 1735–1815.* New York: The Encyclopedia Press, 1922.

Hales, E. E. Y. *The Catholic Church in the Modern World: A Survey from the French Revolution to the Present.* Garden City, N.Y.: Hanover House, 1958.

———. *Pio Nino: A Study in European Politics and Religion in the Nineteenth Century.* New York: P. J. Kenedy & Sons, 1954.

Hayak, F. A. 1944. *The Road to Serfdom: Text and Documents: The Definitive Edition.* Chicago: University of Chicago Press, 2007.

Henze, Paul B. *The Plot to Kill the Pope.* New York: Scribner, 1985.

*Historical Statistics of the United States: Church and Congregations Membership, by Denomination: 1790–1995.* Millennial Edition Online. Cambridge University Press, 2006.

Illing, Robert F. *American and the Vatican: Trading Information after WWII.* Palisades, N.Y.: History Publishing Company, 2011.

Inboden, William. *Religion and American Foreign Policy, 1945–1960: The Soul of Containment.* New York: Cambridge University Press, 2008.

Jefferson, Thomas. *The Writings of Thomas Jefferson: Definitive Edition.* Washington, D.C.: Thomas Jefferson Memorial Association, 1905.

Jenkins, Philip. *The New Anti-Catholicism: The Last Acceptable Prejudice.* New York: Oxford University Press, 2003.

Johnson, Paul. *Modern Times: The World from the Twenties to the Eighties.* New York: Harper & Row, 1983.

Kelly, J. N. D. 1986. *The Oxford Dictionary of Popes.* Oxford: Oxford University Press, 1989.

Kent, Peter C. *The Lonely Cold War of Pope Pius XII: The Roman Catholic Church and the Division of Europe, 1943–1950.* London: McGill-Queens University Press, 2002.

Kent, Peter C., and John F. Pollard, eds. *Papal Diplomacy in the Modern Age.* Westport, Conn.: Praeger, 1994.

Kertzer, David I. *Prisoner of the Vatican.* Boston: Houghton Mifflin, 2004.

Kissinger, Henry. *Diplomacy.* New York: Simon & Schuster, 1994.

———. *On China.* New York: Penguin Press, 2011.

Koehler, John O. *Spies in the Vatican: The Soviet Union's Cold War against the Catholic Church.* New York: Pegasus Books, 2009.

Kurzman, Dan. *A Special Mission: Hitler's Secret Plot to Seize the Vatican and Kidnap Pope Pius XII.* Cambridge, Mass.: Da Capo Press, 2007.

Lansing, Isaac J. *Romanism and the Republic: A Discussion of the Purposes, Assumptions, Principles and Methods of the Roman Catholic Hierarchy*. Boston: Arnold Publishing Company, 1890.

MacCaffrey, James. *History of the Catholic Church from the Renaissance to the French Revolution*. Vol. 1. Whitefish, Mont.: Kessinger Publishing, 2004, Reprint.

Madden, Thomas F. *The New Concise History of the Crusades*. Lanham, Md.: Rowman & Littlefield, 2005.

Manhattan, Avro. *The Vatican in World Politics*. New York: Horizon Press, 1948.

Martin, Benjamin Nicholas, ed. *Choice Specimens of American Literature and Literary Reader*. New York: Sheldon and Company, 1875.

Martin, Malachi. *The Decline and Fall of the Roman Church*. New York: Putnam, 1981.

Marx, Karl, and Friedrich Engels. *On Religion*. Moscow: Progress Publishers, 1975 (1957).

Massa, Mark, ed. *American Catholic History: A Documentary Reader*. With Catherine Osborne, ed. New York: New York University Press, 2008.

McBrien, Richard P. *Lives of the Popes: the Pontiffs from St. Peter to Benedict XVI*. San Francisco: Harper, 1997.

McGreevy, John T. *Catholicism and American Freedom: A History*. New York: W.W. Norton, 2003.

McSorley, Joseph. *An Outline History of the Church by Centuries (From St. Peter to Pius XII)*. New York: B. Herder Book, 1961.

Melady, Thomas Patrick. *The Ambassador's Story: The United States and the Vatican in World Affairs*. Huntington, Ind.: Our Sunday Visitor, 1994.

Moore, John Bassett. *The Works of James Buchanan (1848–1853)*. Vol. 8. Philadelphia: J.P. Lippincott, 1910.

Morgan, Thomas B. *The Listening Post: Eighteen Years on Vatican Hill*. New York: G.P. Putnam's Sons, 1944.

Muñoz, Vincent Phillip. *God and the Founders: Madison, Washington, and Jefferson*. Cambridge: Cambridge University Press, 2009.

Murray, John Courtney. *We Hold These Truths: Catholic Reflections on the American Proposition*. Lanham, Md.: Rowman & Littlefield, 2005 (1960).

———. *Religious Liberty: Catholic Struggles with Pluralism*. Louisville, Ky.: Westminster John Knox Press, 1993.

Muston, Ronald G. *The Catholic Peace Tradition*. Maryknoll, N.Y.: Orbis, 1986.

Nasaw, David. *The Patriarch: The Remarkable Life and Turbulent Times of Joseph P. Kennedy*. New York: Penquin Press, 2012.

Neilsen, Fredrik. *The History of the Papacy in the XIXth Century*. London: John Murray, 1906.

Norwich, John Julius. *Absolute Monarchs: A History of the Papacy*. New York: Random House, 2011.

Novak, Michael. *On Two Wings: Humble Faith and Common Sense at the American Founding*. New York: Encounter Books, 2002.

Nye, Joseph S., Jr. *Soft Power: The Means to Success in World Politics.* New York: Public Affairs, 2004.

O'Sullivan, John. *The President, the Pope, and the Prime Minister: Three Who Changed the World.* Washington, D.C.: Regnery Publishing, 2006.

O'Toole, James M. *The Faithful: A History of Catholics in America.* Cambridge, Mass.: Belknap Press, 2008.

Packard, Jerome M. *Peter's Kingdom: Inside the Papal City.* New York: Charles Scribner's Sons, 1985.

Peters, Walter H. *The Life of Benedict XV.* Milwaukee, Wis.: Bruce Publishing, 1959.

Pollard, John F. *Benedict XV: The Unknown Pope and the Pursuit of Peace.* London: Cassell Academic, 1999.

Pfeffer, Leo. 1953. *Church, State, and Freedom.* Boston: Beacon Press, 1967.

Ratzinger, Joseph (Pope Benedict XVI). *Church, Ecumenism, and Politics: New Endeavors in Ecclesiology.* New York: Crossroads, 1987.

Reese, Thomas J. 1996. *Inside the Vatican: The Politics and Organization of the Catholic Church.* Cambridge, Mass.: Harvard University Press, 1998.

Riccards, Michael P. *Vicars of Christ: Popes, Power, and Politics in the Modern World.* New York: Crossroad, 1998.

Robertson, Geoffrey. *The Case of the Pope: Vatican Accountability for Human Rights Abuse.* London: Penguin Global, 2010.

Rubinstein, William D. *The Myth of Rescue: Why the Democracies Could Not Have Saved More Jews from the Nazis.* London: Routledge, 1999.

Rugoff, Milton. *The Beechers: An American Family in the Nineteenth Century.* New York: Harper & Row, 1981.

Schlesinger, Arthur M., Jr. 1965. *A Thousand Days: John F. Kennedy in the White House.* Boston: Houghton Mifflin, Mariner Books, 2002.

Schofield, Nicholas, ed. *A Roman Miscellany: The English in Rome, 1550–2000.* Herefordshire, UK: Gracewing, 2002.

Schweizer, Peter. *Victory: The Reagan Administration's Secret Strategy That Hastened the Collapse of the Soviet Union.* New York: Atlantic Monthly Press, 1994.

Shea, John Gilmary. *Life and Times of the Most Rev. John Carroll, Bishop and First Archbishop of Baltimore: Embracing the History of the Catholic Church in the United States, 1763–1815.* New York: Edward O. Jenkins' Sons, 1888.

Stock, Leo Francis. *United States Ministers to the Papal States: Instruction and Dispatches, 1848–1868.* Washington, D.C.: Catholic University Press, 1933.

Thomas, Gordon. *Gideon's Spies: The Secret History of the Mossad.* New York: St. Martin's Press, 1999.

Tierney, Brian. *The Idea of Natural Rights: Studies on Natural Rights, Natural Law and Church Law, 1150–1625.* Atlanta: Scholars Press, 1997.

Tittmann, Harold H., Jr., and Harold H. Tittmann III. *Inside the Vatican of Pius XII: The Memoir of an American Diplomat during World War II.* New York: Doubleday, 2004.

Tocqueville, Alexis de: *Democracy in America and Two Essays on America.* Translated by Gerald E. Bevan. New York: Penguin, 2003.

———. *Democracy in America.* Vol. I. Translated by Henry Reeve. New York: D. Appleton and Company, 1904.

Toynbee, Arnold. *A Study of History: Abridgement of Vol. I–VI by D. C. Somervell.* Oxford: Oxford University Press, 1946.

Truman, Harry S. *Dear Bess: The Letters from Harry to Bess Truman, 1910–1959.* Columbia: University of Missouri Press, 1998.

United States Department of State. *Papers Relating to the Foreign Relations of the United States, 1917: Supplement 2: The World War.* Vol. I. Washington, D.C.: U.S. Government Printing Office, 1917.

Van Doren, Charles. *A History of Knowledge: Past, Present, and Future.* New York: Ballantine Books, 1991.

Varacalli, Joseph A. *The Catholic Experience in America.* Westport, Conn.: Greenwood Press, 2006.

Waller, Douglas. *Wild Bill Donovan: The Spymaster Who Created the OSS and Modern American Espionage.* New York: Free Press, 2011.

Weigel, George. *The Courage to Be Catholic: Crisis, Reform, and the Future of the Church.* New York: Basic Books, 2002.

———. *The End and the Beginning: Pope John Paul: The Victory of Freedom, the Last Years, the Legacy.* New York: Doubleday, 2010.

———. *Witness to Hope: The Biography of Pope John Paul II, 1920–2005.* New York: Harper Perennial, 1999.

Weiner, Tim. *Legacy of Ashes: The History of the CIA.* New York: Anchor Books, 2008.

Weiser, Benjamin. *A Secret Life: The Polish Colonel, His Covert Mission, and the Price He Paid to Save His Country.* New York: Public Affairs, 2004.

West, Nigel. *The Third Secret: The CIA, Solidarity and the KGB's Plot to Kill the Pope.* New York: HarperCollins, 2001.

Woods, Thomas E., Jr. *How the Catholic Church Built Western Civilization.* Washington, D.C.: Regnery Publishing, 2005.

Woodward, Bob. *Plan of Attack.* New York: Simon & Schuster, 2004.

Wynn, Wilton. *Keepers of the Keys: John XXIII, Paul VI and John Paul II: Three Who Changed the Church.* New York: Random House, 1988.

Zivojinovic, Dragan R. *The United States and the Vatican Policies, 1914–1918.* Boulder: Colorado Associated University Press, 1978.

## ARCHIVAL SOURCES

Georgetown University Special Collection Research Center, Washington, D.C.
Library of Congress, Washington, D.C.
National Archives, College Park, Maryland.

Propaganda Fide Archives, Rome.
Secretariat of State Archives, Vatican City.
Vatican Secret Archives, Vatican City.


## INTERVIEWS CONDUCTED BY AUTHOR

Claudio Betti, Rome, March 2012.
Monsignor Charles Burns, Rome, March 2012.
Father Drew Christiansen, SJ, New York City, March 2011.
Bishop Frank Dewane, Venice, Florida, January 2011.
Cardinal Timothy M. Dolan, New York City, March 2011.
Professor Gerald P. Fogarty, SJ, Charlottesville, Va., November 2011.
Father James E. Grummer, SJ, Rome, March 2012.
Cardinal James M. Harvey, Vatican City, May 2011.
Cardinal Bernard F. Law, Vatican City, May 2011.
Cardinal William J. Levada, Vatican City, May 2011.
Denis MacShane, by phone, October 2012.
Cardinal Renato Martino, Vatican City, May 2011.
Cardinal Theodore E. McCarrick, Chillum, Md., February 2011; Washington,
    D.C., December 2012.
Archbishop Celestino Migliore, Warsaw, Poland, March 2012.
Bishop William F. Murphy, Rockville Center, Long Island, N.Y., March 2011.
Cardinal Vincenzo Paglia, Rome, March 2012.
Ambassador Georgios F. Poulides, Rome, March 2012.
Father Thomas J. Reese, SJ, Washington, D.C., January 2011.
Ambassador Nikolay Sadchikov, Rome, March 2012.
Archbishop Pietro Sambi, Washington, D.C., January 2011.
Cardinal Leonardo Sandri, Vatican City, May 2011.
Cardinal Jean-Louis Tauran, Vatican City, May 2011
Professor George Weigel, Washington, D.C., February 2011.
Monsignor Peter B. Wells, Vatican City, May 2011; Rome, March 2012.
Prince Hugo Windisch-Graetz, Rome, March 2012.
Cardinal Donald W. Wuerl, Washington, D.C., March 2011.

# INDEX

# ABOUT THE AUTHOR

**Ambassador Francis Rooney** served as the United States ambassador to the Holy See from 2005 through 2008, appointed by President George W. Bush. Currently he is the chief executive officer of Rooney Holdings, Inc., a diversified investment company, and Manhattan Construction Group, a civil and building construction company.

Ambassador Rooney has rejoined the Board of Advisors of the Panama Canal Authority, Republic of Panama, on which he was member prior to resigning in 2005 to enter government service. He is a member of the board of the Florida Gulf Coast University Foundation and serves as chairman of the Board of Visitors of the University of Oklahoma College of International Studies. Ambassador Rooney also currently serves on the boards of directors of Helmerich & Payne, Inc. (NYSE) and Laredo Petroleum, Inc. (NYSE), both in Tulsa, Oklahoma; VETRA Energy Group, Bogota, Colombia; and Mercantil Commercebank, Coral Gables, Florida. He is a trustee of The Center for the Study of the Presidency and Congress and a member of the board of directors of The Trust for the National Mall, both in Washington, D.C., and is a member of the Council of American Ambassadors.

He is a graduate of Georgetown University and Georgetown University Law Center. He is a member of the District of Columbia and Texas Bars, and holds a U.S. Coast Guard 100 Ton Masters License (sailing endorsement). He is married to Kathleen Collins Rooney and they have three children.